I0820448

The Story of the American Civil War

Future Books is an imprint of Future PLC
Quay House, The Ambury, Bath, BA1 1UA

A catalogue record for this book is available from the British Library.

ISBN 978-1-83648-294-9 hardback

The paper holds full FSC certification and accreditation.

Printed in China by C&C Offset Printing Co. Ltd. for Future PLC

GPSR EU RP (for authorities only)
eucomply OÜ Pärnu mnt 139b-14 11317
Tallinn, Estonia
hello@eucompliancepartner.com
+3375690241

Interested in Foreign Rights to publish this title? Email us at:
licensing@futurenet.com

Group Editor
Dan Peel

Senior Art Editor
Andy Downes

History of War Editor-in-Chief
Tim Williamson

History of War Senior Designer
Curtis Fermor-Dunman

Head of Art & Design
Greg Whitaker

Editorial Director
Jon White

Managing Director
Grainne McKenna

Production Project Manager
Matthew Eglinton

Global Business Development Manager
Jennifer Smith

Head of Future International & Bookazines
Tim Mathers

Cover images
Getty Images

STORY OF THE AMERICAN CIVIL WAR

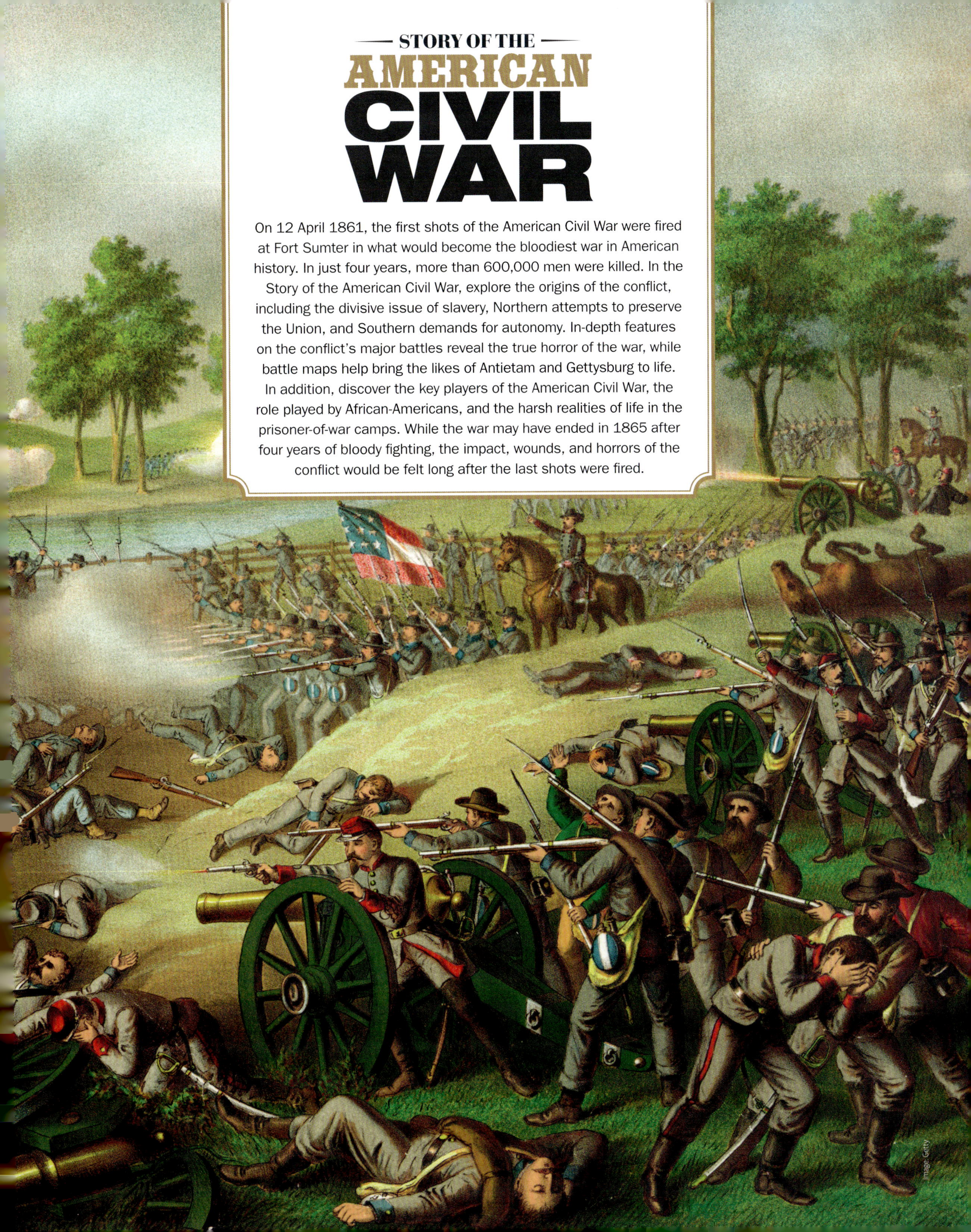

STORY OF THE

AMERICAN CIVIL WAR

On 12 April 1861, the first shots of the American Civil War were fired at Fort Sumter in what would become the bloodiest war in American history. In just four years, more than 600,000 men were killed. In the Story of the American Civil War, explore the origins of the conflict, including the divisive issue of slavery, Northern attempts to preserve the Union, and Southern demands for autonomy. In-depth features on the conflict's major battles reveal the true horror of the war, while battle maps help bring the likes of Antietam and Gettysburg to life. In addition, discover the key players of the American Civil War, the role played by African-Americans, and the harsh realities of life in the prisoner-of-war camps. While the war may have ended in 1865 after four years of bloody fighting, the impact, wounds, and horrors of the conflict would be felt long after the last shots were fired.

Image: Getty

CONTENTS

88

36

60

46

70

140

TIMELINE OF THE AMERICAN CIVIL WAR

Four years of epic struggle and tremendous loss marked a civil war with repercussions still being assessed today

WORDS **MIKE HASKEW**

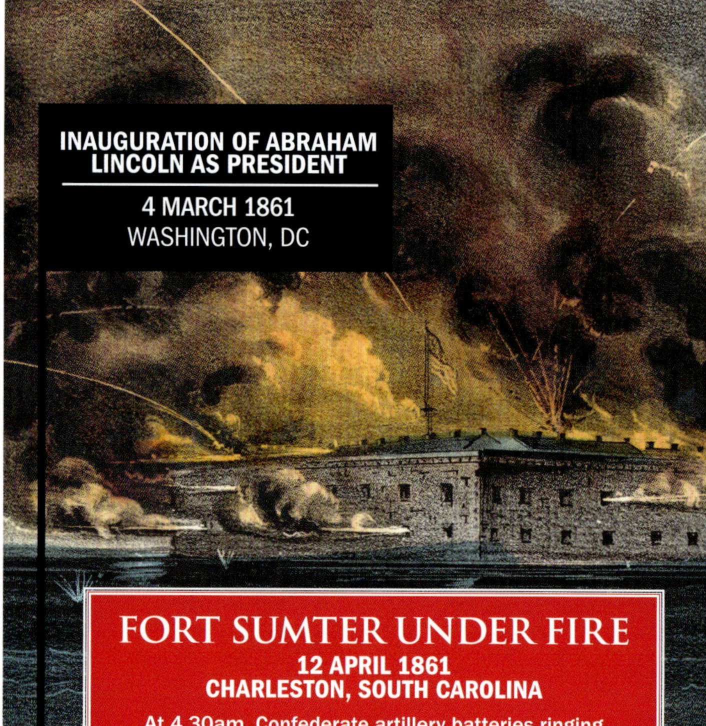

INAUGURATION OF ABRAHAM LINCOLN AS PRESIDENT
4 MARCH 1861
WASHINGTON, DC

FORT SUMTER UNDER FIRE

12 APRIL 1861
CHARLESTON, SOUTH CAROLINA

At 4.30am, Confederate artillery batteries ringing Charleston Harbor open fire on Fort Sumter, situated on a sandbar about a mile from the heart of the city's wharf area. After repeated calls for the surrender of the fort are declined, Confederate general PGT Beauregard orders the 34-hour bombardment to commence. Major Robert Anderson, commanding the Union garrison, surrenders the following day and is proclaimed a hero. The opening shots of the Civil War electrify the American population both North and South.

20 DEC 1860

SOUTH CAROLINA SECEDES

20 DECEMBER 1860
CHARLESTON, SOUTH CAROLINA

Prompted by the election of Republican Abraham Lincoln as the 16th president of the United States, South Carolina adopts an ordinance of secession in Charleston following the unanimous 169-0 vote of the state assembly in Columbia to secede from the Union. South Carolina is the first Southern slave state to leave the Union and earns the nickname 'Mother of Secession'. Eventually, ten other Southern slave states secede and form the Confederate States of America. They include North Carolina, Florida, Georgia, Alabama, Louisiana, Mississippi, Arkansas, Texas, Virginia, and Tennessee. The border states of Maryland, Kentucky, and Missouri remain in the Union.

South Carolina secessionists march through Charleston in support of an ordinance to leave the Union

FIRST BATTLE OF BULL RUN

21 JULY 1861
NEAR THE TOWN OF MANASSAS, NORTHERN VIRGINIA

The first major battle of the American Civil War, also known as First Manassas, ends in Confederate victory after Union forces nearly succeed in routing the Rebels. Confusion reigns during much of the fighting, but a Confederate stand on Henry House Hill, where General Thomas J Jackson earns the nickname 'Stonewall', buys time as Union troops are slow to deploy and Rebel reinforcements arrive by rail, turning the tide of battle. The Union withdrawal from the field toward Washington, DC, turns into a panic, sweeping up many members of the US government and other civilians who have journeyed to the battlefield west of the capital to witness the engagement.

BATTLE OF HAMPTON ROADS

8-9 MARCH 1862
HAMPTON ROADS, VIRGINIA

In the world's first engagement between ironclad warships on 9 March 1862, the Union Monitor and Confederate Virginia fight to a draw after maneuvering and blasting one another with cannon at close range. The previous day, the Virginia had steamed down the Elizabeth River and sunk the Union frigates Congress and Cumberland, shells bouncing harmlessly off its thick iron hull, retiring as the tide ebbed. The battle effectively rendered wooden warships obsolete and compelled navies across the globe to modernize.

■ *The Monitor and Virginia blaze away at close range during the Battle of Hampton Roads*

■ *Fort Sumter is engulfed in smoke and flame during the bombardment that opened the Civil War*

SEVEN DAYS BATTLES

25 JUNE – 1 JULY 1862
VICINITY OF RICHMOND, VIRGINIA

SECOND BATTLE OF BULL RUN

28-30 AUGUST 1862
OLD BULL RUN BATTLEFIELD NEAR MANASSAS, VIRGINIA

30 AUG 1862

FALL OF FORTS HENRY AND DONELSON

6-16 FEBRUARY 1862
CUMBERLAND AND TENNESSEE RIVERS IN TENNESSEE

BATTLE OF SHILOH

6-7 APRIL 1862
PITTSBURG LANDING, HARDIN COUNTY, TENNESSEE

During the great early battle in the West, Confederate general Albert Sidney Johnston launches his Army of Mississippi in a surprise attack against the Union Army of the Tennessee under General Ulysses S Grant. The Confederate onslaught drives the Union troops back toward Pittsburg Landing on the Tennessee River; however, Johnston is killed and Confederate command devolves to General PGT Beauregard, who calls off attacks as daylight fades. Reinforced by a division of his own army and three divisions of the Army of the Ohio, Grant assumes the offensive on the second day, recovering all of the lost ground. Combined casualties approach 24,000.

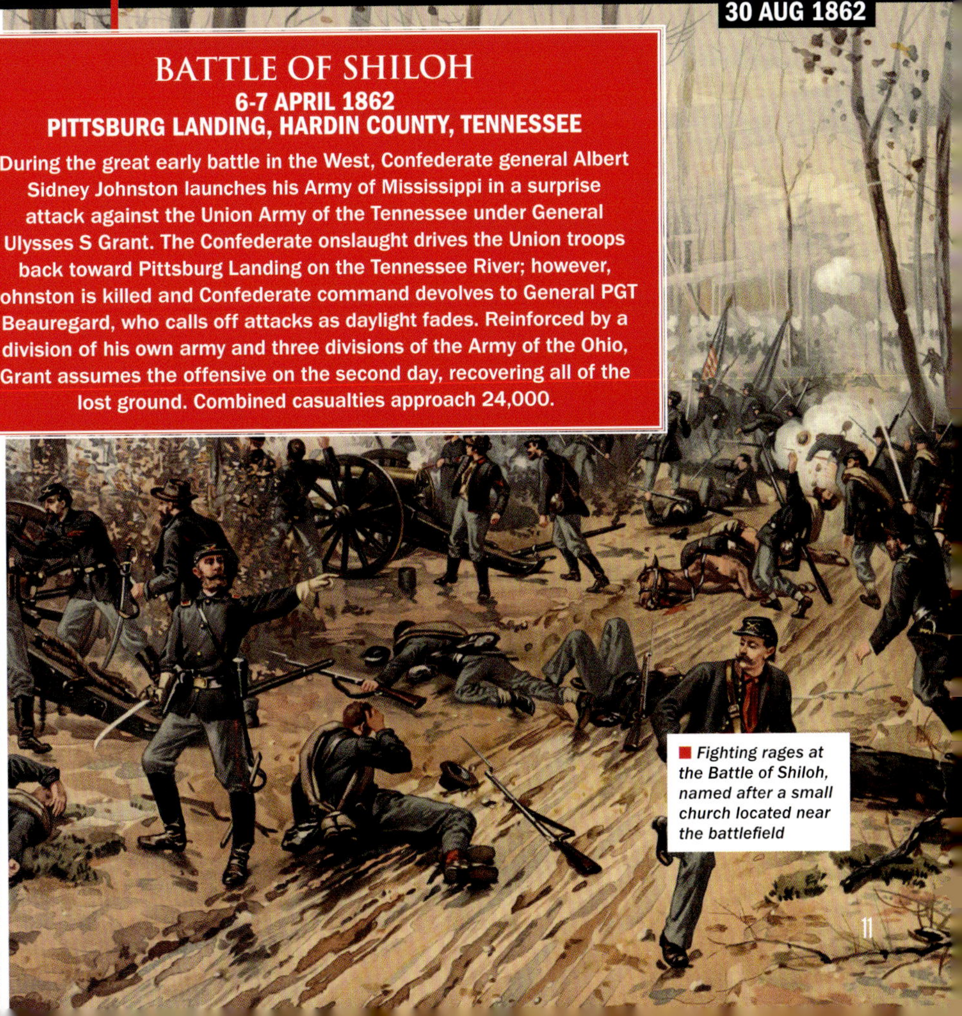

■ *In this Kurz & Allison image of First Bull Run, Union and Confederate soldiers clash*

■ *Fighting rages at the Battle of Shiloh, named after a small church located near the battlefield*

BATTLE OF ANTIETAM

17 SEPTEMBER 1862
ANTIETAM CREEK NEAR SHARPSBURG, MARYLAND

General Robert E Lee's first invasion of the North ends along the banks of Antietam Creek in western Maryland with the bloodiest day in American history. Lee's Confederate Army of Northern Virginia retires across the Potomac River after the Union Army of the Potomac, under General George B McClellan, fights to a tactical draw but gains a strategic Union victory. However, McClellan is criticized for failing to press a substantial numerical advantage. President Abraham Lincoln signs the Emancipation Proclamation after the battle.

■ *Union and Confederate troops fight for control of Burnside Bridge during the Battle of Antietam*

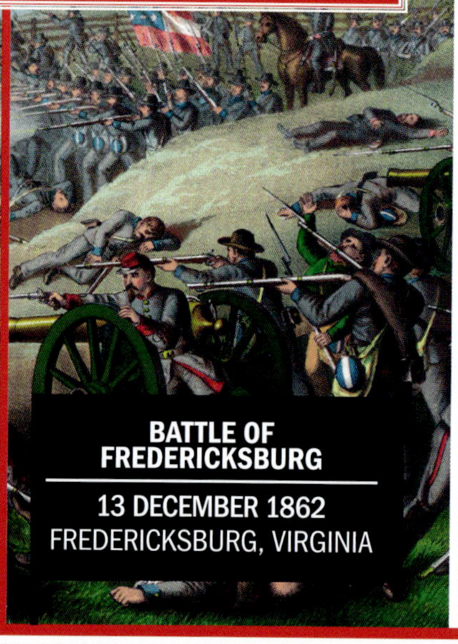

17 SEPT 1862

BATTLE OF FREDERICKSBURG

13 DECEMBER 1862
FREDERICKSBURG, VIRGINIA

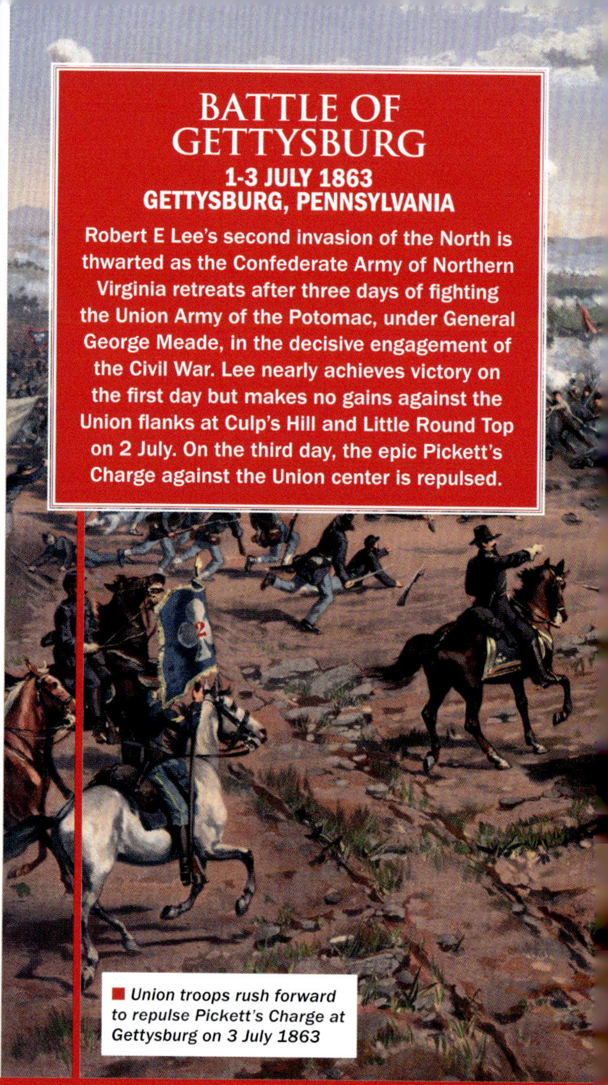

BATTLE OF GETTYSBURG

1-3 JULY 1863
GETTYSBURG, PENNSYLVANIA

Robert E Lee's second invasion of the North is thwarted as the Confederate Army of Northern Virginia retreats after three days of fighting the Union Army of the Potomac, under General George Meade, in the decisive engagement of the Civil War. Lee nearly achieves victory on the first day but makes no gains against the Union flanks at Culp's Hill and Little Round Top on 2 July. On the third day, the epic Pickett's Charge against the Union center is repulsed.

■ *Union troops rush forward to repulse Pickett's Charge at Gettysburg on 3 July 1863*

LINCOLN ISSUES EMANCIPATION PROCLAMATION

1 JANUARY 1863
WASHINGTON, DC

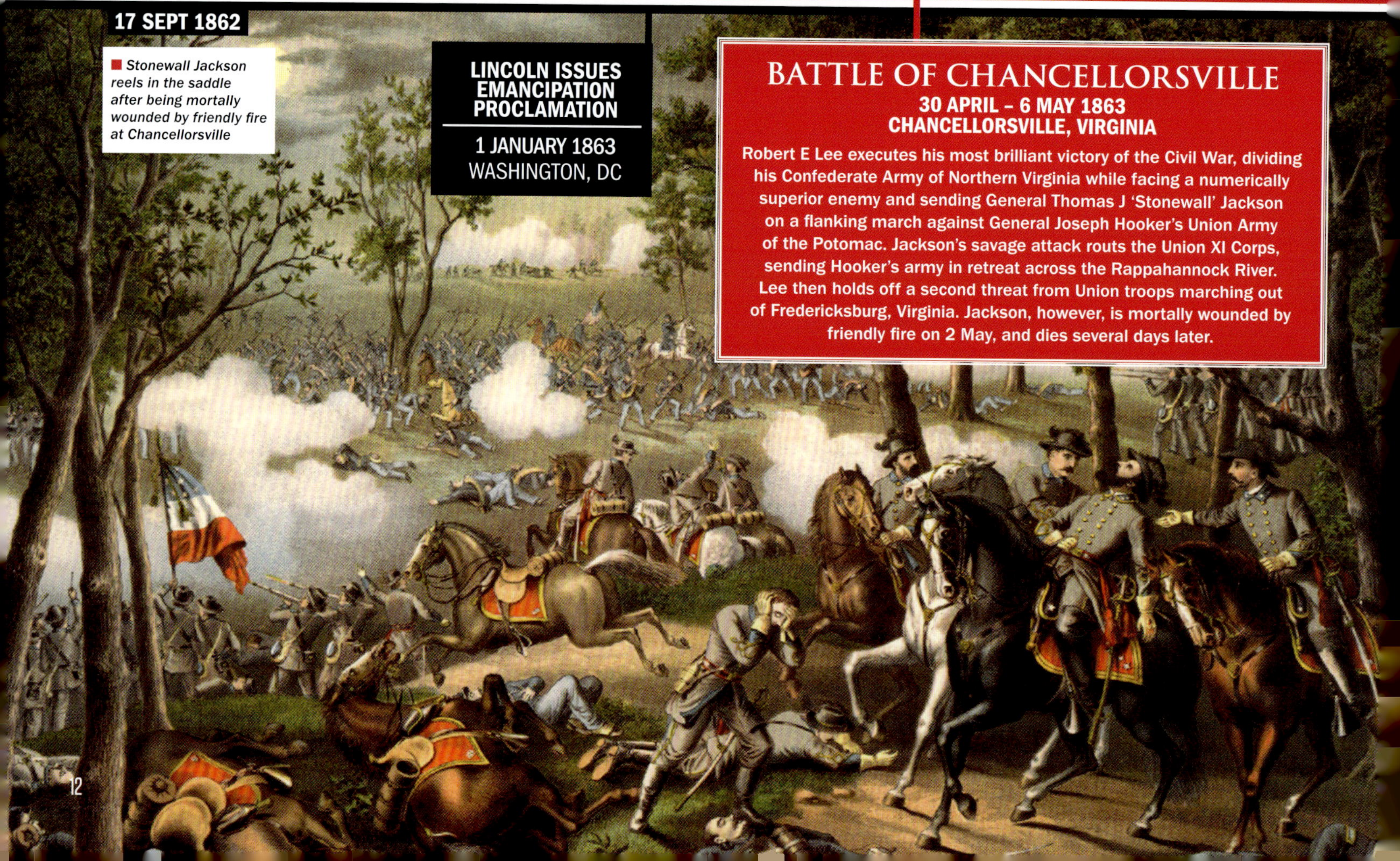

BATTLE OF CHANCELLORSVILLE

30 APRIL – 6 MAY 1863
CHANCELLORSVILLE, VIRGINIA

Robert E Lee executes his most brilliant victory of the Civil War, dividing his Confederate Army of Northern Virginia while facing a numerically superior enemy and sending General Thomas J 'Stonewall' Jackson on a flanking march against General Joseph Hooker's Union Army of the Potomac. Jackson's savage attack routs the Union XI Corps, sending Hooker's army in retreat across the Rappahannock River. Lee then holds off a second threat from Union troops marching out of Fredericksburg, Virginia. Jackson, however, is mortally wounded by friendly fire on 2 May, and dies several days later.

■ *Stonewall Jackson reels in the saddle after being mortally wounded by friendly fire at Chancellorsville*

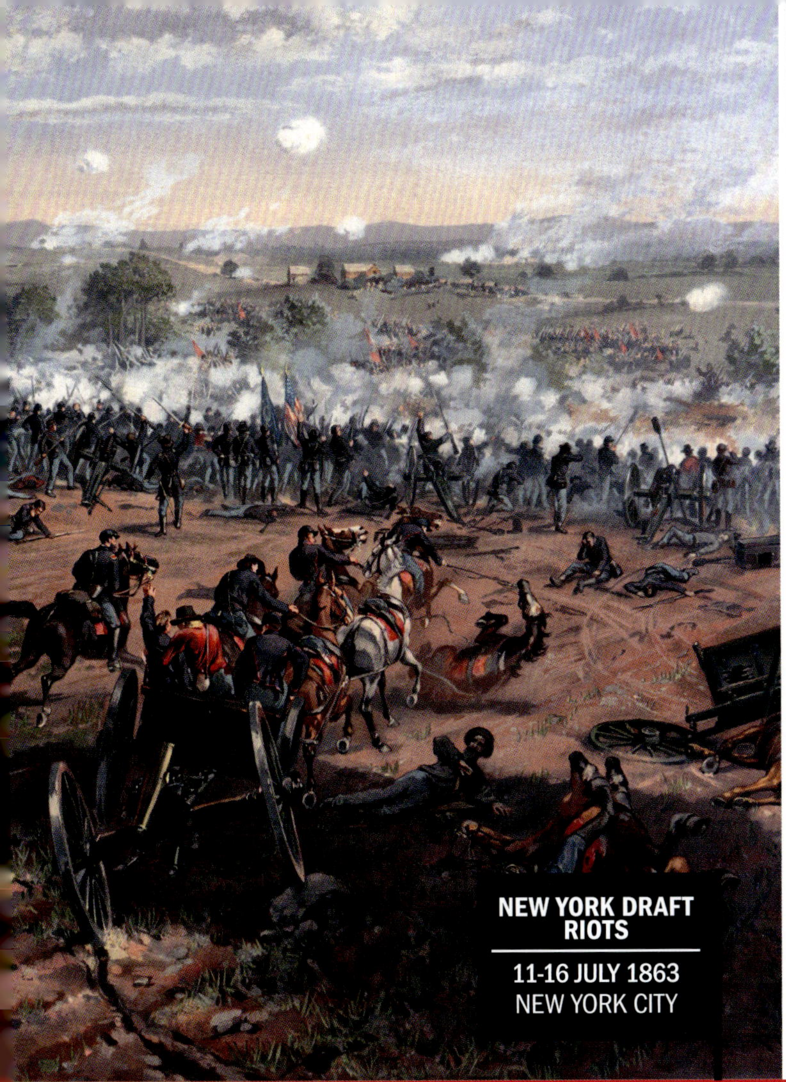

NEW YORK DRAFT RIOTS

11-16 JULY 1863
NEW YORK CITY

BATTLE OF CHICKAMAUGA

19-20 SEPTEMBER 1863
NORTH GEORGIA NEAR CHATTANOOGA, TENNESSEE

General William Rosecrans and the Union Army of the Cumberland confront General Braxton Bragg and the Confederate Army of Tennessee in north Georgia, 20 miles south of Chattanooga. After inconclusive fighting, a mistaken order opens a gap in the Union line. Confederate forces charge through, routing Rosecrans' army, which retreats to Chattanooga. In the largest battle in the Western Theater, nearly 35,000 casualties are sustained, second only to Gettysburg. In November, Union forces raise the siege of Chattanooga in a significant Union victory.

In a combat sketch made during the battle, Confederate infantrymen advance at Chickamauga

FALL OF VICKSBURG

4 JULY 1863
VICKSBURG, MISSISSIPPI

After weeks of siege warfare, the city of Vicksburg, Mississippi, falls to Union forces under the command of General Ulysses S Grant. Situated on the bluffs above the Mississippi River, Vicksburg controls the waterway for miles. Confederate general John Pemberton surrenders the city on 4 July, Independence Day. Coupled with the earlier capture of New Orleans, the Union now controls the length of the great river and the Confederacy is split in two. President Lincoln proclaims that the "father of waters again goes unvexed to the sea". Along with Gettysburg, the defeat at Vicksburg seals the fate of the Confederacy.

19 NOV 1863

LINCOLN DELIVERS GETTYSBURG ADDRESS

19 NOVEMBER 1863
GETTYSBURG, PENNSYLVANIA

Shirley's House stands prominently among makeshift dwellings during the siege of Vicksburg

Months after the Battle of Cold Harbor, workers collect remains of soldiers killed in action

THE OVERLAND CAMPAIGN

4 MAY – 24 JUNE 1864
NORTHERN AND CENTRAL VIRGINIA

Appointed to command all Union armies in the field in the spring of 1864, General Ulysses S Grant embarks on a campaign of maneuver and attrition against General Robert E Lee and the Confederate Army of Northern Virginia. Although the Union suffers tremendous casualties at the Battles of the Wilderness, Spotsylvania, and Cold Harbor, the Confederates lose thousands of casualties as well. However, Lee's losses are irreplaceable. Grant exploits his adversary's dwindling resources and ultimately threatens the city of Petersburg, a vital rail link to the South. A ten-month siege ensues, and eventually leads to Union victory in the Civil War.

FALL OF RICHMOND

3 APRIL 1865
RICHMOND, VIRGINIA

Union General Ulysses S Grant's final offensive against Petersburg leads to victory at the Battle of Five Forks, and General Robert E Lee's defensive lines collapse. Union troops sever the rail arteries from Petersburg and Richmond to the South, which were vital to the resupply of the Confederate capital. The city can no longer be defended, and the government of President Jefferson Davis flees by rail toward the city of Danville, Virginia. The remnants of the defending force evacuate as well. Union troops enter the city and begin restoring order, fighting raging fires. President Abraham Lincoln visits Richmond the following day.

4 MAY 1864

FALL OF ATLANTA
2 SEPTEMBER 1864
ATLANTA, GEORGIA

SHERMAN'S MARCH TO THE SEA

15 NOVEMBER – 21 DECEMBER 1864
ATLANTA TO SAVANNAH, GEORGIA

Utilizing the city of Chattanooga, Tennessee, General William T Sherman, commander of the Union armies in the West, concludes the costly Atlanta campaign with the fall of the city on 2 September 1864. Two months later, he begins the famous March to the Sea, cutting a wide swath of destruction through the countryside and ending with the capture of the port of Savannah, Georgia, in December. He then turns northward into the Carolinas in pursuit of Confederate General Joseph Johnston's Army of Tennessee.

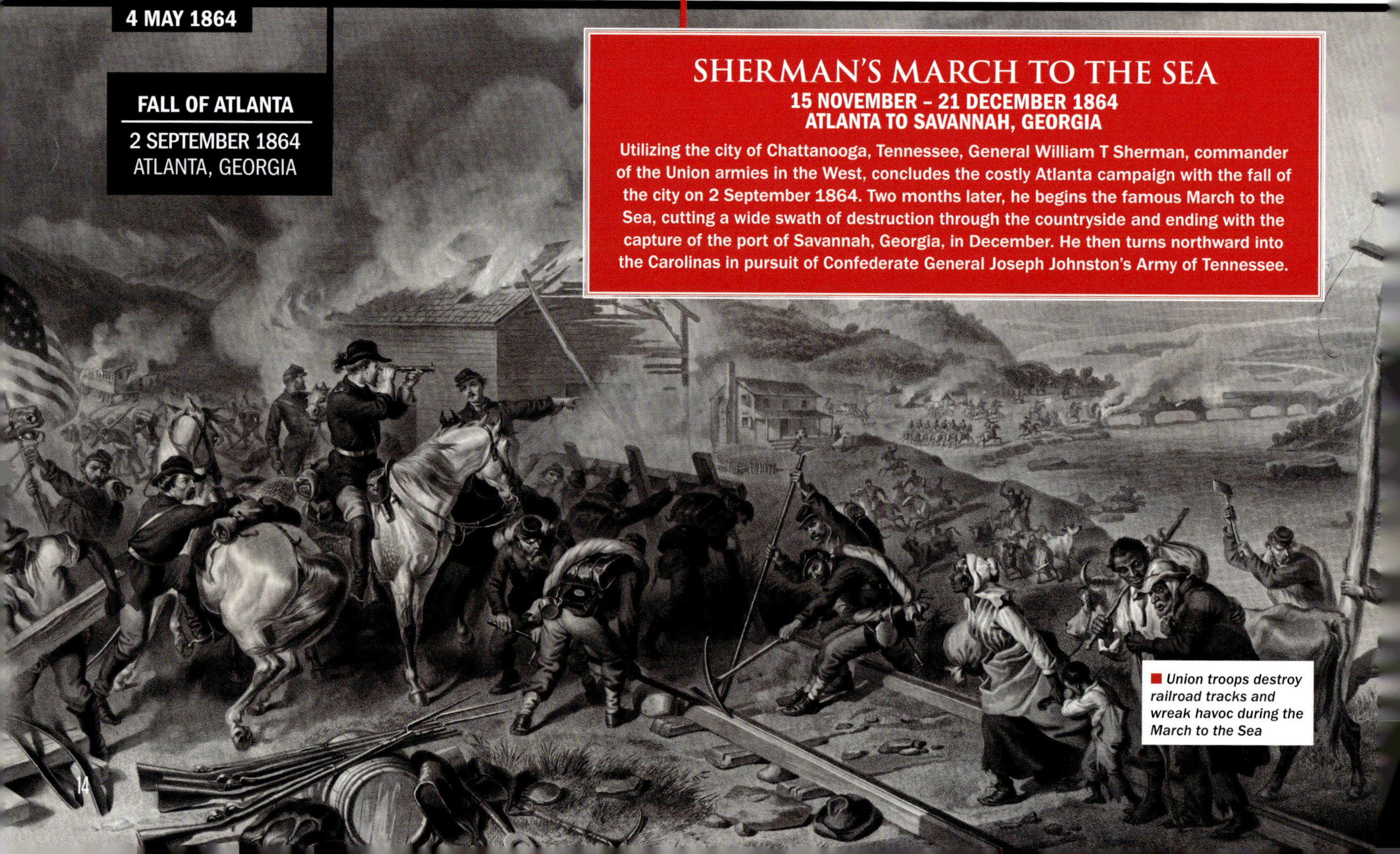

Union troops destroy railroad tracks and wreak havoc during the March to the Sea

Union soldiers inspect some of the devastation in Richmond after the city is occupied

John Wilkes Booth fires the fatal shot at President Lincoln on 14 April 1865

ASSASSINATION OF PRESIDENT LINCOLN

14-15 APRIL 1865
WASHINGTON, DC

While attending a performance of the play *Our American Cousin* at Ford's Theater in Washington, DC, President Abraham Lincoln is shot in the head by disgruntled actor John Wilkes Booth, a Southern sympathizer. Lincoln is carried to a boarding house across the street, where he dies at 7.22 the following morning. A young officer who accompanies the president and First Lady Mary Todd Lincoln is slashed with a knife as Booth jumps from the presidential box to the stage and makes his escape, setting off a manhunt that ends in his death days later. Conspirators also attempt to assassinate other government officials.

JOHNSTON SURRENDERS TO SHERMAN

26 APRIL 1865
BENNETT PLACE, NORTH CAROLINA

LINCOLN CONSPIRATORS HANGED

7 JULY 1865
WASHINGTON, DC

ANDERSONVILLE PRISON COMMANDANT HENRY WIRZ HANGED

10 NOVEMBER 1865
WASHINGTON, DC

20 AUG 1866

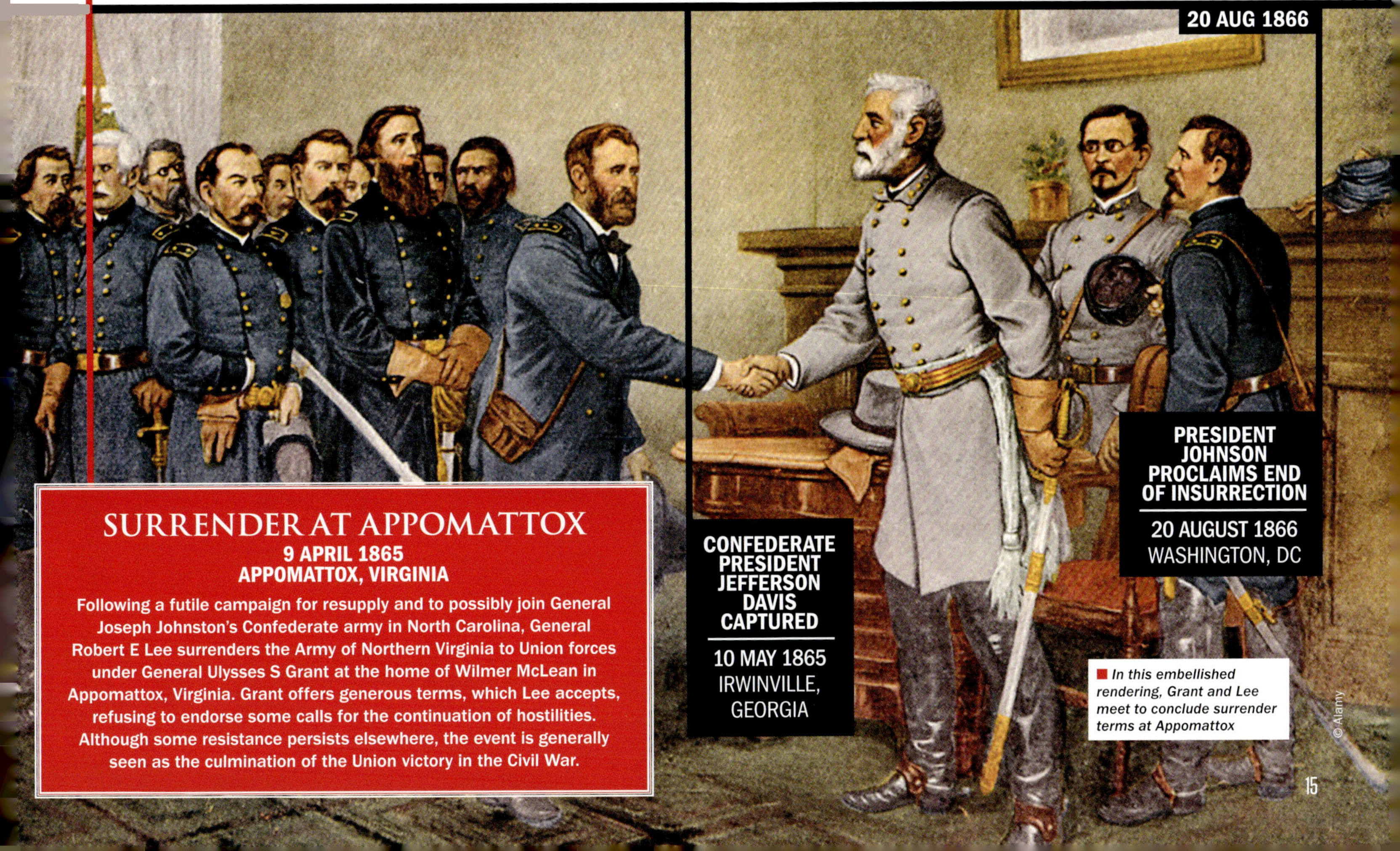

SURRENDER AT APPOMATTOX

9 APRIL 1865
APPOMATTOX, VIRGINIA

Following a futile campaign for resupply and to possibly join General Joseph Johnston's Confederate army in North Carolina, General Robert E Lee surrenders the Army of Northern Virginia to Union forces under General Ulysses S Grant at the home of Wilmer McLean in Appomattox, Virginia. Grant offers generous terms, which Lee accepts, refusing to endorse some calls for the continuation of hostilities. Although some resistance persists elsewhere, the event is generally seen as the culmination of the Union victory in the Civil War.

CONFEDERATE PRESIDENT JEFFERSON DAVIS CAPTURED

10 MAY 1865
IRWINVILLE, GEORGIA

PRESIDENT JOHNSON PROCLAIMS END OF INSURRECTION

20 AUGUST 1866
WASHINGTON, DC

In this embellished rendering, Grant and Lee meet to conclude surrender terms at Appomattox

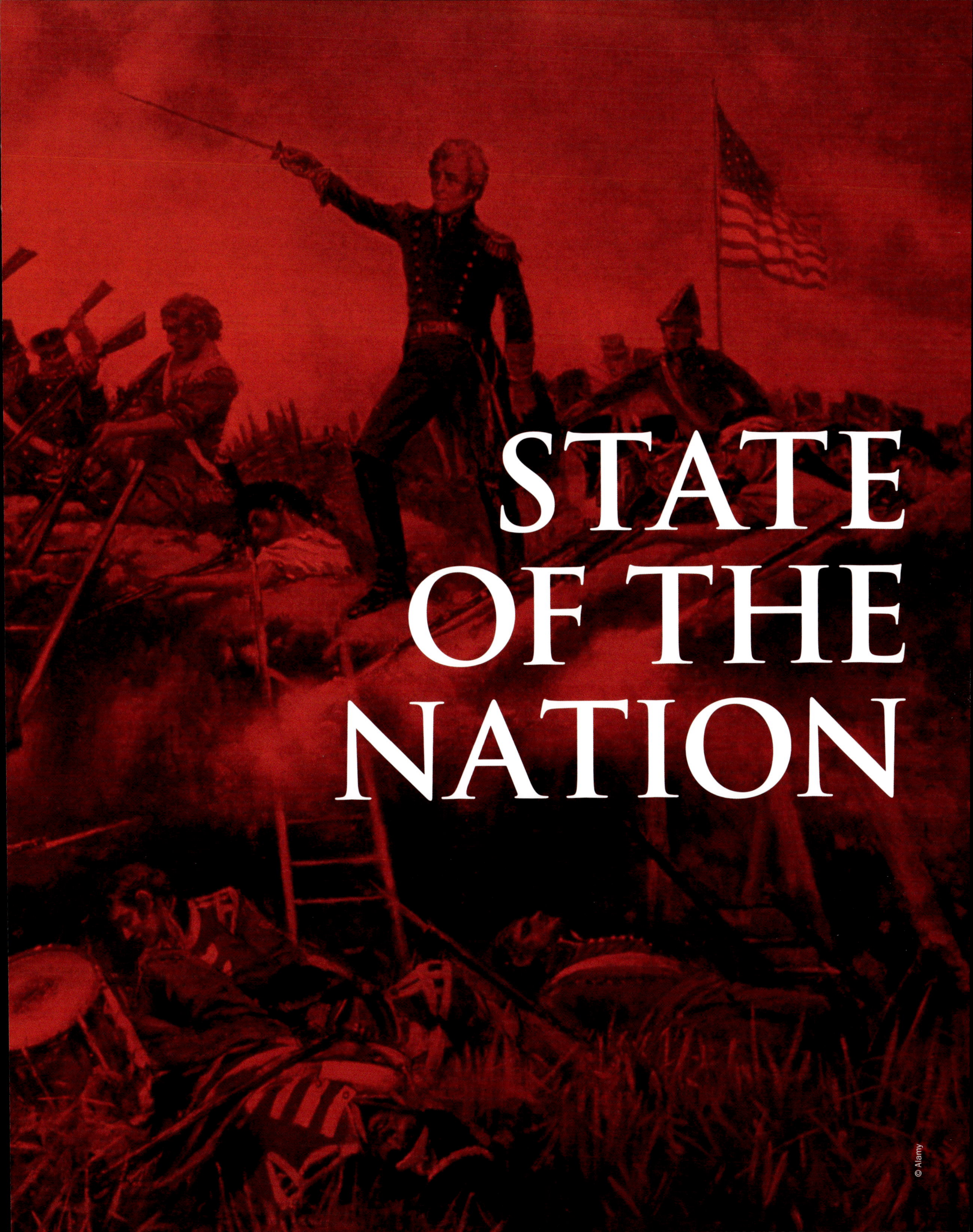

STATE OF THE NATION

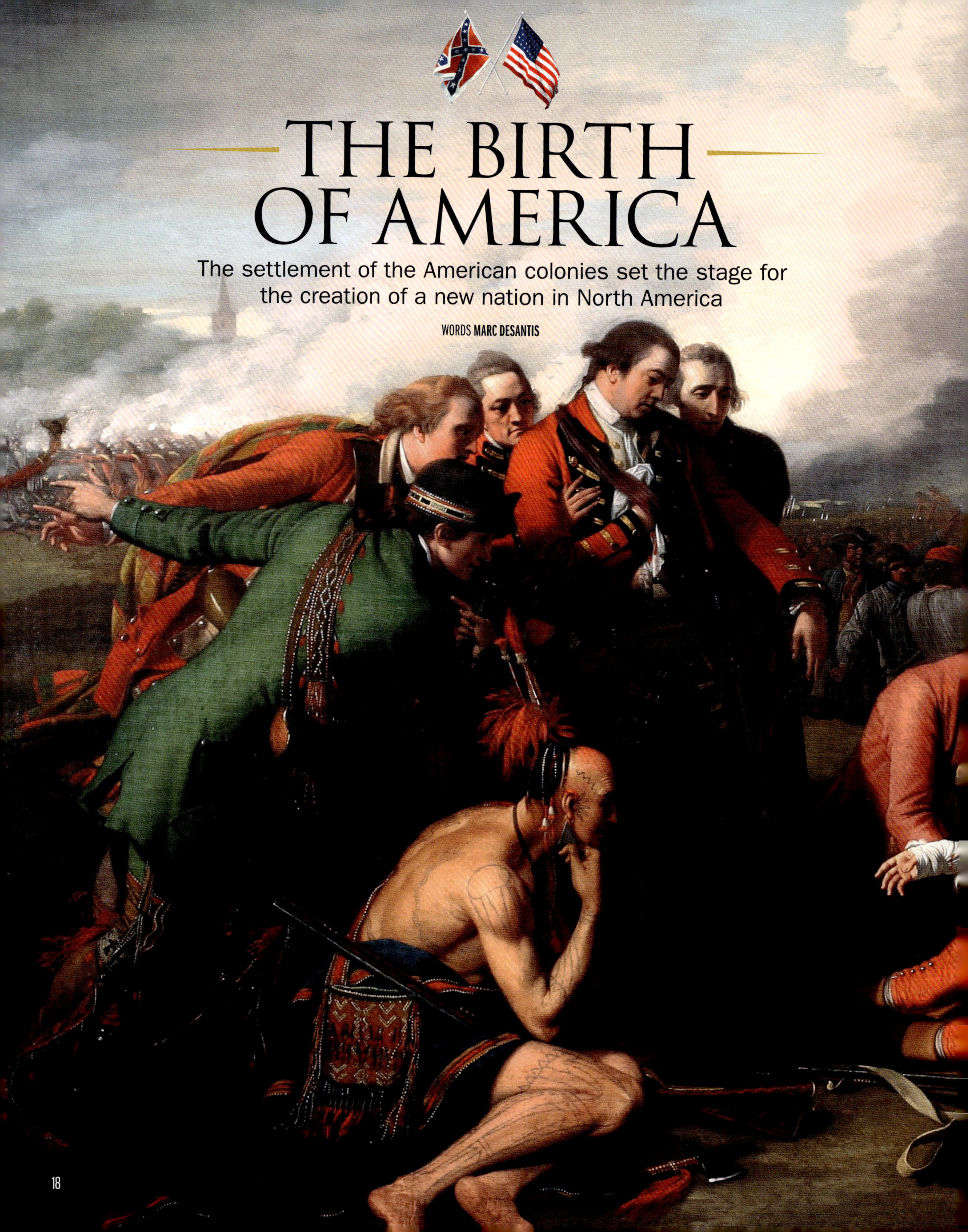

THE BIRTH OF AMERICA

The settlement of the American colonies set the stage for the creation of a new nation in North America

WORDS **MARC DESANTIS**

Below: *General James Wolfe died in the victorious Battle of the Plains of Abraham outside of Quebec City during the French and Indian War*

The first successful British settlement in the New World was at Jamestown, Virginia, founded in 1607. This was followed a few years later by the Pilgrim settlement at Plymouth, Massachusetts, in 1620. British North America would become peopled by a diverse group of settlers drawn from around the British Isles and beyond. In New England, the Puritans predominated, while in Virginia's Tidewater country, society was dominated by the cavalier aristocracy coming from southern England.

The Thirteen Colonies were mostly peopled in a series of four great migrations from different parts of Britain and Ireland. The earliest of the big waves was that of the Puritans, originating mainly in East Anglia in the first half of the 17th century. The next wave was that of Royalists of southern England who sailed to Virginia, accompanied by their servants, between 1642 and 1675. Another large migration left from the North Midlands, making their way to the Delaware Valley between the last quarter of the 17th century and the first quarter of the 18th. The last of the four major migrations was that out of northern Britain and northern Ireland to the colonial backcountry Appalachia that took place throughout the 18th century.

The majority of all these migrants were English in language and Protestant in religion. There were also many differences between them in customs, dialects, religious views, and outlook, and these often had their roots in the specific regions of Britain from which they originally hailed. Each of these four groups brought with them their varied but staunch traditions of English liberty, and these would set them in conflict with the Crown when these ancient rights were ignored.

Apart from these four major groups the American colonies also received smaller migrations. Maryland was settled by British Catholics, while Quakers founded Pennsylvania. New York had a large population of Dutch inhabitants from when it was a Dutch colony known as New Amsterdam. The North Carolina backcountry saw a huge influx of Scottish Highlanders starting in the early 18th century. Despite the troubles that the Highlanders had with the royal government in their own country, in America, when the Revolution came, they would by and large stay loyal to the Crown. Germans could be found in significant numbers in various colonies.

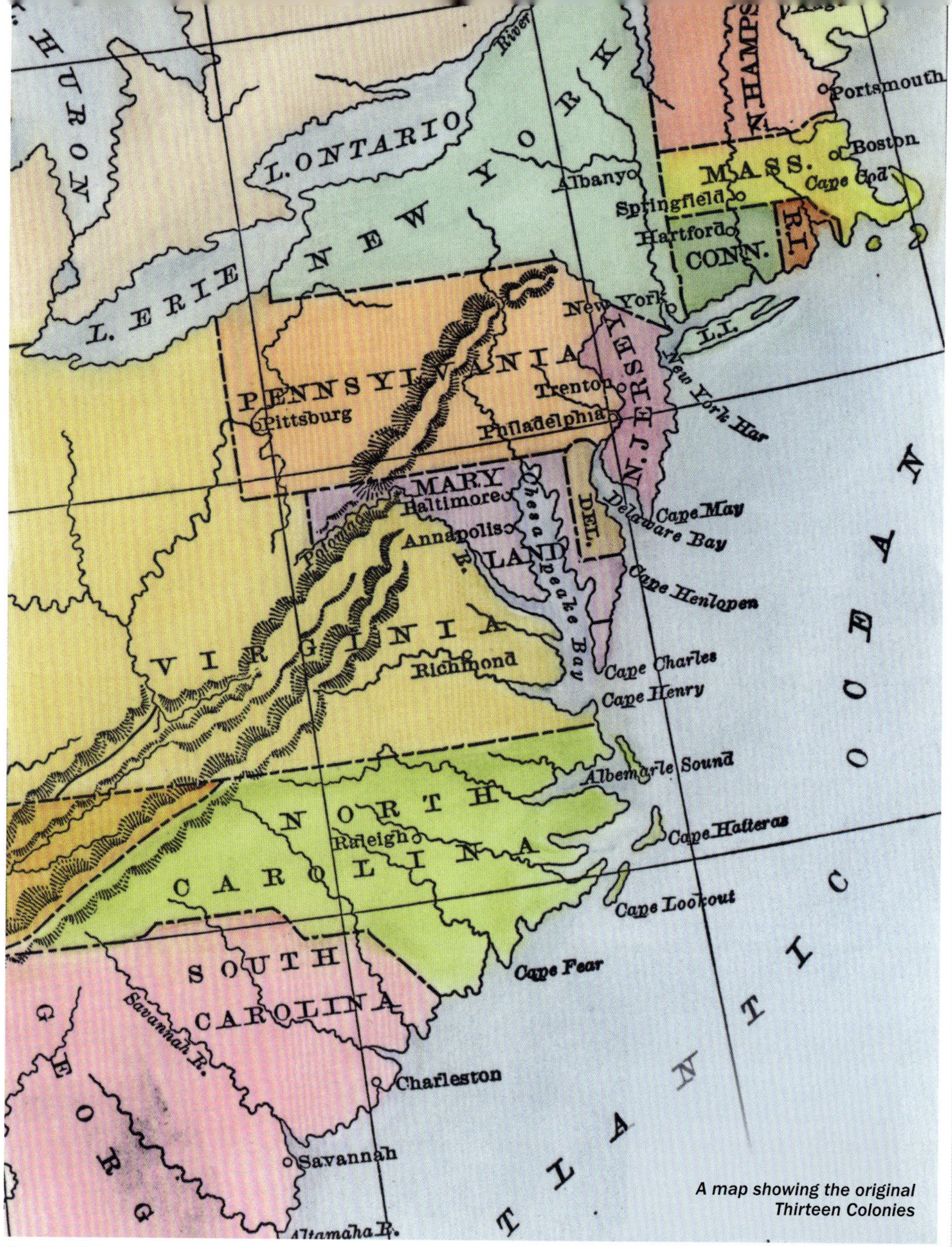

A map showing the original Thirteen Colonies

Trouble in the colonies

The American colonies were drawn into the great power struggles between Britain and her European rivals. Chief among these was the French and Indian War of 1756-63, as the Seven Years' War was known in America. It was ironic then that Britain's overwhelming victory in the French and Indian War, which saw the French ejected from North America, was the beginning of the end for its relatively untroubled reign over its American colonies. An extensive British army had to be stationed permanently in the colonies for their defense, but the presence of Redcoats dismayed many of the colonists that they were there ostensibly to protect. Some of these soldiers were quartered in civilian homes, an unwelcome and costly burden on the colonists.

The Marquis de Montcalm was the French general at the Battle of the Plains of Abraham, and like his opposite number, General Wolfe, was also killed in the battle

"THE ANTAGONISM BETWEEN DISGRUNTLED AMERICANS AND AN UNCOMPREHENDING ROYAL GOVERNMENT ONLY GREW"

The British landing outside Quebec City, just before the Battle of the Plains of Abraham

Further, a serious uprising of Native American tribes in 1760 had seen many settlers forced back from the frontier and this had also shaken British confidence. To placate the Native Americans, King George III decreed that no further settlement would be allowed beyond the Appalachian Mountains. This proclamation hemmed in the white settlers closer to the coast, the reasoning being that there thus would be less friction with the Native Americans. However, many colonists were deeply unhappy with this restriction.

Other actions by Parliament in London also angered the American colonists. The Stamp Act of 1765 placed a tax on all official documents that had to be paid to have them legally recognized. This new imposition, justified as a means to make the colonists pay for their own defense, was met by howls of protest by the Americans. For many colonists, this represented taxation without representation, which meant that they had no say in the government that presumed to tax them. The antagonism between disgruntled Americans and an uncomprehending royal government only grew. In Boston in March 1770, a force of Redcoats shot and killed four Americans in what became known as the Boston Massacre, highlighting the emotional distance that had begun to stretch between Britain and its American subjects.

British troops open fire on a group of protestors in Boston in 1770, killing four

Image: Alamy, Getty

Above: *Boston citizens, some disguised as Native Americans, dump British tea into the city's harbor*

From rebellion to revolution

A hugely unpopular tax on tea led to the dumping, in protest, of East India Company tea chests into Boston Harbor in December 1773 by colonists dressed as Native Americans. The Quebec Act of 1774 gave legal equality to French Catholics in Canada and granted tolerance to the Roman Catholic religion. The Act also expanded the territory of Quebec, which now encompassed lands to the west of the colonies that the colonists were forbidden to settle in. These awards infuriated the extremely anti-Catholic American colonists, who feared a surge of 'popery' on the North American continent.

Also in 1774, in retaliation for the destruction of the tea in the 'Tea Party' in Boston, Parliament leveled the Coercive Acts against Massachusetts as punishment, which shut down Boston's port to trade. The other colonies, though very different in situation towards the Mother Country, rallied around the stricken New England colony. Agitation against royal rule had been growing steadily for several years, with many colonists forming Committees of Correspondence to defend colonial rights. The Coercive Acts did nothing to quell the rebellious spirit; instead it only added fuel to the thirst for independence. The First Continental Congress convened in Philadelphia in September 1774, in which the colonies' representatives agreed to a trade embargo on imports from Britain.

"A HUGELY UNPOPULAR TAX ON TEA LED TO THE DUMPING OF EAST INDIA COMPANY TEA CHESTS INTO BOSTON HARBOR"

No resolution was to be had between King George III and his unhappy American subjects. The next year, on 19 April 1775, the first shots of the American Revolution were fired at Lexington and Concord in Massachusetts.

A Second Continental Congress met again in Philadelphia in May. Among other notable acts, in June 1775 it appointed George Washington as the commander of the Continental Army tasked with the defense of 'American liberty'. The war for America had begun, and the colonies were firmly on the road to independence. ★

Founded in 1607, Jamestown was the first successful British settlement in the Americas

The French and Indian War

BRITAIN EXPELLED THE FRENCH FROM NORTH AMERICA AND BECAME THE DOMINANT EUROPEAN POWER ON THE CONTINENT

In America, the Seven Years' War was known as the French and Indian War. The bone of contention in North America was over the western lands of the interior, to which both Britain and France had laid claim. English settlers had penetrated into the Ohio Valley and had even reached the Mississippi River by the middle of the 18th century.

To safeguard the route between French Canada and Louisiana, far to the south on the Gulf of Mexico, the French constructed several forts, at Presque Isle, Rouillé, Duquesne and Le Boeuf. These were meant to stop the British going any further west. Troops from colonial Virginia, commanded by future American president George Washington, were despatched to build Fort Necessity near to Fort Duquesne in 1754, but this operation miscarried badly and Washington and his men capitulated to the French. The war revolved very much around the possession of forts that controlled the depths of the unsettled wilderness. In 1755, British general Edward Braddock made an assault against Fort Duquesne, but was defeated at the Battle of the Monongahela River on 9 July 1755. Fighting in northern New York saw the capture of forts by the French at Oswego in 1756 and William Henry in 1757. Louisbourg fell to the British in July 1758. Fort Duquesne followed in November 1758, and Ticonderoga and Niagara in July the following year.

On 13 September 1759, a British attack was made against Quebec. At the Battle of the Plains of Abraham outside the city, a British army under the command of General James Wolfe defeated a French force under General Louis-Joseph de Montcalm. All of Canada fell soon after, and under the Treaty of Paris of 1763, Britain's control was formally recognized, along with Florida and formerly French possessions to the east of the Mississippi River. Britain was now the dominant European power in North America.

"WASHINGTON AND HIS MEN CAPITULATED TO THE FRENCH AT THE BATTLE OF FORT DUQUESNE"

In 1754, a young George Washington led Virginia colonial troops westward to demand that the French evacuate lands claimed by Virginia

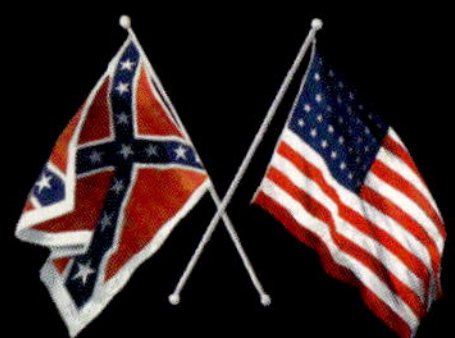

AMERICA WINS ITS INDEPENDENCE

It had won its nationhood after a long and costly war, but the problem of slavery was unresolved, leaving the North at loggerheads with the South

WORDS **MARC DESANTIS**

The American Revolution was the outcome of a long process of estrangement between Britain and her American colonists. To many Americans, the crux of the problem was King George III's failure to respect their rights as Englishmen. The high-handed actions of the royal ministers, especially the imposition of taxes on the colonists in contravention of traditional rights – taxation without representation – were extremely annoying.

From the perspective of the Crown, as well as many other Britons besides, the royal demand that colonists pay their share of the costs of their own defense was only fair and proper. Still, there was no sense in the 1760s and early 1770s that the bonds between Crown and subjects were irretrievably broken. Britain was the 'Mother Country', the ethnic wellspring of the greater part of the colonists.

Foremost among these were such men as Benjamin Franklin and George Washington. Franklin, the Philadelphia polymath and inventor, would try to make royal ministers understand the American viewpoint as the colonies slid towards open rebellion, but his efforts were in vain. George Washington, a wealthy Virginia planter, had served alongside British regulars against the French some two decades before the outbreak of the Revolution. He had even

George Washington was the commanding general of the Continental Army during the American Revolution and subsequently became the first president of the United States

Image: Alamy

Redoubt No 10 is captured by American troops at the Battle of Yorktown, 1781

hoped for a commission in the British Army, but as a mere colonial, he was denied one.

That such men found their way into the revolutionary camp throws into stark relief the frustration of many American colonists with the Crown. There had been much to fuel the growth of that antagonism. The taxes imposed by London caused American protests and this brought about harsh reactions of Britain. This caused even more American dismay and ever harsher responses by the government.

By 1775, after a series of provocations, including the shutdown of Boston's port to trade, the colonies had become a veritable powder keg waiting only for a spark to ignite a general war.

The War of Independence begins

That spark came on 19 April 1775 at Lexington, Massachusetts, when American militiamen traded shots with British regulars. A shooting war was now under way, but actual independence took some time to declare. In the meantime, George Washington was named commander-in-chief of the Continental Army, the fighting force raised by the First Continental Congress to defend the colonies from Britain.

Washington's presence and prior military experience made him a logical choice for the position, and he scored an early success at Boston when, after he surrounded the place with artillery dragged from Fort Ticonderoga hundreds of miles away, he trapped and forced the evacuation of British forces in the city.

Though Boston was now in Patriot (as the rebels called themselves) hands, New York City was captured by the British in July 1776. Washington was badly beaten at the Battle of Long Island and driven all the way to Pennsylvania where his bedraggled army spent a bitterly cold winter at Valley Forge. A daring crossing of the Delaware River on Christmas morning 1776 allowed Washington to surprise the Hessian garrison at Trenton, but the Patriot cause would also suffer its share of reverses. A bid to conquer Canada in late 1775 had failed miserably and Washington had himself been defeated at the Battle of White Plains in October 1776.

A bright spot arrived in the form of Baron von Steuben, a professional soldier who instructed the untrained American regulars in modern European military drill and tactics. Contrary to popular belief, the Americans would fight the war in the same way as the British, in long, thin lines in which soldiers in their first rank would discharge their weapons and then retire behind rear ranks to reload and wait to fire again.

Benjamin Franklin was one of the leading lights of the American Revolution, and served as the United States' wartime ambassador to France

The success at Trenton was followed by a victory at Princeton in January 1777. This would prove to be the crucial year of the war. The rebel colonists had struggled to gain recognition from other European powers but these had balked, giving the colonists little chance of success.

Saratoga

This all changed with the Saratoga campaign. The British plan formulated by General Sir John Burgoyne called for a three-pronged attack that would sever New England from the other colonies. He himself would lead an army south from Canada, seize Fort Ticonderoga, and then take Albany. At the same time, forces under Colonel Barry St Leger would move down the Mohawk Valley, while William Howe would march north to Albany in order to link up with Burgoyne.

The plan encountered problems from the moment Burgoyne began his southward trek. Movement through the northern New York wilderness was extremely difficult and the Loyalists in the region whom Burgoyne counted on to flock to his colors never materialized. Though he would capture Fort Ticonderoga in July 1777, St Leger's force was checked at the Battle of Oriskany that August. Howe, in the meantime, instead of moving north in support of Burgoyne, decided to move against Philadelphia. He fought Washington at Brandywine on 11 September and had the victory, but Washington retreated with his army still in fighting condition. Howe then took Philadelphia on 26 September, and then defeated Washington once more at Germantown on 4 October. By this time, Burgoyne was already in deep trouble. General Sir Henry Clinton, in command at New York City in Howe's place, advanced up the Hudson River but did little more than take two forts.

After an extremely slow march, Burgoyne had encountered the Americans in a strong position at Bemis Heights under General Horatio Gates in the vicinity of Saratoga, New York. At the Battle of Freeman's Farm on 19 September, Burgoyne held the field, but the Americans had inflicted heavy losses on him. With supplies running low, Burgoyne next assaulted the entrenched Americans on Bemis Heights on 7 October and was rebuffed. Soon the Americans had forced the surrender of the whole of Burgoyne's army.

The Battle of Saratoga, as the twin battles became known, convinced the French that the American cause stood a chance, and a formal alliance was concluded in 1778. The intervention of France, as well as Spain, changed the war for Britain. It was now not only her North American colonies at risk, but also the extremely valuable sugar islands of the Caribbean too.

The Battle of New Orleans in 1815, a major American victory, was fought only after the peace treaty ending the war had been signed in Europe

The United States Constitution is signed in Philadelphia, 17 September 1787

"CONTRARY TO POPULAR BELIEF, THE AMERICANS WOULD FIGHT THE WAR IN THE SAME WAY AS THE BRITISH"

Image: Alamy, Getty

General John Burgoyne surrenders British forces after the Battle of Saratoga, 1777. The battle opened the way for a Patriot alliance with France

The War in the South

In response, the British devised the 'Southern strategy' that would focus their military efforts on the Southern colonies where, it was thought, there were better prospects for victory. Savannah, Georgia, was captured in 1778 and Charleston, South Carolina, was taken in 1780, via amphibious attacks, but the Loyalist upswell the British expected in the South proved a mirage. Instead, the South became a battleground between the bitterly divided Patriots and Loyalists, with their conflict bearing many of the characteristics of a civil war.

The over-confident General John Burgoyne met defeat at the Battle of Saratoga

Despite a victory at Camden in August 1780 and at Guilford Courthouse in March 1781, Lord Cornwallis, the commander of British forces in the South, could make no real headway in South Carolina, and then moved back north to try to achieve victory in Virginia. This proved just as illusory as in other parts of the South. Cornwallis found himself besieged at Yorktown, Virginia, with the Royal Navy, defeated at the Battle of the Chesapeake by a French fleet, unable to sail to his rescue.

Washington's men and their French allies constructed extensive siegeworks around Yorktown, and Cornwallis, with no avenue of escape, surrendered his army on 19 October 1781. Peace between the United States and Britain was formally concluded with the Treaty of Paris in 1783.

Postwar America

Internally, the United States suffered from political weakness. The Articles of Confederation were considered insufficient for the formation of a strong central government, which was thought a prerequisite of national power. In 1787, delegates from the various states met in Philadelphia to hold a Constitutional Convention to draft a new charter for the country. The new United States Constitution that resulted created a stronger national government, with three branches – legislative, executive and judicial – that is still in effect today. The first president of the country under the new constitution was none other than George Washington himself.

There were also still serious challenges from abroad. The US was a small nation among the powers of the world. Despite recognizing the United States as a free and sovereign nation in the 1783 Treaty of Paris that ended the War of Independence, Britain had difficulty truly accepting that it had lost its American colonies for good. It therefore also had trouble viewing the Americans as no longer being British subjects. During the Napoleonic Wars, British naval actions, such as the stopping of United States merchant ships on the high seas and the forcible impressment of their sailors into the Royal Navy, outraged Americans. The Royal Navy was beset by a crushing need for bodies to man their warships in the wars with France, and was often not too particular about grabbing Americans to crew them. One of the most egregious incidents occurred in 1807 when HMS Leopard fired on USS Chesapeake.

Americans were further angered by the British blockade of Europe, which was designed to strangle the Napoleon-dominated European economy. Americans championed the rights of neutral nations to trade with whomever they would. British economic measures spurred the United States to declare war on Britain, and the resulting War of 1812 was for the

Americans as much a matter of national pride and sovereignty. It would probably not have occurred at all if the British had been more considerate of American feelings.

The War of 1812

The war was a distraction for Britain while it was consumed with the struggle against Napoleon. With Napoleon's exile to Elba in 1814, Britain was able to devote more resources to the war, and the US reeled when Washington, DC, was burned by British troops. Yet neither side was able to gain the upper hand in the war, and both sides were willing to make peace by the end of 1814. Ironically, the largest battle of the war, the Battle of New Orleans, an American victory, was fought after peace had been signed at Ghent but before news could travel across the Atlantic Ocean to the soldiers on the front lines.

Though the war had scant effect on the map of North America, as each side retained what it held prior to its start, the United States came out of the conflict with the sense that it had won its independence from Britain for a second time. It was now ready to embark upon the great westward expansion that would eventually carry the American flag all the way to the Pacific Ocean. Yet slavery would also expand westward into the newly won territories, and the problem of slavery would haunt the nation for decades until the fiery outbreak of the Civil War in April 1861. ★

King George III, the last British king of America

America's First Civil War

DURING THE AMERICAN REVOLUTION, IN A FORESHADOWING OF THE CIVIL WAR, PATRIOTS AND LOYALISTS FOUGHT BITTERLY OVER THE QUESTION OF REMAINING PART OF THE BRITISH EMPIRE

Though it is seldom remarked upon today, the American Revolution was as much a civil war between Americans as it was a war between Americans and the British. Though Patriots, those who supported the cause of independence, outnumbered those who wished to remain part of the British Empire, known variously as Loyalists and Tories, neither represented a majority among the colonial populace, of which a substantial number held ambivalent feelings towards both independence and the Crown.

The Patriots, however, controlled the much larger portion of the geographic extent of the country. There were few places where Loyalists were in the majority. One such area was New York City. After its capture in mid-1776, New York became a haven for Loyalists fleeing violence and oppression. Like the American Civil War nearly a century later, the War of Independence set brother against brother, and fathers against sons. Though Benjamin Franklin would be one of the leading Revolutionary figures, his son, William, remained staunchly loyal to King George III. Father and son would be estranged forever.

The Americans who remained loyal to their king served under British colors in large numbers. At the Battle of Kings Mountain in 1780, every participant on either side, was an American, be he Patriot or Loyalist, but for the single exception of the British commander of the Loyalist force. The Patriots won the day, the battle being a microcosm of the larger conflict between Americans with irreconcilable political views.

Despite their valor, the Loyalists were unable to sway the war in favor of the Crown. Their numbers were too few relative to the rest of the American population, and the desire for independence burned too fiercely in the hearts of their countrymen to turn them back to allegiance to the king. Many Loyalists went into exile in other parts of the British Empire after the war.

William Franklin, the son of Patriot leader Benjamin Franklin, defied his father and remained loyal to the Crown during the American Revolution

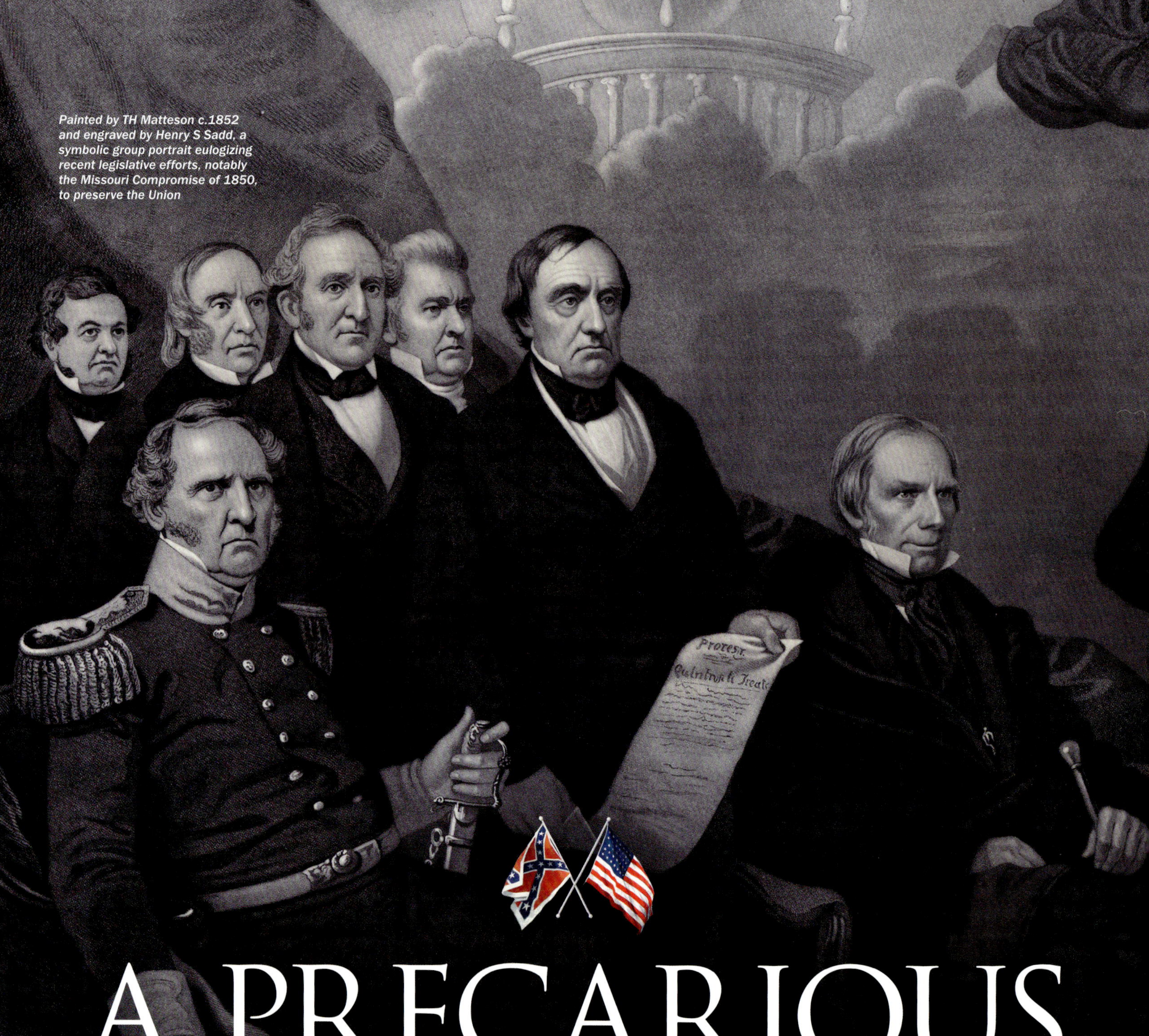
Painted by TH Matteson c.1852 and engraved by Henry S Sadd, a symbolic group portrait eulogizing recent legislative efforts, notably the Missouri Compromise of 1850, to preserve the Union

A PRECARIOUS UNION

A mingling of ideological difference, radical social upheaval, and westward expansion steered a nation towards the 19th century's bloodiest war

WORDS **WILL LAWRENCE**

Image: Getty

At the time of the Louisiana Purchase in 1803, the United States was granted little regard among the European powerhouses. Its population was akin to Ireland's. And yet, a little over two generations later, by 1860, it had surpassed Great Britain to become the third most populous nation in the Western world (behind Russia and France) with almost 32 million inhabitants. Four million of those were slaves.

With the population boom came a shifting economy, a surge in industrialization and manufacturing, fueled by the exploitation of vast coal reserves and the nation's sprawling forests. The great rivers of New England, Pennsylvania, and New York were harnessed to turn water wheels, while improvements in transportation – the laying of all-weather roads, the building of canal networks, and, crucially, the coming of the railroad – brought the vast country closer together.

The great cities boomed. Chicago, for example, saw its population rise from 5,000 in 1840 to 110,000 by 1860. An ever-growing number of workers moved from the fields to the cities, surrendering subsistence farming in a bid to earn a working wage.

A North-South divide

As the century progressed, an economic geography emerged with the North becoming increasingly industrialized in contrast to the South. By 1850 the proportion of farmworkers in the North had fallen below 40 percent; in the South it remained above 80 percent. If a line were drawn between St Louis in Missouri, Louisville in Kentucky, and Baltimore in Maryland, every industrial center would have stood to the north.

Southern cities were small compared to their Northern counterparts. New Orleans was four times larger than any other Southern city, and Montgomery, Alabama, the first Confederate capital, had only 36,000 people at a time when St Louis and Cincinnati each had more than 160,000. At secession, the combined population of Richmond and Petersburg was less than 60,000, and there were no large towns at all between the lower Mississippi and the Atlantic seaboard.

In the face of this stark divide, the South made a virtue of its rural life, believing it to be closer in keeping to the ideals of the Founding Fathers than the urban life of the North. Southern life did indeed mirror that of the preceding century, with the vast majority living as subsistence farmers, growing corn and raising pigs even as Northerners were already flooding to the cities.

As the North's economy outstripped the South's, so too did its literacy rates, further widening the gulf. New England, for example, boasted 95 percent literacy rates, compared to an average of just 20 percent in the South. Three-quarters of New England's children attended schools. In the South it was no more than a third.

The most striking difference between North and South in the first half of the 19th century was, of course, slavery,

Above: The Nullification Crisis sought to give states the powers to void measures passed by Congress

Left: These slaves belonged to James Hopkinson of South Carolina, a major plantation owner with more than 50 slaves

"AS THE CENTURY PROGRESSED, AN ECONOMIC GEOGRAPHY EMERGED WITH THE NORTH BECOMING INCREASINGLY INDUSTRIALIZED IN CONTRAST TO THE SOUTH"

which permeated all aspects of Southern economic and social life, though the great plantations were fewer than sentimental remembrance might declare. Of a total population in the South of eight million, fewer than 50,000 were considered planters, or property holders owning more than 20 slaves. Fewer than 3,000 planters owned more than 100 slaves and only 11 men, it is said, held more than 500 slaves.

Most Southern farms had just a handful of slaves or none at all, hence the ubiquity of the phrase among Confederate soldiers in the ensuing fight that they were engaged in "a rich man's war but a poor man's fight".

Slave owners, however, dominated Southern politics and while many members of the lower classes looked at the planters with resentment and envy, it was to such positions that most aspired. To climb the social ladder in the South required the acquisition of slaves and it was through the slave-manned cotton plantations that many Southerners earned their great fortunes.

This owed much to the invention of the cotton gin in 1793, a technological innovation that radically reduced the manpower required to separate cotton fibres from their seeds. It revolutionized the industry, which had prospered in the richer soils of the Southern states. Soaring demand from Europe led to massive exponential growth. In 1790, American cotton production stood at 3,000 bales per annum. By 1810 it had leapt to 178,000; by 1830 it stood at 732,000 and by 1860 it had grown to 4.5 million bales.

Uprising and rebellion

In certain areas – notably South Carolina and Alabama – slaves outnumbered whites, and any talk of emancipation filled the white population with dread. Surely, they thought, freedom for the slaves would release their savage energies. Southern fears became reality when in 1822, the freed slave Denmark Vesey, an urban artisan of Charleston, South Carolina, was thought to be planning an uprising comprising, said

American victory in the Mexican War of 1846-1847 helped edge the US towards civil war

some, up to 9,000 slaves. His 'conspiracy' was betrayed and 130 blacks were arrested, of whom 35 (including Vesey) were hanged.

Nine years later, in 1831, Nat Turner led his rebellion, murdering almost 100 whites, and though these incidents were, in the words of one historian, "trifling affairs", they lived long in the Southern imagination and cast long shadows. It was in the interest of all Southerners to keep the black population shackled, or so it was claimed.

In truth, an event of even wider significance unfolded in the aftermath of Turner's uprising. This was the beginning of the Nullification Crisis precipitated by South Carolina in 1832, which sought to give the state's legislature the powers to nullify measures passed by Congress if they deemed them harmful to the interests of their state. The crisis was averted but it set the stage for the tussle between Unionism and state's rights. In many ways it became a rehearsal for the secession crisis of 1860-61. Charleston, the state's primary urban center, became a cradle of secession. It perhaps comes as no surprise to consider that it was in Charleston that the first shots of the war were fired.

Indeed, it is important to note that separatism was a permanent topic of discussion during the first half of the 19th century; secessionism lurked perennially on the shoulder of federal governance. Any sense of national unity was tenuous. "The sinews of federal power were feeble," notes one historian, pointing to the fact that it was the state government that maintained law and order and which raised direct taxes.

Secession from the Union had, for example, raised its head during the Missouri Compromise of 1820, when the federal government debated the new state's entrance to the Union. The South wanted it admitted as a slave state, and the North only agreed if Maine was accepted as a free state, thereby maintaining the balance in Congress between slave and free states. Neither would have a majority vote. The balance endured. In 1847 there were 14 free and 14 slave states.

A volatile union

The Missouri Compromise's legacy, however, was negative, says one leading historian, fomenting, "Southern unity of action in the halls of Congress." This unity tightened during the 1840s, not least when Massachusetts and eight other states passed personal liberty laws under which state officials were forbidden to assist in the capture of fugitive slaves.

During the 1850s, the population boomed as more and more immigrants crossed the Atlantic to join the native-born in pushing into the farmlands of the Midwest. It was during this decade that slavery became a key point of political discussion. The South lobbied for slavery to become legal in the new territories – not only so slaveholders could profit from selling their chattels to the settlers, but also so that the political balance in the Senate, once new states joined the Union, would not swing against them.

The vast Southwest – comprising modern-day California, Texas, Arizona, Nevada, Utah, and New Mexico – soon saw a trickle of settlement, though the area was the sovereign property of Mexico.

The Dred Scott Case

THE SUPREME COURT'S RULING IN THIS LANDMARK CASE NUDGED THE CRISIS IN AMERICA TOWARDS ITS VIOLENT CONCLUSION

Scott was sold after the Supreme Court's 1857 ruling against his case and was freed immediately by his new owner, though he died the following year

Dred Scott, a slave owned by army surgeon John Emerson, launched a legal case that dragged on for 11 years and escalated into what one commentator describes as "the most notorious cause célèbre in American constitutional history." In 1846 Scott sued for his freedom on the grounds that his master had removed him for several years to military bases in the free state of Illinois and the Wisconsin Territory before returning him to the slave state of Missouri.

The case was lost and won on several occasions, leading to claims that it is the most overturned case in America's legal history, before it landed with the Supreme Court in 1856. In March 1857 it was announced by the majority decision of six judges (five of whom were Southerners) that Scott had no case for, as a negro, he was not a citizen of the United States and thus had no recourse in a federal court.

The abolitionists, who had secretly sponsored his suit, were outraged. But the case had further repercussions, as the presiding judge went on to declare that the Missouri Compromise was unconstitutional as Congress had no rights to exclude slaves from any state as they were private property. Slavery was now a political hot potato and there was talk of secession from the Union among Northerners as well as Southerners. New England witnessed secessionist meetings across the state.

The Dred Scott case had placed the Supreme Court, the common guarantor of both North and South in the midst of sectional conflict. The bonds of Union strained further under the weight of the court's decision.

Trouble arose in 1836 when the American population of Texas rebelled. This eventually led to the Mexican War of 1846-1847, in which the US emerged victorious.

An immediate repercussion of America's victory was the opportunity for settlers to forge new states from the conquered territory, and even before the war's end, the anti-slavery congressman David Wilmot introduced a measure to outlaw slavery in all new territory. Southern politicians annulled the 'Wilmot Proviso' in the Senate, but the issue reappeared in 1850 when California petitioned to join the Union.

The Gold Rush in the West had seen a surge in the state's population and these predominantly Northern settlers were vehemently opposed to the legalization of slavery on soil they planned to work themselves. Eventually, California was admitted as a free state with New Mexico and Utah permitted to choose. Both voted for slavery though the institution never took hold. This became known as the 1850 Compromise, but it would leave a lasting, negative legacy on the increasingly volatile Union.

On the verge

The most malignant legacy of the Compromise was the inclusion of the Southern-backed Fugitive Slave Act, which granted slave owners federal backing to enter free states to reclaim runaway slaves. The abolitionists in the North were furious and many anti-slavery proponents, from the mild to the radical, objected. This in turn led to indignation from Southerners who, in their minds, were simply trying to reclaim their legal property. The 1852 publication of the anti-slavery novel *Uncle Tom's Cabin* in book form further fanned the flames of unrest in both North and South.

This rivalry began to coalesce and in 1854 Southern politicians challenged the Northern states over the issue of slavery, seeking repeal of the Missouri Compromise. This led to the Kansas-Nebraska Act, which admitted both states, with the former accepting slavery and the second refusing. This paved the way for growing conflict within what became known as Bloody Kansas.

Ideological differences hardened between North and South and in the words of a leading writer on the Civil War: "By 1860 most Southerners agreed that they had, in an incredibly short period of time, developed a distinct civilization, and were culturally different from other Americans." This sentiment was reinforced by the actions of the radical abolitionist John Brown in his attack on Harper's Ferry and the judgment on the Dred Scott case. As 1860 loomed, and presidential nominations were put forward, the South was sitting on a tinderbox of secessionist feeling. It would not take much to ignite the fires of rebellion and war. ★

Many Southerners felt that slaves could not be freed given their violent actions during Nat Turner's 1831 uprising

Abolitionist leader Harriet Tubman (left) helped found the 'Underground Railroad' for escaping slaves, which were targeted by the Fugitive Slave Act of 1850

Images: Getty

Abolitionist John Brown, who led a raid on a federal armory in Harpers Ferry, Virginia, is led to his execution

A LAND OF HOPE BUILT ON SUFFERING

For millions of people, the American Dream had a horrendous flip side: the living nightmare of slavery

WORDS **EDOARDO ALBERT**

Slavery looms large in the history of the United States. But there should be little surprise that slavery was practiced – first in the British colonies and then, after the War of Independence – in the new United States of America, for slavery has been a universal human institution, carried out throughout history and in pretty well every civilization. What is unusual about slavery in America was that it eventually became the great political, moral, and religious issue of its day, finally dragging the country into the bloodiest war in its history. In the end, America baptized itself in blood over a principle: that no man might own another.

The first African slaves were landed in the British colony of Virginia in 1619. They were brought there by Dutch traders who had captured a Spanish slave ship. However, the Spaniards had already baptized the Africans so, according to English common law, they were treated as indentured servants, a condition shared by many of the poor white colonists who could not afford to pay their own passage across the Atlantic. As indentured servants, they were bound to an employer for a fixed period, but after that time had expired they were entitled to their freedom. But over the next century the distinction between black and white, and the institution of slavery, was gradually put into law, with Massachusetts the first state to authorize slavery in law. In 1662, in response to a case where a mixed-race woman, Elizabeth Key Grinstead, had successfully won her freedom and that of her son on the grounds that she was a Christian and the daughter of an Englishman, Virginia changed its statutes so that children took their status from their mother, not their father. This meant that the child of a slave woman would be born into slavery and it also freed male white slave owners from the responsibility of raising children fathered on slave women.

Image: Alamy

NAT TURNER'S REBELLION

Virginian slave Nat Turner had learned to read and write when he was very young and had immersed himself in the Bible, seeing visions and hearing messages that convinced him that God had appointed to him a great mission. These visions had coalesced into the belief that, "I should arise and prepare myself, and slay my enemies with their own weapons."

He would lead a great slave uprising against the white masters. The signs from heaven throughout the year of 1831 had convinced him the time had come. Now, standing in front of a small group of men gathered in the woods of Southampton County, Turner told them what they had to do. This would be no gentle revolt but one born of decades of cruel treatment.

The first to die were Turner's owners. In the early hours of 22 August, the seven men made their way to the Travis farmstead. Turner had become the property of Joseph Travis when the widow of his previous owner had married Travis. Turner entered the house and let the other rebels in, before they filed silently into the room where Travis lay sleeping. Turner struck the first blow but it served only to wake Travis, who rose, yelling for his wife. Another slave killed Travis with an axe, before turning the weapon on Travis's wife, her nine-year-old son, and a farmworker.

Gathering men as they went, the rebels attacked other farmsteads, killing everyone they found, but soon the alarm was spread, church bells ringing through the district and the white militia arming itself. In two days, the rebels killed 60 men, women, and children, before the group was overwhelmed, although Turner managed to escape, hiding out in the woods for two months before he was finally discovered. He was tried on 5 November and executed on 11 November 1831, his body flayed and beheaded. The bloodiest slave rebellion in US history was over – but not forgotten.

On Sunday 30 October 1831, farmer Benjamin Phipps, armed with a loaded gun, spotted some out-of-place fence rails and discovered Nat Turner after he had eluded searchers for two months

Although slavery existed throughout the colonies, by the 18th century there was a significant difference in how slaves were employed, with those in the North usually working as servants, craftsmen, and laborers in cities, while those in the South largely worked the land, on crops such as tobacco and rice. For such labor-intensive work, Southern plantation owners invested heavily in slaves. However, voices were already being raised against slavery throughout the British Empire and the North American colonies. Individual colonies, and later states, would outlaw slavery outright during the United States' fledgling years of independence, but the transatlantic slave trade would not formally be prohibited until the passing of a federal act in 1807. Conditions for slaves in the British colonies were comparatively better than elsewhere in the New World, and the population of slaves expanded rapidly.

During the American War of Independence, both British Loyalists and American Patriots promised freedom to slaves who fought on their side, but despite the Revolutionary army being between one fifth and one quarter black, the new Constitution of the United States required free states to return escaped slaves to slave states. Already, the divide between the Northern 'free' and the Southern 'slave' states was deepening. By 1804, every Northern state had outlawed slavery, while the economy of the Southern states was becoming tied ever more closely to slavery, in particular following the invention of the cotton gin. Tobacco growing exhausts the soil but when Eli Whitney invented the cotton gin in 1793, making it much easier to remove the seeds from cotton fibre, the Southern states quickly moved to growing cotton to supply the rapidly growing demand for cotton from the newly mechanized textile industry in England. Slavery, which might have declined, was reinforced and although Congress outlawed the importation of African slaves in 1807, the domestic population expanded rapidly, reaching nearly four million by 1860.

Growing abolitionism

Slaves in the South were not allowed to learn to read and write. In order to control a population that amounted to a third of the populace, slave owners pursued a policy of creating a hierarchy among their slaves, with the more privileged house slaves lording it over agricultural workers. While slaves did marry, these marriages had no legal basis and slave owners could sell off children and split husbands from wives. Punishments for misbehavior were severe and when rebellions did occur, they were dealt with savagely.

In the face of what Southerners came to call their 'peculiar institution', a growing abolitionist movement spread in the Northern states. Quakers were prominent early opponents of slavery, and they formed the core of the first abolitionist society, the Society for the Relief of Free Negroes Unlawfully Held in Bondage, founded in 1775 and renamed the Pennsylvania Abolition Society in 1784. No less a figure than Benjamin Franklin became its president.

However, political power in Congress was evenly split between 'free' and 'slave' states, with 11 states in each camp. But as the United States spread westward, and new territories petitioned to be admitted to the union, the question of whether these new states would be 'free' or 'slave' states became ever more pressing. When Missouri asked to join the union as a slave state, a compromise was effected whereby Maine simultaneously became part of the United States as a free state, maintaining the uneasy balance. But the Missouri Compromise also stipulated that any future states north of the line of latitude at 36 degrees and 30 minutes would be free states, while those south of it would be slave states, extending slavery westwards with the same North/South divide.

A further effort at a solution was made in 1854 when the Kansas-Nebraska Act stipulated that whether new states should be free or slave should be decided by a popular vote. Many politicians, seeing this as an effort by the slavery-supporting Democratic Party to expand the 'peculiar institution', left the party to join the new anti-slavery party, the Republicans. When Kansas came to vote on whether it should be free or slave, many natives of Missouri came across the border to vote for slavery, skewing the results and leading to growing anger among Kansas abolitionists. The conflict grew increasingly nasty, with a rash of murders and lynchings committed by both sides, leading to the new state being given the nickname 'bleeding Kansas'.

Harpers Ferry

Some abolitionists became increasingly impatient at the slow pace of reform, chief among these being John Brown. He had come to see the conflict in apocalyptic terms, and slavery as so heinous a sin that it could only be redeemed by a great blood sacrifice. To that end he led an attack at the armory at Harpers Ferry in West Virginia with the aim of raising a general slave revolt. The attack failed, and Brown and most of his followers were either killed or

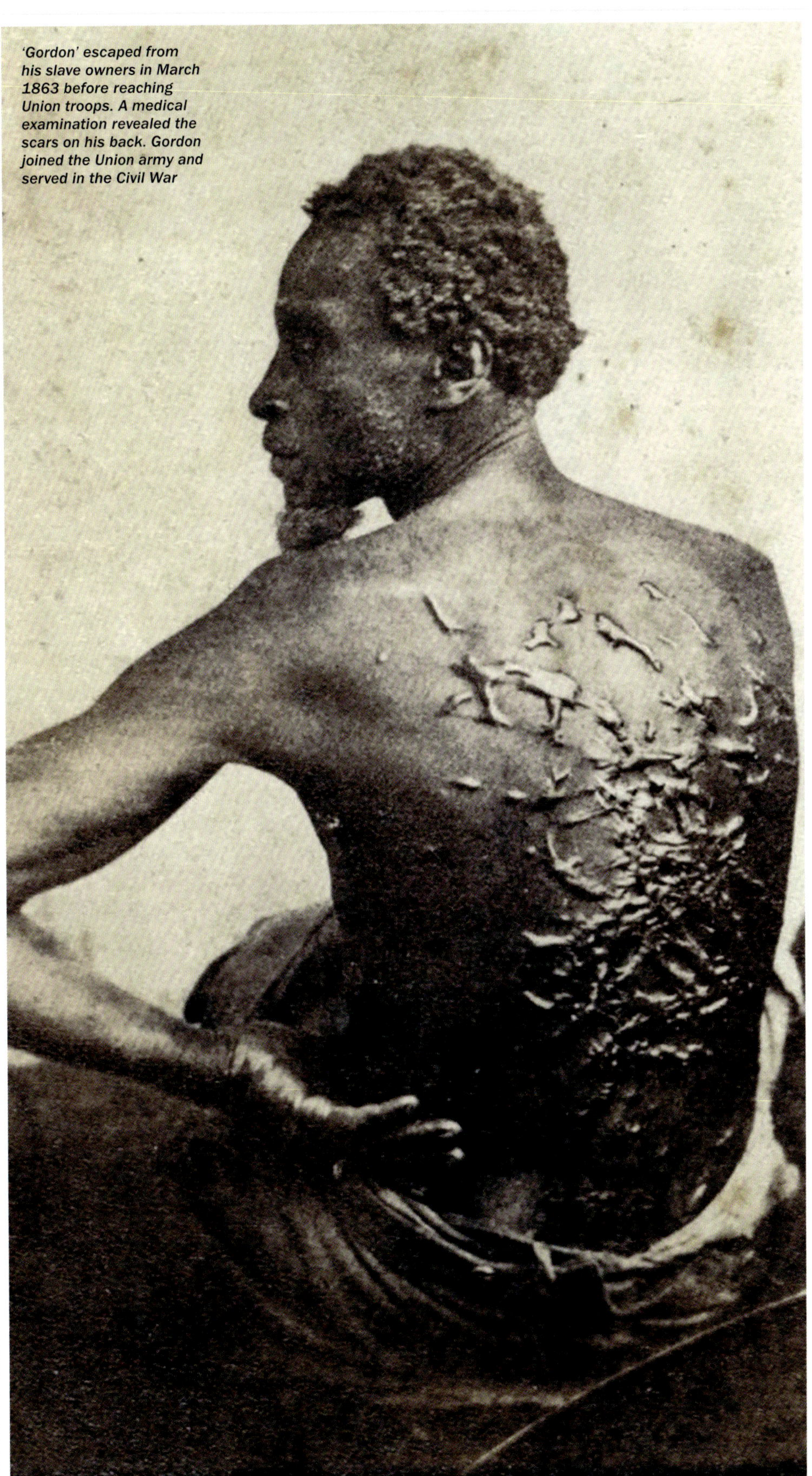

'Gordon' escaped from his slave owners in March 1863 before reaching Union troops. A medical examination revealed the scars on his back. Gordon joined the Union army and served in the Civil War

Image: Alamy, Getty

executed, but the incident further inflamed the tensions between free and slave states.

In 1852, Harriet Beecher Stowe published *Uncle Tom's Cabin*, an anti-slavery novel that became the bestseller of the 19th century, further convincing the Northern free states of the immorality of slavery. In response, outraged Southerners produced a stream of anti-Tom novels, attempting to show how slavery was a necessary institution for a race that was unable to look after itself.

Then, in 1857, the Supreme Court made its infamous Dred Scott decision, which declared that the descendants of Africans imported into the United States as a slave could not be American citizens and that the federal government had no power to outlaw slavery in the new territories being acquired with westward expansion. Thinking to end the political debate over slavery by making it a matter of settled law, the Supreme Court's decision had the opposite effect, enraging Northern opposition to slavery and splitting the Democratic Party into two. In 1860, Abraham Lincoln, of the new abolitionist political party, the Republicans, took advantage of the split among the Democrats and was elected president. In response, the Southern slave states withdrew from the Union, forming the Confederate States of America on 4 February 1861. There would be no more talking. The great moral question of America's founding would be answered in blood. ★

FRANK LESLIE'S ILLUSTRATED NEWSPAPER

NEW YORK, SATURDAY, JUNE 27, 1857.

A newspaper report on the Supreme Court's Dred Scott decision, which enraged abolitionists

Slaves planting sweet potatoes. The majority of Southern slaves worked the land

Image: Getty, Source: Wiki/Henry P. Moore

A clash between pro-slavery and anti-slavery groups in Fort Scott, Kansas, 1850s

THE ABOLITIONIST MOVEMENT IN AMERICA

The abolitionists grew from marginal lobbyists to a major voice for change, helping to spark Lincoln's famous Emancipation Proclamation

WORDS **WILL LAWRENCE**

Human bondage was anathema to many Americans in the early 19th century. After all, how could a country founded on the principle of liberty and the pursuit of happiness for all still allow the enslavement of several million men and women? Those who had fought the Revolutionary War had abolished slavery above the Mason-Dixon line, with the new states north of the Ohio River entering the Union without bondage – they were free states.

In spite of that sentiment and the act passed on 1 January 1808, which abolished the African slave trade in America, serious political debate about the continuation of slavery in the South remained scarce. In the early decades of the 19th century, many people in both the North and South remained convinced that slavery would, given time, just wither away.

A bill abolishing slavery in the British Empire, passed by the House of Commons in 1833, as well as the suppression of the international slave trade enforced by the powerful British Navy, appeared to support this view. However, this position was counter-balanced by a boom in cotton production that went on to transform the economy of the Southern states, making rich men of many planters.

These men and their politicians (often one and the same) soon found words to defend the perpetuation of slavery. As a response, many Northern liberals found words to condemn it. A polarization crept into American politics and the world of letters.

Religious reformers

Around the same time, a wave of Protestant revivalism swept the country, finding its most fertile ground in New England and upstate New York. Known as the Second Great Awakening, these Puritan enthusiasts recognized temperance and accountability. They also considered black souls to be as valuable as white – and it was from their stock that many of the most fervent abolitionists emerged.

Chief among the reformers, and a man who demanded the immediate abolition of slavery, was William Lloyd Garrison, from Newburyport, Massachusetts. In 1831, he established *The Liberator*, a newspaper mouthpiece for his movement. In 1837, he helped found

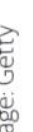
Image: Getty

Abolition officers drive black enslaved people from the plantations

the American Anti-Slavery Society. He enjoyed some support from the likes of Theodore Weld, Angelina Grimké, Wendell Phillips, and brothers Benjamin and Lewis Tappan, as well as from the tenacious former runaway slave, Frederick Douglass.

For all the abolitionists' fervor, however, they nevertheless inspired only small-scale support in the Northern states and, contrary to the view of many Southerners, they were often pilloried for their views. Several publishers of abolitionist literature were attacked and one unfortunate soul, Reverend Elijah P Lovejoy, was killed, in 1837, in Alton, Illinois.

Strength of argument

Even as late as 1850, the abolitionists remained a marginal force. In the words of one historian, however, "They lurked incorrigibly on the flanks of American politics." Their strength lay not in the number of voters that rallied to their cause, but in their ability to promote articulate and consistent argument.

This found particular voice in a popular novel by Harriet Beecher Stowe, who in 1852 published *Uncle Tom's Cabin*, drawing upon the book *American Slavery As It Is*, by fellow abolitionist Theodore Weld, for several prominent scenes. *Uncle Tom's Cabin* used the notion of family to pluck at the heartstrings of

"EVEN IN 1850, THE ABOLITIONISTS REMAINED A MARGINAL FORCE. THEIR STRENGTH LAY NOT IN THE NUMBER OF VOTERS THEY RALLIED, BUT IN THEIR ABILITY TO PROMOTE ARGUMENT"

Elijah P Lovejoy, a Presbyterian minister, was killed by a pro-slavery mob during an attack on Godfrey and Gillman's warehouse

its middle-class, family-orientated readership, and scenes such as Eliza's fleeing over the icy Ohio River to save her son, or Tom crying over his children left behind in Kentucky after his sale, stand among the most celebrated in American literature.

Free at last?

During the 1850s, the abolitionists began to gain ground, thanks in large part to newspaper coverage of fugitive slave cases. In 1850, Congress had passed an even more rigorous Fugitive Slave Law, which gave owners the right to repossess their runaway slaves with federal assistance. As the decade unfolded, more and more cases came to the fore and slave owners soon found themselves confronted by local anti-slavery activists.

There was great diversity within the movement, of course, with John Brown representing the most radical of reformers, bent on insurrection in the name of his cause. Still, by the 1860s, the tide appeared to have turned in the North, with many beginning to feel shame that they alone, among the great constitutional civilizations of the Western world, still permitted slavery.

As the Civil War unfolded, the abolitionists' voices grew louder. Recognizing that racism and a love of the Constitution might hinder plans to make emancipation an aim of the war, the abolitionists urged it instead as a military necessity. They pointed to the use of black people as a powerful rebel force. "The very stomach of this rebellion is the negro in the form of the slave," wrote Douglass. With the Emancipation Proclamation of 1863, the abolitionists finally won their victory. ★

Born into slavery, abolitionist Frederick Douglass became a man of letters whose sons fought in the Civil War

An anti-slavery meeting takes place in Boston in 1835, with free blacks seen among the crowd

METEOR OF THE WAR

THE MOST RADICAL OF ABOLITIONISTS, JOHN BROWN, CAUSED PANIC IN THE SOUTH WITH HIS BID TO SPARK A SLAVE REVOLT...

It was *Moby Dick* author Herman Melville who wrote in one of his poems that "weird John Brown" was the "meteor of the war". This abolitionist and his bold, if ill-conceived, bid in 1859 to sequester the arsenal at Harpers Ferry in Virginia certainly did much to ignite the tinderbox of secession. Brown hoped his raid would spark a slave uprising, an eventuality that was prominent in the minds of many Southerners, particularly in Mississippi and South Carolina where black people outnumbered white.

"Harpers Ferry," wrote the *Richmond Enquirer*, "coupled with the expression of Northern sentiment in support… have shaken and disrupted all regard for the Union; and there are but few men who do not look to a certain and not distant day when the dissolution must ensue."

Brown was a wild and ferocious man, who with his associates in Kansas had in 1856 murdered five pro-slavery settlers in what became known as the Pottawatomie massacre. On 16 October, his band of 13 white and five black abolitionists took Harpers Ferry. Their victory, however, was short-lived – the insurrection he had dreamed of failed to materialize, and he was swiftly defeated by federal troops under Colonel Robert E Lee.

Along with six followers, Brown was hanged for treason and murder, his name seized upon by both pro-slavery supporters and abolitionists. To many of the former he was a symbol of Northern intent, while to many in the North he was a martyr. In a prophetic note found after his death, he'd written that the "crimes of this guilty land will never be purged away but with blood".

Abraham Lincoln, 16th president of the United States of America

THE ELECTION OF 1860

The election of Abraham Lincoln in November 1860 was a victory for the anti-slavery Republicans and spurred the slave-holding South to secede from the Union

WORDS **MARC DESANTIS**

No other election in American history, before or since, has been so fraught with peril and more laden with consequences for the nation than that of 1860. There were several candidates running for the land's highest elective office, a consequence of the split among the pre-war parties that had dominated political life for decades.

One of the candidates, the eventual winner, Abraham Lincoln, failed to make it onto the election ballots of ten Southern states. The future president, to many the greatest that the US has ever had, saw six out of every ten voters cast their votes for some other candidate. Yet he still prevailed, and would go on to serve as the United States' 16th president during the most trying four years of its existence.

Lincoln's chief opponent for the election to be held on 6 November 1860 was John C Breckinridge of Kentucky, the candidate for the Southern Democrats. Stephen Douglas of Illinois, was the standard bearer of the Northern Democrats, who had splintered from the Southern Democrats. The newly formed Constitutional Union Party put forth John Bell of Tennessee as its nominee.

Stephen Douglas constantly inveighed against disunion while campaigning. In these times, a candidate would ordinarily not travel about to solicit votes, but Douglas visited no fewer than 23 states while the election campaign was ongoing.

He had realized early on that he had no path to victory. He saw that Lincoln's Republicans already won state elections taking place that October, and thus that victory for him in the presidential election in November was almost certainly out of reach.

His motive in campaigning in person was to preserve the unity of the United States. "Mr Lincoln is the next president," he acknowledged. "We must try to save the Union. I will go South."

Douglas was tireless in his bid to convince Southerners not to secede. His message to Southern voters was, by and large, poorly received. One hostile newspaper in Memphis, Tennessee, made note of his "bloated visage" that was now "turned toward the South." The same paper derided him an "itinerant peddler of Yankee notions," who would "soon be hawking his pinchback principles over the South. He comes in our midst with no worthier motives than the incendiary."

Talk of secession was rife in the South, particularly in states where slave-worked cotton plantations dominated the economy. There was a fear among them that the Republicans would wrest away their slaves, and this had to be avoided at all costs. Slavery had been one of the most divisive issues confronting America during the first half of the 19th century, and had made incorporating new states in the West into the Union problematic because neither the free North nor the slave South wanted an imbalance in free and slave

John C Breckinridge was Vice President of the United States under President James Buchanan and the Southern Democrats' candidate for the presidency in the 1860 election

John Bell was the 1860 presidential candidate for the Constitutional Union Party

Stephen Douglas was the Northern Democrat nominee for the presidency in the 1860 election

Lincoln's Secret Entry to Washington

RUMORS OF AN ASSASSINATION PLOT AGAINST LINCOLN'S LIFE FORCED HIM TO ENTER THE CAPITAL IN DISGUISE

Anti-Lincoln sentiment was so profound that there were fears that president-elect Abraham Lincoln would come to harm before he made it to Washington, DC. Lincoln had received death threats emanating from the Washington area before he ever left Springfield, Illinois, for the capital. He forwarded these threats to General Winfield Scott, who assured the president that he would emplace cannons on Pennsylvania Avenue. If any secessionist sympathizers made any untoward move, he would "blow them to hell."

Lincoln left Springfield by train on 11 February 1861, and made speeches at stops along the route. In the meantime, Allan Pinkerton, founder of the Pinkerton Detective Agency, had uncovered an assassination plot against Lincoln centered on the city of Baltimore, which lay close to Washington, on the route that Lincoln would be taking.

Allan Pinkerton, founder of the Pinkerton National Detective Agency

Pinkerton's first corporate logo

Pretending to be one John H Hutchinson, a contact had told Pinkerton that Lincoln might be attacked as he made his way through Baltimore. Pinkerton next questioned Cipriano Ferrandini, an Italian who was an earnest supporter of the South. Ferrandini insisted that Lincoln must not become president and that he was ready to kill the president-elect himself.

Other evidence came to light concerning Lincoln's peril. Both Winfield Scott and William Seward in Washington had learned of a putative Baltimore attack and their own investigators had confirmed that an assassination plot was afoot.

Lincoln was disguised by Pinkerton as an invalid, with the president-elect bent over to obscure his hard-to-miss height, and in the dark of the night of 22 February was put aboard a special sleeping car on the train leaving Harrisburg, Pennsylvania, for the capital. With the help of the railroad, the telegraph lines between Harrisburg and Washington were cut, and other trains were moved over to sidings. Lincoln's train chugged through Baltimore without incident at 3.30am and arrived safely in Washington at around 6.00am on 23 February.

Jefferson Davis of Mississippi was elected provisional president of the Confederate States of America in February 1861

states to result to the detriment of their respective blocs.

Electoral politics

In 1860, there were 33 states in the Union, all of which participated in the election. 18 of these were free states, where slavery was prohibited, and 15 were slave states, where it was fully legal. The philosophical split over the issue of slavery had only widened since independence and had become unbridgeable. Though slavery was legal under the Constitution, the institution itself had become utterly unacceptable to many Americans, especially Northern abolitionists who wanted to do away with slavery altogether.

Southerners were by and large terrified of the projected consequences of abolition, thinking that a war between the races, as well as racial mixing, would result. There could be no compromise between the abolitionists and the great mass of Southerners who wanted slavery to remain legal.

The 1860 election was also remarkable because it showcased the relatively newly formed Republican Party as the dominant political force in the free Northern states. The Republicans had emerged out of the collapse of the so-called second American party system that had prevailed from the early 1830s until the middle of the 1850s. The two predominant parties had been the Whigs and the Democrats. The Whigs had fallen to pieces completely over the issue of slavery. Northern Whigs had opposed it, while those in the South had supported it.

The implosion of the Whigs left the Democratic Party as the largest national party. The Democrats, however, were also split over slavery. Many Northern Democrats were extremely anti-Southern in outlook, believing that their party had been torn from them by slavery-friendly Southern Democrats.

The disaffected Northern Democrats and politically homeless Northern Whigs combined with others who were fiercely anti-slavery in their beliefs. This new political alliance became the Republican Party, which was formed in 1854. Though these Republicans were divided over any number of other issues that vexed the mid-19th-century Republic, they were united by their hostility to the South.

For most Republicans, slavery would eventually have to be eliminated. They were firmly opposed to the excessive power of the Southern slave states. The US Constitution allowed slave states to count their slaves as three-fifths of a free person for the purposes of representation in Congress, and this served to inflate Southern political power beyond what it would be on the basis of free persons alone. The free states of the North had a total population of 18.8 million while the slave states of the South had just 8.3 million free persons. With the three-fifths counting of the South's approximately four million slaves, however, Southern political representation was boosted to 10.4 million.

The Republican Party convention that nominated Abraham Lincoln for the presidency in 1860

Notwithstanding this, the Northern states, on account of their far larger aggregate populations, offered many more votes in the Electoral College, 180 to 120, which formally voted the president into office under the US Constitution. In theory, a candidate could win the presidency by polling strongly enough to Northern voters that he would not need to win a single Southern electoral vote. Accordingly, the Republicans appealed exclusively to Northern voters with a pledge to defend the Republic against slave interests. They were adamantly against allowing the legalization of slavery in the Western territories being settled as the nation expanded towards the Pacific Ocean.

On 18 May 1860, the Republican Party held its national convention in Chicago, and nominated Abraham Lincoln, a lawyer from Springfield, Illinois. His governmental experience was limited; he had not held political office since his single term in the House of Representatives had ended in 1849. Yet Lincoln was nominated because party politicians didn't think that the too-radical William Seward, the Republicans' other main potential nominee, could win with the voters of critical states such as Pennsylvania, Illinois, and Indiana. Lincoln was himself adamantly opposed to slavery. He would say at another time that "if slavery is not wrong, then nothing is wrong." He was thoroughly opposed to the expansion of slavery into the West.

Election Day arrives

Election Day was 6 November 1860. In Springfield, Lincoln anxiously awaited the returns that day as state after state reported their tallies via telegraph. It was past midnight when New York reported its tally, putting Lincoln over the top. Unsurprisingly, Lincoln did not win a single electoral vote from any of the 15 slave states.

"THIS NEW POLITICAL ALLIANCE BECAME THE REPUBLICAN PARTY, WHICH WAS FORMED IN 1854"

John C Breckinridge won 11 of the 15 slave states, but he did so by winning just 848,356 popular votes. The Democratic Party vote was hopelessly riven by the failure of the party to put forward a single candidate for the presidency.

Lincoln obtained the most votes out of all four candidates, despite not being on the ballots of ten Southern states. He won the Electoral College with 180 electoral votes. His closest rival, Breckinridge, garnered 72, and Bell took 39. Douglas gained a mere 12 electoral votes, even though his overall popular vote tally was 1,363,876, far higher than Breckenridge's. Unfortunately, this sizable number only netted him the states of Missouri and New Jersey.

A 1958 US postage stamp commemorating the 1858 Lincoln-Douglas debates

Lincoln would become the 16th president of the United States of America, and would be inaugurated in the next year on 4 March 1861. Many Southerners were appalled by Lincoln's victory. There ensued ever more insistent cries for secession, especially among the 'fire-eaters' who wanted to leave the Union immediately. In their minds, the South was now in profound peril with Lincoln on the way to the White House. South Carolina, a hotbed of secessionist feeling, seceded from the Union on 20 December 1860. In addition to South Carolina, the Deep South Cotton States of Georgia, Alabama, Florida, and Texas seceded by the following February.

The breakaway states wasted no time in organizing their own country. On 9 February 1861, Southern delegates elected Jefferson Davis of Mississippi as provisional president of the Confederate States of America, with its capital in Montgomery, Alabama.

The secession, heretofore peaceful, would soon turn into an armed conflict. On 9 April, Confederate forces opened fire on Fort Sumter, an island fort in the harbor of Charleston, South Carolina. Four years of bloody civil war would follow. ★

Image: Wiki, Alamy

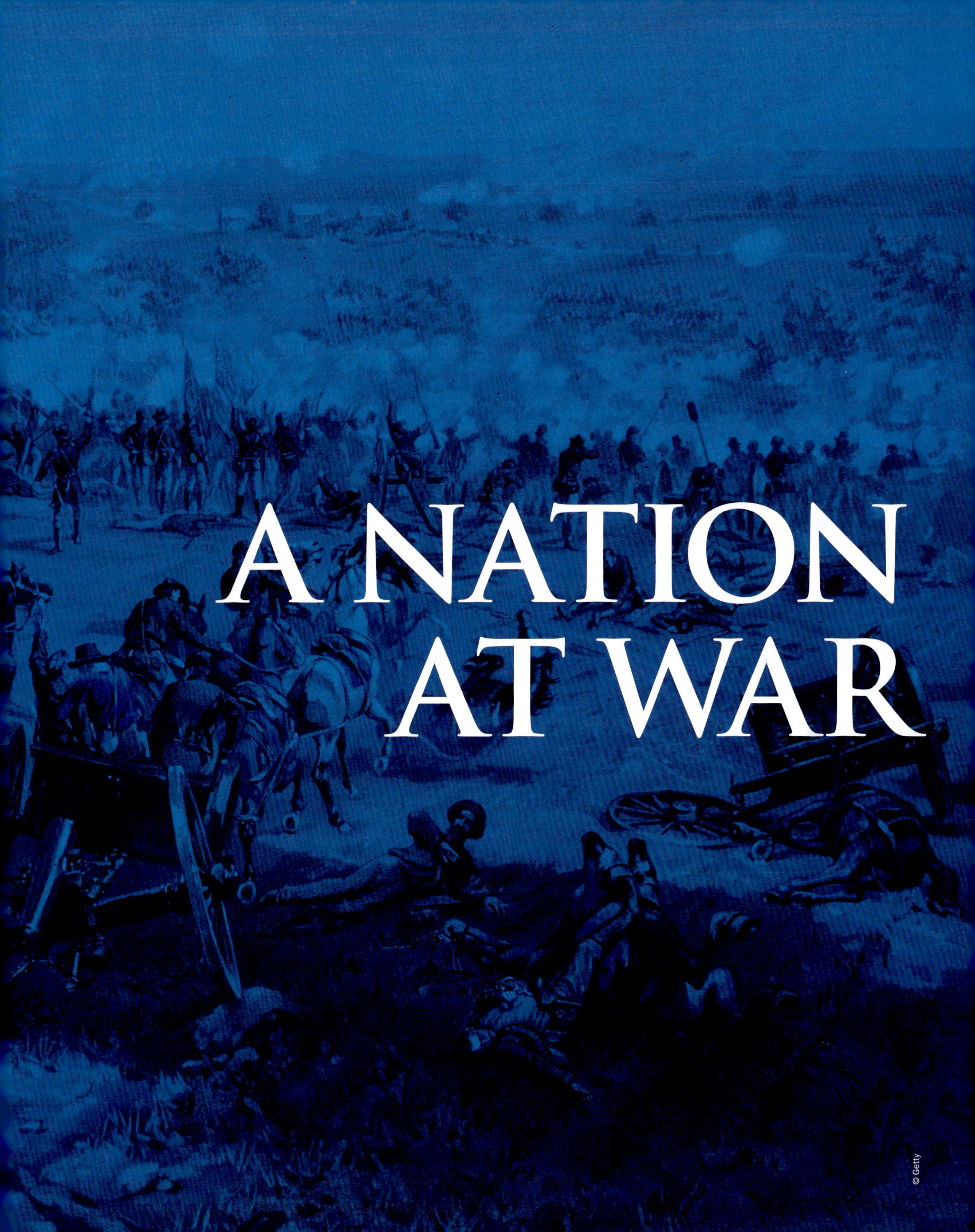

A NATION AT WAR

STATE OF PLAY 1861-1862

Marshaling men and materiel, the Union and Confederacy embark on four years of costly conflict that transforms a nation

Two months after Jefferson Davis is sworn in as president of the Confederacy, rebel guns fire on Fort Sumter in Charleston, South Carolina, on 12 April 1861. The Union and Confederacy have reached the point of no return. Within a week, President Abraham Lincoln issues a call for 75,000 volunteers of short duration to put down the rebellion and the Union begins to enact its grand strategy, the Anaconda Plan, envisioned by General-in-Chief Winfield Scott.

Early battles quickly dispel the belief that the Civil War will end swiftly. In the east, the First Battle of Bull Run, fought on 21 July 1861, ends with a Confederate victory as the Union army is routed. The Confederate press derides the North's performance, calling the retreat the "Great Skedaddle". A second Union defeat is then suffered in August, at Wilson's Creek, Missouri, during the first major battle of the Trans-Mississippi Theater. In November, the Trent Affair, involving the arrest of two Confederate envoys on the high seas, raises the specter of a war with Great Britain.

By the spring of 1862, the killing has begun to reach a massive scale. At Shiloh in West Tennessee, the two sides suffer about 20,000 casualties, but Union forces under General Ulysses S Grant win a victory. In August, at Second Bull Run, the Union army suffers a stinging defeat at the hands of General Thomas J 'Stonewall' Jackson's Confederates, and the bloodiest day in American history occurs at Antietam, in western Maryland, in September. Then, at the end of the bloody year, the Union's Army of the Potomac takes horrendous casualties in the Battle of Fredericksburg. ★

Fighting rages along Stones River, near the town of Murfreesboro, Tennessee, during a three-day battle beginning on 31 December 1862

Image: Wiki, Alamy

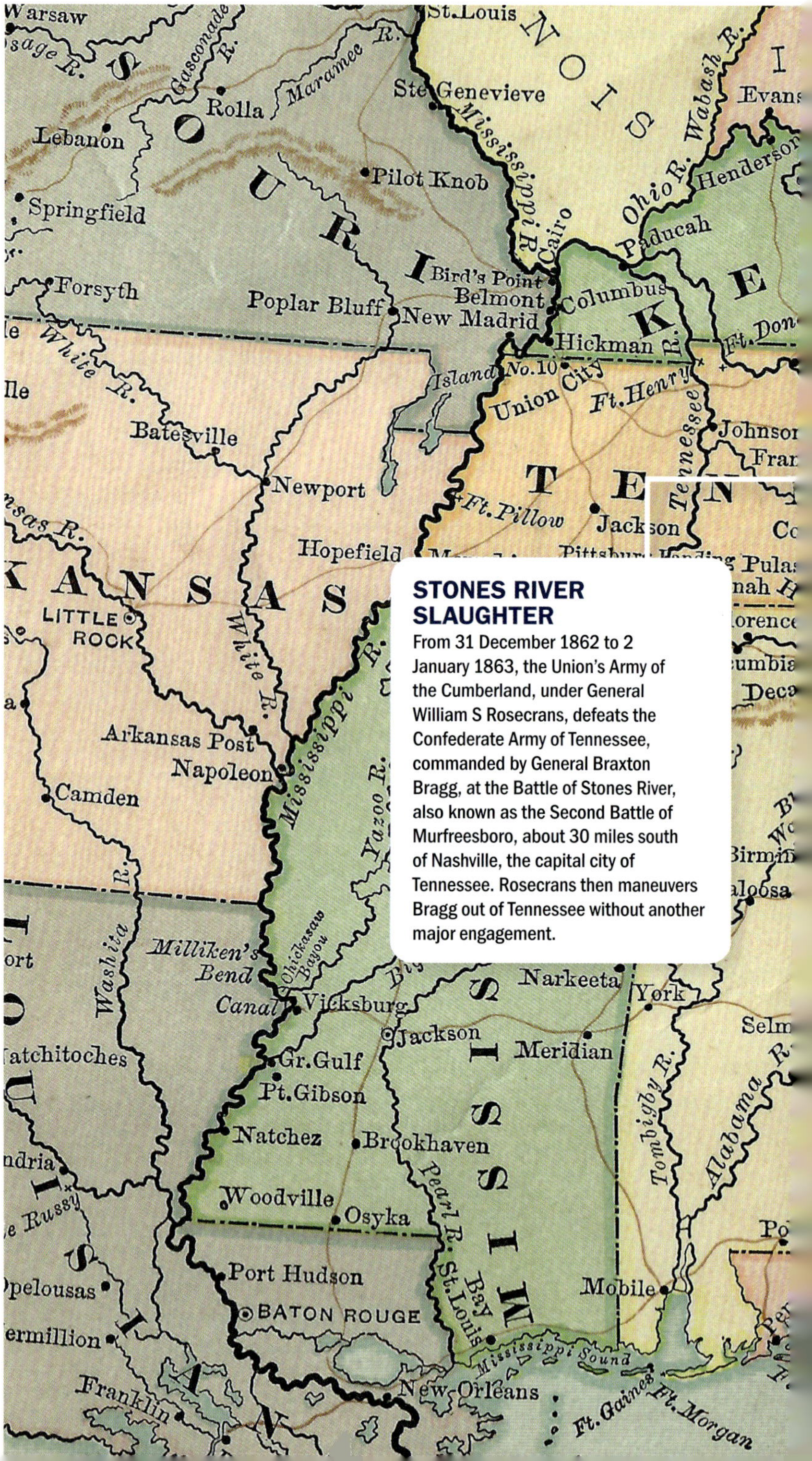

STONES RIVER SLAUGHTER

From 31 December 1862 to 2 January 1863, the Union's Army of the Cumberland, under General William S Rosecrans, defeats the Confederate Army of Tennessee, commanded by General Braxton Bragg, at the Battle of Stones River, also known as the Second Battle of Murfreesboro, about 30 miles south of Nashville, the capital city of Tennessee. Rosecrans then maneuvers Bragg out of Tennessee without another major engagement.

Jefferson Davis takes the oath of office as president of the Confederacy, at Montgomery, Alabama, on 18 February 1861

Confederate and Union troops blaze away during the Battle of Wilson's Creek, in Missouri, the first major battle in the Trans-Mississippi West

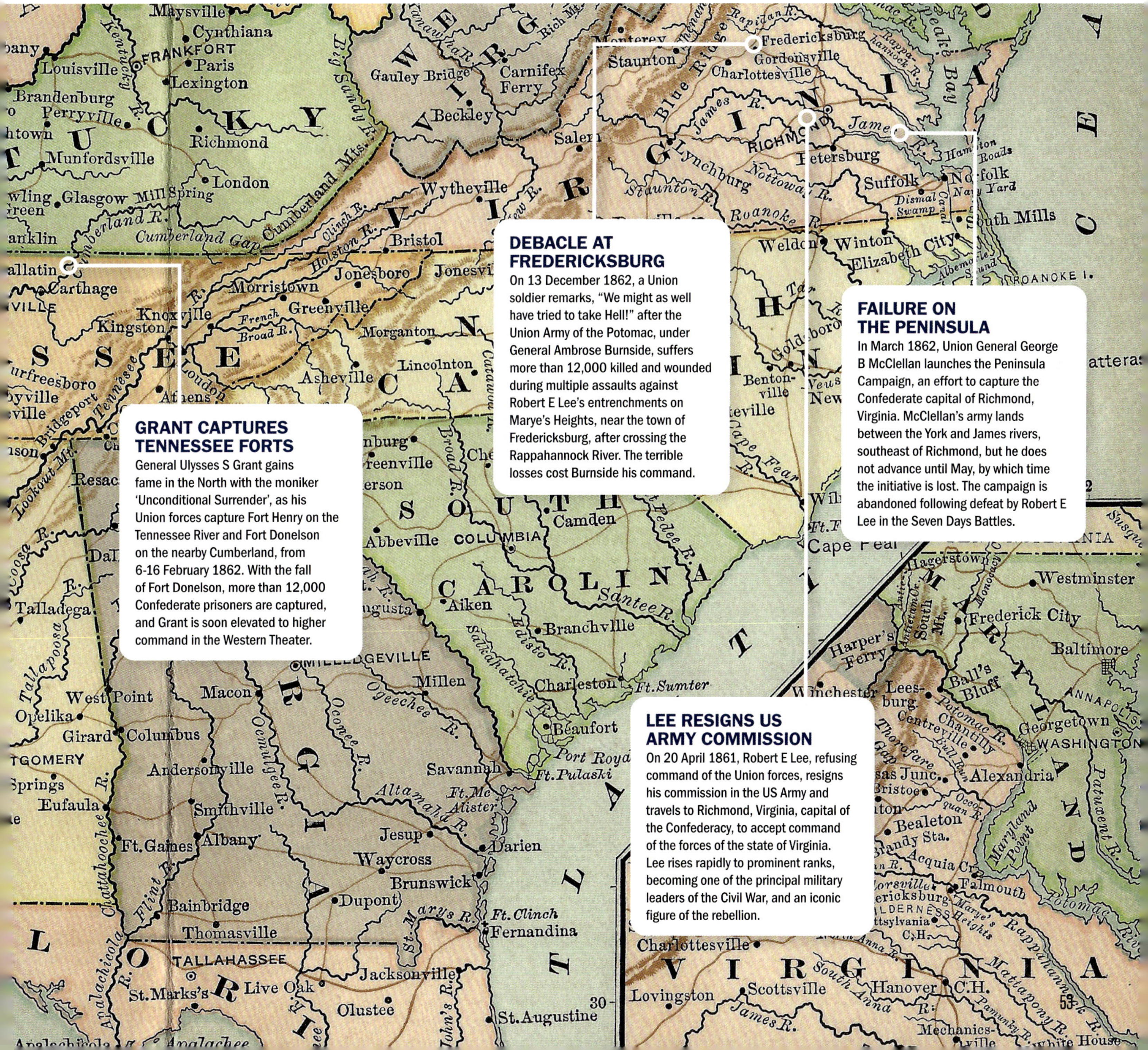

GRANT CAPTURES TENNESSEE FORTS

General Ulysses S Grant gains fame in the North with the moniker 'Unconditional Surrender', as his Union forces capture Fort Henry on the Tennessee River and Fort Donelson on the nearby Cumberland, from 6-16 February 1862. With the fall of Fort Donelson, more than 12,000 Confederate prisoners are captured, and Grant is soon elevated to higher command in the Western Theater.

DEBACLE AT FREDERICKSBURG

On 13 December 1862, a Union soldier remarks, "We might as well have tried to take Hell!" after the Union Army of the Potomac, under General Ambrose Burnside, suffers more than 12,000 killed and wounded during multiple assaults against Robert E Lee's entrenchments on Marye's Heights, near the town of Fredericksburg, after crossing the Rappahannock River. The terrible losses cost Burnside his command.

FAILURE ON THE PENINSULA

In March 1862, Union General George B McClellan launches the Peninsula Campaign, an effort to capture the Confederate capital of Richmond, Virginia. McClellan's army lands between the York and James rivers, southeast of Richmond, but he does not advance until May, by which time the initiative is lost. The campaign is abandoned following defeat by Robert E Lee in the Seven Days Battles.

LEE RESIGNS US ARMY COMMISSION

On 20 April 1861, Robert E Lee, refusing command of the Union forces, resigns his commission in the US Army and travels to Richmond, Virginia, capital of the Confederacy, to accept command of the forces of the state of Virginia. Lee rises rapidly to prominent ranks, becoming one of the principal military leaders of the Civil War, and an iconic figure of the rebellion.

FIRST BLOW AT FORT SUMTER

A tiny garrison of Union troops, in an unfinished fort, would receive the first hostile shot of the American Civil War

WORDS **DAVID SMITH**

The American Civil War began on 12 April 1861 with the bombardment of Fort Sumter

A casemate attempts to defend Fort Sumter during the attack

Although war appeared increasingly likely, neither side wanted to be the one to draw first blood. Being seen as the aggressor would have been politically damaging, and in the North, a lame-duck president added to the complications. James Buchanan, quite understandably, wanted to get through the remaining days of his presidency without the nation erupting into open conflict, so he planned to let the incoming Abraham Lincoln deal with the crisis after his inauguration.

The situation was tense, and flashpoints were easy to identify. Most obvious were the Union-occupied forts in the South's territory – including Fort Moultrie at Charleston and Fort Pickens at Pensacola Bay, in Florida. These became points of intense debate.

The garrison commander at Fort Moultrie, Major Robert Anderson, had an impressive lineage. His father had defended the position against the British during the War of Independence and now he had the responsibility of holding the line against a potential new attacker. The problem, however, was that Fort Moultrie was in no fit state to be effectively defended. So, on 29 December 1860, Anderson decided to shift his garrison across a mile of water and instead take up residence at Fort Sumter.

It was a bold move and an unauthorized one, but Anderson had been asking for instructions for a long time and had received nothing back. The South viewed his move as an act of aggression, while Buchanan wished it could have waited until he was out of office. The overriding question instantly became: should the North hold on to the fort (which would mean sending reinforcements), or let it go? There was to be no easy answer.

Manning the guns

Anderson, a Kentuckian who had married a Georgia girl, had been expected to turn to the Confederate cause, but his loyalty to the Union proved stronger than family ties. He now set about organizing his limited resources.

Sumter was an impressive structure, with three decks of gun emplacements, but it was unfinished and required 650 troops to man fully. Anderson had just 85, as well as a number of laborers. The fort could also theoretically mount 146 guns, but only 81 were in place. Of those, just 15 were properly mounted in their emplacements.

Major Robert Anderson, commander of Fort Sumter, remained loyal to the Union despite strong Southern connections

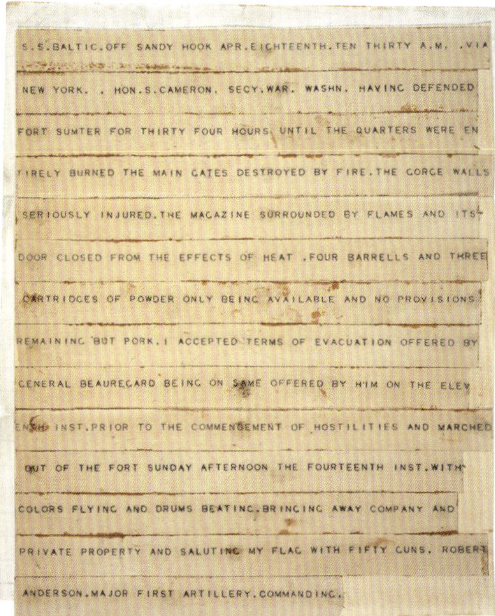

S.S.BALTIC.OFF SANDY HOOK APR.EIGHTEENTH.TEN THIRTY A.M. .VIA
NEW YORK. . HON.S.CAMERON. SECY.WAR. WASHN. HAVING DEFENDED
FORT SUMTER FOR THIRTY FOUR HOURS UNTIL THE QUARTERS WERE EN
TIRELY BURNED THE MAIN GATES DESTROYED BY FIRE.THE GORGE WALLS
SERIOUSLY INJURED.THE MAGAZINE SURROUNDED BY FLAMES AND ITS
DOOR CLOSED FROM THE EFFECTS OF HEAT .FOUR BARRELLS AND THREE
CARTRIDGES OF POWDER ONLY BEING AVAILABLE AND NO PROVISIONS
REMAINING BUT PORK.I ACCEPTED TERMS OF EVACUATION OFFERED BY
GENERAL BEAUREGARD BEING ON SAME OFFERED BY HIM ON THE ELEV
ENTH INST.PRIOR TO THE COMMENCEMENT OF HOSTILITIES AND MARCHED
OUT OF THE FORT SUNDAY AFTERNOON THE FOURTEENTH INST.WITH
COLORS FLYING AND DRUMS BEATING.BRINGING AWAY COMPANY AND
PRIVATE PROPERTY AND SALUTING MY FLAG WITH FIFTY GUNS. ROBERT
ANDERSON.MAJOR FIRST ARTILLERY.COMMANDING.

***Above** The telegram sent by Major Anderson explaining his surrender of Fort Sumter*

"WITH A RELIEF FLEET ON THE WAY, SOUTH CAROLINA'S GOVERNOR WAS FORCED INTO ACTION"

Anderson immediately set to work wrestling more of the 66 unmounted guns into position. Due to the lack of men, Anderson decided to occupy only the casemate tier of the fort, the most heavily protected deck. Meanwhile, South Carolinian forces continued to gather outside.

The first attempt to reinforce Fort Sumter came on 9 January 1861, when a merchant ship carrying supplies and 200 men appeared off the coast and attempted to reach the fort. It was driven away by land batteries, with Anderson unwilling to open fire in defense of the ship for fear of inadvertently starting a war.

The situation became more tense with Lincoln's inauguration. In his speech, he promised to "hold, occupy and possess the property and places belonging to the government". This obviously included Fort Sumter, but three commissioners from the South were in Washington to negotiate for its handover. Complicating the situation, Lincoln's designated secretary of state, William H Seward, took it upon himself to assure the commissioners that Fort Sumter would be given up without a fuss.

By this point, the fort had less than six weeks' provisions left and Lincoln was dealing with the reality that a relief effort was essential. Having sent Captain Gustavus Fox to visit the fort and report back, Lincoln made his decision. The fort would be resupplied.

Recognizing how provocative this would be, Lincoln informed the authorities in Charleston that he would not attempt to "throw in men, arms or ammunition", unless an attack was made upon the fort. The resupply would be strictly limited to provisions for the existing garrison. On 6 April 1861, the relief fleet was ordered to set sail.

Both sides were tip-toeing around the issue, each hoping the other would make the first aggressive move. Senator Robert Toombs, who later served as secretary of state in the Confederate government, was among the many men who recognized that the nation was poised on a knife edge. "The firing on that fort," he warned, "will inaugurate a civil war greater than the world has yet seen." Others wanted violence to explode to solidify the rift caused by secession, and to convince the border or upper Southern states to secede as well.

South Carolina's governor, Francis Wilkinson Pickens, had hoped to avoid making the first move in the Fort Sumter affair, but with the

***Above** Edmund Ruffin is reputed to have fired the first shot on Fort Sumter. At the end of the war, he committed suicide*

knowledge that a relief fleet was on its way, he was forced into action.

The race to resupply

General Pierre Gustave Toutant-Beauregard was given orders to demand the surrender of the fort. Beauregard, an energetic character known as the 'little Frenchman', had been a student of Anderson at West Point, adding a layer of awkwardness to the situation. The steady approach of the fleet added a further element, a ticking clock that demanded action. There was now little chance of avoiding violence.

Beauregard offered Anderson generous terms if he would abandon the fort, but the major refused, knowing that the resupply fleet was on its way. He did, however, let Beauregard know that he was near to running out of food and offered to surrender if he hadn't been resupplied by 15 April. Whether this was an attempt to buy time is uncertain, but Beauregard was not in the mood to wait. At 3.30am on 12 April, Anderson was given one hour's notice that a bombardment of the fort was about to start.

Exactly who fired the first shot of the war is debated (and some argue that the honor should actually go to whoever fired against the ship attempting to resupply Fort Sumter in January). A signal shot went up from Fort Johnson on James Island, and the first shot aimed at Fort Sumter was fired at 4.30am, from the ironclad battery moored off Morris Island. The shot came from an eight-inch Columbiad gun and was reputedly fired by Edmund Ruffin. The American Civil War had started.

There is no doubt over who fired the first shot in reply. Anderson's second-in-command, Captain Abner Doubleday, was granted the honor and fired a shot back at the ironclad battery.

It was the start of an uneven duel. Anderson's men could bring only 21 guns into action and the majority were mere 32-pounders, loaded with roundshot. They had no mortars and no shells to respond to the Confederate bombardment. The besieging forces had 30 large guns and 18 mortars, splitting them between six batteries, some of which were out of range of Fort Sumter's guns. The fire of the beleaguered Union garrison

A photograph taken in April 1861 after the attack, shows the Confederate flag flying over Fort Sumter

was more defiance than anything, and they threw only 1,000 shots back in response to the 4,000 they received over a 33-hour period.

The start of the war was not greeted with the sober reflection it deserved. Many locals came out to watch, some bringing picnics and settling down for a long day's entertainment. There was no doubt about the eventual outcome. The relief fleet, which had been scattered by a gale, was spotted off the coast but did not dare to run up to the fort while it was under such a fearful bombardment. Briefly heartened when they had first seen the ships on the horizon, the forces at Fort Sumter quickly realized they were not going to enjoy any sort of rescue.

The Confederate shots set fire to the barracks in the fort and did significant damage to the brick walls, but apart from a few injuries there was little effect. Remarkably, the first action of the war caused no fatalities.

***Above** The Confederates bombarded the fort from artillery batteries surrounding the harbor*

The fall of the fort

By the following morning, the guns of Fort Sumter were unleashing just one shot every ten minutes as ammunition ran low. Anderson eventually bowed to the inevitable. With only three shots remaining, he agreed to enter into talks. At 1.30pm on 13 April, he agreed to surrender his exhausted garrison. A 50-gun salute, to honor the Union flag as it was struck the next day, sent an ember into what was left of the fort's supply of gunpowder, with the resulting explosion claiming the life of Private Daniel Hough. The first person to die in the American Civil War did so by accident.

Controversy has swirled over the build-up to the assault. It is clear that both sides would have preferred the other to have struck first. Lincoln certainly maneuvered to ensure it was the Confederates who fired first, but in reality, all were spoiling for a fight.

There was no turning back once shots had been fired. Within days of Sumter's surrender, both sides began building their armies. ★

AN APPETITE FOR WAR

THE VIOLENCE AT FORT SUMTER BROUGHT FORTH POWERFUL EMOTIONS ON BOTH SIDES OF THE GREAT DIVIDE

The fall of Fort Sumter had a galvanizing effect on both sides. Perversely, there was almost a sense of relief that the tension had been broken. North and South were each confident of victory, both sure that the war would be brief and decisive. Few people seemed to consider the possibility that it would be anything other than a glorious crusade.

Leading the jubilation after the outbreak of hostilities were the newspapers. Northern publications crowed that "all squeamish sentimentality should be discarded, and bloody vengeance wreaked upon the heads of the contemptible traitors who have provoked it by their dastardly impertinence and rebellious acts". Southern papers were equally bullish.

Neither side had any doubt that their cause was just, and neither seemed to notice that there had been no fatalities during the capture of the fort.

"The Nation has been defiled," an Indianapolis newspaper railed. "The National Government has been assailed. If either can be done with impunity... we are not a nation, and our Government is a sham."

Many private citizens also committed their thoughts to diaries and letters, and there was a common theme – outrage at the actions of the other side. "I had rather be dead than see the Yanks rule this country," wrote one citizen from North Carolina.

The inability of either side to consider events from the other's perspective was summed up neatly in the adoption of the same song as an anthem for the civil war causes of both North and South. Each heard their own story echoed in the strains of the George Frederick Root composition, 'Battle Cry of Freedom'.

THE SECESSION MOVEMENT. 833

two days which had elapsed since its adjournment hither from Columbia, had been deliberating in secret session. A little after midday of December 20th, the streets of Charleston were filled with the following placards, giving the public the first notice of its action:

CHARLESTON
MERCURY
EXTRA:

Passed unanimously at 1.15 o'clock, P.M., December 20th, 1860.

AN ORDINANCE

To dissolve the Union between the State of South Carolina and other States united with her under the compact entitled "The Constitution of the United States of America."

THE
UNION
IS
DISSOLVED!

The usual jubilations immediately followed,—ringing of bells, salutes of cannon, and the noise and display of street parades. The convention resolved to celebrate the event further by a public ceremonial to which it invited the governor, the legislature, and other dignitaries; and both branches of the legislature also sent a committee to Caleb Cushing to give him an official invitation to attend. At half-past 6 that evening the members of the convention marched in procession to Institute Hall, where the public signing of the ordinance of secession was performed with appropriate solemnities, and at its close the President announced: "The ordinance of secession has been signed and ratified, and I proclaim the State of South Carolina an Independent Commonwealth."

ATTORNEY-GENERAL JEREMIAH S. BLACK. (FROM A PHOTOGRAPH BY BRADY.)

The city and the State joined in general exultation as if a great work had been accomplished, as if the efforts of a generation had been crowned with fulfillment, and nothing remained but to rest and enjoy the ripened fruit of independence. There seemed to be no dream, amid all this rejoicing, that nothing definite had as yet been effected; that the reckless day's act was but the prelude to the most terrible tragedy of the age, the unchaining of a storm which should shake the continent with terror and devastation, leaving every Southern State a wreck, and sweeping from the face of the earth the institution in whose behalf the fatal work was done.

The secession ordinance having been passed, signed, and proclaimed, the convention busied itself for the next few days in making up a public statement of its reasons for the anomalous procedure. The discussion showed a wide divergence of opinion as to the causes which had produced the act. One ascribed it to the election of Lincoln, another to the failure of the Northern States to execute the fugitive-slave law, a third to the antislavery sentiment of the free States, a fourth to the tariff, a fifth to unconstitutional appropriations by Congress, and so on. On the 24th of December the convention adopted a "Declaration of Causes," and an "Address to the Slave-holding States," the two papers together em-

The Charleston Mercury was the first Confederate newspaper to be published following secession

IN THE RANKS

One nation produced two armies when the American Civil War broke out, but despite their common heritage they became markedly different

WORDS **DAVID SMITH**

Colorful depictions of the Civil War armies in action fail to capture the usually horrific nature of the battlefield

An army officer takes roll call in a Confederate camp

The standard image of the armies of the American Civil War is not entirely correct. Blue-coated Union troops did indeed take the field against grey-uniformed Confederates, but this familiar picture is only partially accurate. In reality, the armies were not always easily distinguished from each other, whether by the soldiers standing in the ranks, the weapons they were using, or even the uniforms they wore. The Civil War armies were complex creations, and they had much more in common than is generally assumed.

To start with, these were two armies drawn from one nation. The sense of unity in that nation had obviously become increasingly strained, but the men who faced each other at Bull Run, Gettysburg and Nashville were more alike than not. It has become a cliché to describe the American Civil War as pitting brother against brother and father against son, but that doesn't make it any less important.

Despite the armies' many similarities, however, each opposing force had its own characteristics, and many of these developed and intensified as the war progressed. By the close of hostilities, soldiers from opposite sides of the battlefield could often look on each other as genuinely different.

Sons of the land

Both North and South were still predominantly agricultural nations at the opening of the war. Industrialization in the North was advancing at a far more rapid pace, but the men who made up the Union army were overwhelmingly from rural backgrounds, with only a quarter of the soldiers coming from towns of greater than 2,000 people. In the South, the picture was even starker. Only ten percent of the population of the Confederate states lived in towns of greater than 2,000.

There was a tiny regular army when war broke out. Just 16,000 strong, it reflected the nation's suspicion of standing armies, which dated back to the days of the Revolution. The regular army was expanded slightly, but it was instead a huge temporary army that would do the fighting for the North.

On 15 April 1861, Abraham Lincoln called for a militia army of 75,000 volunteers, to serve for just three months. Nothing better encapsulates the misapprehensions about the nature of the coming war than the modest numbers and short term of enlistment specified by the president, but it was a start. Just months later, half a million more volunteers were authorized by Congress. By May 1865, more than a million men would be under arms, with around two million in total serving the Union over the course of the war, including around 180,000 African-Americans.

Artillery had lost its dominance on the battlefield, but still played a key role in defensive works

Recruitment was a local affair. A prominent citizen would raise a company, which would then be incorporated into a regiment, alongside other independently raised companies, by the state governor. Most men joined up with a sense of fighting for a worthwhile cause (although some were just looking for adventure), but that cause was the preservation of self-government and the Union. The issue of slavery was not a major motivation at the start of the war. Conscription was introduced in March 1863 under the terms of the Enrolment Act (a militia draft had been in place since the previous year, for states that did not fill their militia quotas).

More than 110,000 of the two million men who served in the Union Army died from wounds received on the battlefield. Another quarter of a million perished from other causes.

The numbers game

In the South, there was a similar underestimation of the scale of the war. On 6 March 1861, the Confederate Congress authorized an army of 100,000 for an enlistment period of 12 months. In just the same way that figures were hastily revised in the North, after war actually broke out, authorization was quickly passed for up to 400,000 men on three-year enlistments.

With the South's population being roughly a third that of the North's, the army was necessarily smaller. It hit its high water mark in June 1863, when 475,000 men were under arms. By that time the Confederate States Army had adopted a conscription system, but it was seldom needed as most eligible men volunteered rather than suffer the stigma of being drafted. Around a quarter of a million of those soldiers would die in service, with disease responsible for two or three times as many deaths as the battles themselves.

The Confederates did raise a tiny regular army, just seven regiments strong, but for the most part they did their fighting with regiments raised by the individual states.

Those regiments, as was the case in the North, were the basic building blocks of the

Union Army generals Wesley Merritt, Philip Sheridan, George Crook, James William Forsyth, and George Armstrong Custer discuss strategy

Image: Alamy, Getty

army. In both the Union and Confederate armies, regiments were grouped into brigades, brigades into divisions, divisions into army corps and corps into armies. In the North, armies were named after major rivers, while Southern armies took their names from the states where they were raised.

A changing battlefield

When those armies went into battle, they fought in the same way. This is unsurprising, as they used the same instruction manual. With the infantryman being by far the most important soldier on the battlefields of the American Civil War, it was *Rifle and Light Infantry Tactics* by Lieutenant Colonel William J Hardee that both sides turned to for instruction. It was heavy reading, with more than 500 pages devoted almost entirely to battlefield evolutions for maneuvering and taking up formations in the face of the enemy. It was almost all hopelessly out-dated, and the adoption of revised editions did little but confuse matters, as different officers drew from passages in different versions.

The instruction to form square when menaced by cavalry, for example, was particularly obsolete. A throwback to the days of Napoleon, it was no longer necessary, as the increased range and accuracy of rifled muskets had made a line of infantrymen far too dangerous for cavalry to charge.

Each side was familiar with the other's weapons as well, as they were for the most part the same. Breech-loading rifles did give the North an advantage in the latter stages of the conflict, but the rifled musket was the signature weapon of the war. New tactics were adopted to exploit advantages and limit risk on the new battlefield. The 'advance by rushes' replaced the near-suicidal advance in packed ranks, but there were still far too many costly frontal assaults against prepared defenses. At the Battle of Franklin, in November 1864, the Confederates' General John Bell Hood sent his troops headlong against Union positions and lost 7,000 in a matter of hours.

The performance of the officer corps played a huge part in the course of the conflict and here at least the South had an advantage (even allowing for men such as Hood). Seven of the eight military academies in the United States at the outbreak of war were based in the Southern states.

The North could counter with a better logistical system, better supply chains, and more plentiful food, ammunition and other materiel. These advantages would increase as the years passed, gradually becoming overwhelming. In November 1864, Lincoln gave

a speech that must have struck despondency into the hearts of the wilting Confederate States. "We have more men now than we had when the war began," he stated to Congress. "We are gaining strength and may, if need be, maintain the contest indefinitely."

Southern comfort

The North may have held most of the aces, but the Confederates had an enduring faith in the quality of their men. Importantly, the North shared that belief. The idea (part mythology, part romance, but with at least an element of truth) that the South was a land of noble warriors was a powerful one. As such, morale remained high in the South, even after they had suffered defeats. Southern troops also tended to be more proficient with firearms before joining the army, though experience soon brought the Union fighters up to speed.

In terms of cavalry, the Confederates enjoyed an early advantage, but they insisted on their troopers providing their own horses, and this led to a steady decline in their numbers. Men who had their horses shot from under them either had to buy a replacement or join the infantry. In any event, cavalry was in decline and useful mostly for scouting or harassing fleeing foes.

Artillery saw guns (most often the standard 12-pounder smoothbores known as 'Napoleons') arranged in batteries of six or so pieces. Their days of lording it over the battlefield had passed as increased infantry firepower made it lethal for them to approach to close range. The use of canister shot (metal cylinders packed with musket balls) was much less effective than during the Napoleonic era as gun crews risked annihilation if they allowed enemy infantry to get close enough to employ the short-range ammunition.

Life in each army would therefore have been very familiar to men from the opposite ranks, but that does not mean the armies thought or acted in the same way. Southern troops were notoriously harder to manage and freer in spirit, and after five years of bitter fighting, felt themselves distinctly different to men who had once been fellow citizens. The Confederate cavalry commander Nathan Bedford Forrest summed up such sentiments as the war ground to its inevitable conclusion.

"Be not allured by the siren song of peace," he exhorted his men. "You can never again unite with those who have murdered your sons, outraged your helpless families, and with demonic malice wantonly destroyed your property, and now seek to make slaves of you." The armies of North and South had started out from much the same position, but they had journeyed to very different destinations. ★

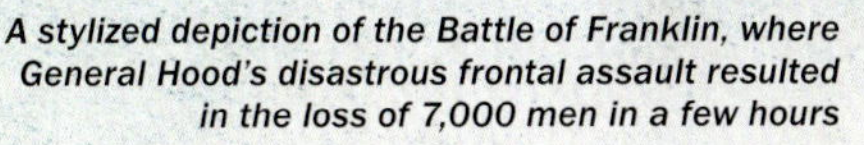

A stylized depiction of the Battle of Franklin, where General Hood's disastrous frontal assault resulted in the loss of 7,000 men in a few hours

SUPPLY AND DEMAND

CLOTHING AND FEEDING THE HUGE ARMIES OF THE CIVIL WAR PUSHED BOTH NORTH AND SOUTH TO THE LIMIT

Supplying the armies of the Civil War was a monumental undertaking. As well as the scale of the armies themselves, there were huge areas of territory to be covered. Many commanders, especially in the South, preferred to let their men live off the land, although this meant moving on quickly to avoid devastating the area.

Rations were strikingly similar for both sides - pork or bacon with bread or flour, along with coffee and sugar, were the staples. Depending on availability, a soldier might also get rice, crackers, or peas, but the diet was poor enough that scurvy was not uncommon.

All too often, a soldier had almost nothing at all to eat unless he found it himself. The hungry men in the Army of Tennessee, trudging their way towards Nashville in December 1864, often had nothing more than a couple of ears of corn per man. Union troops tended to be better fed, and generally enjoyed superior clothes. Southern soldiers were theoretically provided with smart uniforms, but often a man had to provide his own clothing, which would become increasingly disheveled over time.

Late in the war, Union forces also deliberately targeted the South's infrastructure, most infamously during General Sherman's marches through Confederate territory. The destruction of the railways, factories, and mills of Georgia and South Carolina severely damaged the Confederates' already struggling supply system.

Sherman's march through Georgia deliberately targeted the South's supplies

KEY MEN IN THE UNION ARMY

The men who commanded the forces of the North came from a variety of backgrounds and enjoyed differing fortunes during the war

WORDS **DAVID SMITH**

After the war, Grant rode his wartime record to the White House, serving as the 18th President of the United States

ULYSSES S GRANT

TENACIOUS GENERAL WHO BROKE THE CONFEDERACY

YEARS: 1822-85 **BIRTHPLACE:** POINT PLEASANT, OHIO

Christened Hiram, Grant's birth name was dropped when it was mistakenly omitted on his application to West Point. The name he became known for is more impressive, although he was a man of small stature. His first command was of the 21st Illinois regiment, where he did a good job of instilling discipline. His initials made a nickname inevitable after he demanded the 'unconditional surrender' of the garrison of Fort Donelson in 1862. Having blotted his copybook at Shiloh, Grant found himself commanding the Army of the Tennessee when Henry Halleck was promoted to overall commander of Union forces. Grant captured Vicksburg and won other victories, earning the position of commander of Union forces in the Western Theater. Further victories at Lookout Mountain and Missionary Ridge got him promoted to lieutenant general in the regular army and given overall command. Tackling the Confederates' leading general, Robert E Lee, in a series of battles, Grant showed a tenacity that had been missing in previous commanders. Having forced Lee out of Petersburg, he maintained the pursuit and forced the Confederates to surrender at Appomattox. Grant's great gift was to recognize that pressure needed to be applied to the enemy, even at great cost. This would puzzle those who knew him, who struggled to reconcile the slight, gentle man in front of them with the ruthless commander who brought the Confederacy to its knees.

Lincoln, as presented by the artist George P A Healy in his painting *The Peacemakers* of 1868

ABRAHAM LINCOLN

PRESIDENT AND COMMANDER-IN-CHIEF

YEARS: 1809-65 **BIRTHPLACE:** HARDIN COUNTY, KENTUCKY

Although most famous for his decision to emancipate the slave population of the Southern states, Lincoln's initial goal on the outbreak of war was simply to preserve the Union. In fact, his election campaign had been clear that he did not intend to attack the institution of slavery where it already existed. Once convinced of the need to abolish slavery, however, Lincoln was resolute and even described the Civil War as God's punishment for the vile trade. Aware of the demands of politics, he was sometimes forced to appoint generals with political connections, and this led to problems, especially early in the war. Lincoln had a keen military mind, and recognized that decisive victories were hard to come by. He did, however, struggle to get his generals to act with vigor, such as in the case of George B McClellan. As the war hardened his commanders, he gradually saw victory approach, although his murder at Ford's Theater cut short his satisfaction of guiding the nation back toward unity.

George P A Healy's portrait of Sherman captures a much softer side of the man than his many wild-eyed photographic portraits

William Tecumseh Sherman

Advocate of 'Total War'

YEARS: 1820-91 **BIRTHPLACE:** LANCASTER, OHIO

Sherman was adopted by US Senator Thomas Ewing, and rechristened William at the age of ten, having originally been named after the famed Native American chief. Exuding nervous energy, the restless Sherman plodded his way through an unremarkable life until the war revealed his true calling. Scornful of attempts to maintain an air of civility, he saw warfare as nothing more than an evil that needed to be brought to an end as quickly as possible. On his famous march through Georgia, South Carolina, and North Carolina, he fulfilled his intention to make the civilian population face the reality of war by driving an army of 60,000 through the helpless states. Having unleashed a chilling version of 'total war', he then offered generous terms to his defeated foe, General Johnston, and was even accused of treason by some in the North. Hero, war criminal, or ultimate realist, Sherman is still a bitterly divisive figure to this day.

McClellan adopted a self-conscious imitation of Napoleon in this portrait, but failed to bring the great French general's dash to the battlefield

George B McClellan

'The Young Napoleon'

YEARS: 1826-85 **BIRTHPLACE:** PHILADELPHIA, PENNSYLVANIA

Having graduated from West Point second in his class, McClellan distinguished himself in battle during the Mexican War, but then left to pursue a career in the railroad industry. Called back on the eve of war, he was quickly elevated to overall command, where he displayed a genius for organization but also a timidity that drove Lincoln to distraction. Failing to show the drive and aggression that might have ended the war earlier, McClellan still performed valuable service in transforming and reinvigorating the Army of the Potomac on two occasions. He also deserves credit for recognizing that painstaking preparation would be required to earn victory and for resisting the goading of politicians who would not have to witness the results of a premature commitment of forces. He stood for President in 1864 and stood a chance until the war swung in the North's favor with the fall of Atlanta, which secured victory for Lincoln.

A solid, unfussy commander, Thomas nonetheless won the most one-sided victory of the entire war at Nashville

George H Thomas

'The Rock of Chickamauga'

YEARS: 1816-70 **BIRTHPLACE:** SOUTHAMPTON COUNTY, VIRGINIA

After attending West Point with Sherman, and then serving in the Seminole War and Mexican War, Thomas became an instructor back at West Point in 1851. He was disowned by his family after remaining loyal to the Union on the outbreak of war – he was offered a commission by the State of Virginia – and he was best known for his stubborn defensive qualities. Those qualities were displayed when he saved the Army of the Cumberland in 1863 at the battle where he won his famous nickname. Despite this, and a reputation for being ponderous and overly cautious, Thomas won one of the Union's greatest victories, decisively defeating John Bell Hood (whom he had instructed at West Point) at the two-day Battle of Nashville. Recognized as the only decisive victory of the entire war, the Confederate Army of Tennessee was almost completely destroyed and never went into battle again. Thomas, however, refused to indulge in self-promotion and was largely overlooked in the back-slapping after the war.

KEY MEN IN THE CONFEDERATE STATES ARMY

With a superior officer corps, the CSA was generally well led, which helped to compensate for its smaller numbers

WORDS **DAVID SMITH**

Lee on his most famous horse, Traveller, a grey American Saddlebred

ROBERT E LEE

SYMBOL OF THE SOUTH

YEARS: 1807-70 **BIRTHPLACE:** STRATFORD, VIRGINIA

Few men emerged from the war with a reputation as glowing as that of General Lee. Respected as a commander, he came to epitomize the notions of civility and urbanity associated with the South. An excellent student at West Point, he served with distinction in the US Army prior to the war and resigned his commission on the outbreak of hostilities, going on to command the Army of Northern Virginia with great success. He was also close to the equivalent of American royalty, being directly descended from Martha Washington and son of legendary Revolutionary War cavalry commander Henry 'Light Horse Harry' Lee.

If Lee had a flaw, it was his preference for offensive action. He may have fared better by dragging the war out to induce war-weariness in his opponent. Instead, Lee looked for the eye-catching victory that he felt was vital to secure independence. This aggressive approach led to high casualties, which the Southern states were ill-equipped to absorb. This quest for glory echoed that of the Continental Army in its struggle with the British almost a century earlier. But where the Americans had won such a victory at Saratoga, Lee's push for a decisive victory led to the costly defeat at Gettysburg.

Having danced around his Union counterparts early in the war, Lee therefore found himself increasingly constricted as his numbers dwindled, and he was eventually penned in, besieged in the antithesis of the sort of warfare he championed. After the war he became the president of Washington College.

An aged and war-weary Davis, painted after the war by Daniel Huntington

JEFFERSON DAVIS

ONLY PRESIDENT OF THE CONFEDERATE STATES

YEARS: 1808-89 **BIRTHPLACE:** FAIRVIEW, KENTUCKY

As the first and last president of the Confederate States, and commander-in-chief of Confederate forces, Jefferson Davis had a monumental task on his hands and the enormity of it eventually broke his health. A gifted military man, Davis returned from the Mexican War as a wounded hero and used that distinction to full advantage in his political career. He believed in the necessity to expand the number of slave-owning states to balance with the Northern free states. In terms of military strategy, Davis believed the South needed to resist the North at every point. Aware that he could not muster as many men as his Union opponents, he advocated dispersing forces and keeping two large concentrations to be moved rapidly to the point of crisis. It was a sensible and workable plan, but eventually crumbled as the North was able to mount multiple incursions into Confederate territory.

After the war, Davis remained defiant and was briefly imprisoned, until released due to his poor health. He never swore allegiance to the Union.

Johnston, as captured in a portrait by Benjamin Franklin Reinhart in 1860

JOSEPH E JOHNSTON

THE BEST GENERAL IN THE CSA

YEARS: 1807-91 **BIRTHPLACE:** FARMVILLE, VIRGINIA

Johnston graduated from West Point in the same class as Robert E Lee – he finished 13th out of 46, while Lee topped the class – and went on to establish a reputation for bad luck. "Johnston is a great soldier," commented General Winfield Scott, "but he had an unfortunate knack of getting himself shot in nearly every engagement."

Evolving into an exceedingly cautious general, Johnston took the same approach to commanding an army as he did to hunting – he never committed himself to aggressive action unless assured of success. This inevitably meant he did not initiate many offensive moves, but instead he was skillful and dogged on the defensive, especially when holding General Sherman at bay before Atlanta.

When he did order an attack, his men were buoyed by confidence that the odds must truly be in their favor and as a result, he became beloved by his men and was later described by many fellow officers as the greatest general of all the ones on the Confederate side.

A somber, mournful-looking man, Hood only really understood offensive operations and his men suffered greatly as a result

JOHN BELL HOOD

TRAGIC REPRESENTATION OF THE SOUTH

YEARS: 1831-79 **BIRTHPLACE:** OWINGSVILLE, KENTUCKY

Hood saw his star rise and fall in dramatic fashion during the war. Always an aggressive commander, his approach won him attention and promotion, but also exacted a terrible price before the end.

He was an undistinguished student – graduating 44th out of a class of 52 at West Point – and never got to grips with the intricacies of military logistics and organization.

After catching the eye at the Seven Days' Battle, Antietam, and Fredericksburg, he climbed the ranks quickly, but he lost the use of his left arm at Gettysburg and most of his right leg at Chickamauga. Having undermined his superior Joseph E Johnston during the defense of Atlanta, he was given command of the Army of Tennessee at the age of 33. He instantly attacked and was soundly defeated by General Sherman. Hood then took his army into Tennessee, taking heavy casualties in a frontal assault at Franklin and then suffering a cataclysmic defeat at Nashville while Sherman marched his men unopposed through Georgia to start his successful but controversial 'total war' march.

A highly intelligent man, Forrest is credited with coining the military phrase, 'get there firstest with the mostest'

NATHAN BEDFORD FORREST

CAVALRY GENIUS

YEARS: 1821-77 **BIRTHPLACE:** BEDFORD COUNTRY, TENNESSEE

In contrast to the West Point graduates who packed the officer ranks of both armies, Forrest did not attend military school and had little formal education. He was, however, a superb cavalry commander, often cited as the best such soldier in his nation's history. Something of a firebrand, he was reputed to have killed 30 men as well as having almost as many horses shot out from under him, and he chafed under any sort of authority, demanding independent commands. One of the few men to escape from Grant at Fort Donelson, Forrest rose through the ranks and was in charge of a cavalry brigade in the Army of Tennessee by 1862. A specialist in raiding tactics, especially behind enemy lines, he covered Hood's offensive into Tennessee and then the inevitable retreat. After the war, he sullied his reputation by becoming the first Grand Wizard of the Ku Klux Klan.

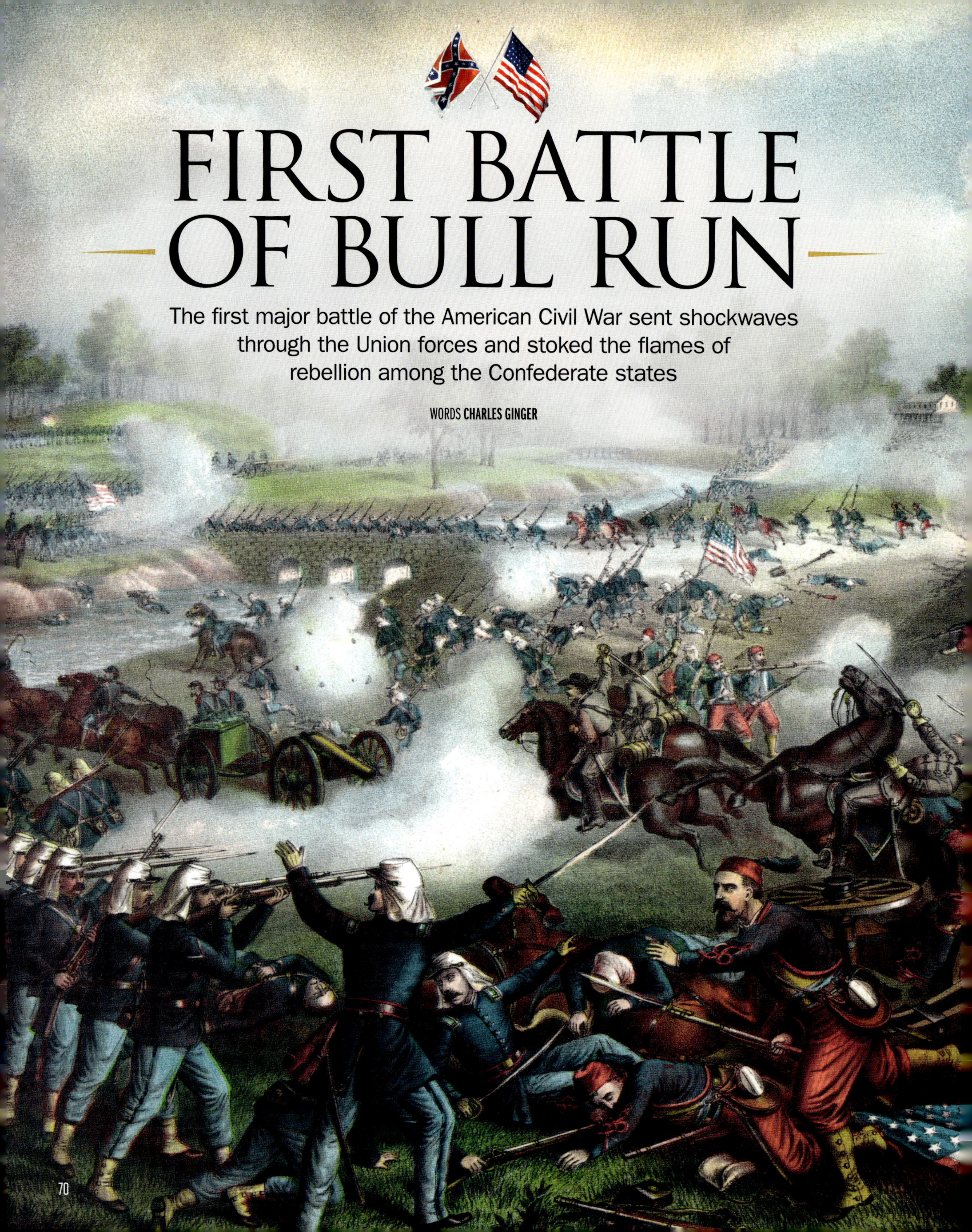

FIRST BATTLE OF BULL RUN

The first major battle of the American Civil War sent shockwaves through the Union forces and stoked the flames of rebellion among the Confederate states

WORDS **CHARLES GINGER**

Image: Getty

The first major clash of the American Civil War, the First Battle of Bull Run provided a harsh wake-up call to anyone who had anticipated a swift conclusion to the rebellion, claiming the lives of approximately 850 men and horribly maiming countless more besides.

The Civil War had escalated quickly. After Abraham Lincoln won the presidential election in November 1860, vowing to keep slavery out of the Western territories that were yet to become states, many in the South felt threatened. Despite Lincoln's assurances in his inaugural address that he had "no purpose to interfere with the institution of slavery where it exists in the United States," these states feared the North would eventually seek to abolish all slavery, which was the cornerstone of the South's agricultural economy. South Carolina, Mississippi, Florida, Alabama, Georgia, Louisiana, and Texas seceded from the United States, but the war itself didn't break out until 12 April 1861. Confederate forces bombarded Fort Sumter, an island fortress that controlled Charleston harbor, in South Carolina. Lincoln replied by calling for 75,000 volunteers to support the US Army in crushing the uprising. In response to this show of force, another four states (Virginia, Arkansas, North Carolina and Tennessee) joined the Confederacy.

With the stage set for a confrontation, the Union Army's Major McDowell was promoted to the post of Brigadier General and placed in charge of the Department of North-Eastern Virginia. Though McDowell felt that his 35,000 recruits would require extensive training, political pressure forced him to go on the offensive.

He devised a plan to outflank the Confederates stationed at Bull Run (around 25 miles from Washington, DC) and embarked from the capital on 16 July 1861. Unfortunately for the Unionist

"IT PROVIDED A HARSH WAKE-UP CALL TO ANYONE WHO HAD ANTICIPATED A SWIFT CONCLUSION TO THE REBELLION"

general, a Confederate spy named Rose O'Neal Greenhow had obtained his plans and passed them on to General Beauregard. Aware that reinforcements were headed via rail from the Shenandoah Valley to Beauregard's position, McDowell launched a pre-emptive attack on Beauregard's army.

Crushing defeat

The attack began with an artillery barrage at 5.15am on the morning of 21 July. Alerted by projectiles striking alarmingly close to where he was eating breakfast, Beauregard countered the Unionist attack by trying to defend his exposed left flank. He also waited to hear how the planned attack on the Union's left flank was going. But these plans actually failed to materialize, as the troops had not received Beauregard's order. When a brigade under the command of Colonel William T Sherman forded the Bull Run tributary to attack the enemy's right flank, the Confederate lines began to buckle. Only fierce resistance led by the likes of Thomas Jackson (earning him the infamous nickname 'Stonewall') prevented the Unionists from closing in for the kill.

Fortunately for the Confederates, reinforcements soon began to arrive, enabling them to establish a defensive line on the slopes of Henry House Hill. Having held McDowell's advance, the Southern army turned the tide in the mid-afternoon when the 33rd Virginians stormed an artillery battery, earning a foothold that eventually led to the Confederates putting their adversaries to flight around an hour later.

The crushing Unionist defeat sent shockwaves across the previously confident Northern states, with anyone who had harbored ideas of a rapid end to the conflict instantly disabused of such notions. Instead of the battle extinguishing the Confederate cause, it stoked the flames of rebellion that would engulf the United States for four long years and claim over 620,000 lives. ★

"THE CRUSHING UNIONIST DEFEAT SENT SHOCKWAVES ACROSS THE PREVIOUSLY CONFIDENT NORTHERN STATES"

FIRST BATTLE OF BULL RUN

21 JULY 1861

05 MCDOWELL'S FATAL ERROR

Confident that he has the Confederates hopelessly trapped on the hill, McDowell commits the critical error of deciding to obliterate his enemy with a relentless artillery bombardment instead of seizing the ground before him.

09 FORCED FROM THE HILL

At around 4pm the remaining Unionist troops are finally rushed off Henry House Hill and sent into a scattered retreat. At the same time, Colonel Oliver O'Howard's brigade finds itself on the wrong end of an assault on Chinn Ridge (west of the main battle) from two Confederate brigades recently arrived from Shenandoah Valley. At the sight of the enemy's collapse, General Beauregard commands his entire army to move forward. Total victory is within his grasp.

07 TURNING THE TIDE

Having held their ground, the Confederates spot a chance to put the enemy batteries out of action. In a charge that will take a horrendous toll, the 33rd Virginians overrun the guns of Captain Charles Griffin, who had moved two of his guns to the southern end of his line with the aim of enveloping the enemy in a hailstorm of cannon fire. This success is then compounded by the capture of Captain James Ricketts' battery of the 1st US Artillery.

06 STONEWALL ARRIVES

Further reinforcement arrives for the Confederates in the form of Thomas Jackson, who earns his famous nickname during a determined defense of the Southerners' position from around noon until 2pm. It is alleged that when Jackson vowed, "We will give them (the Unionists) the bayonet", Brigadier General Barnard Bee (who died during the battle) exclaimed to his men, "There is Jackson standing like a stone wall. Let us determine to die here, and we will conquer."

08 A FIERY EXCHANGE

Desperate to plug the holes torn in their flank by the Confederate onslaught, Unionist infantrymen rush to engage the triumphant captors of the guns. A ferocious fight ensues that results in the Union artillery exchanging hands several times. Implored to "Yell like furies!" by Jackson, the cry of the Confederates' 'rebel yell' fills the sky as they smash into the Union ranks.

01 OPENING SALVO

Intent on harassing the Confederates' right flank in order to draw fire away from the main attack, McDowell directs Colonel Israel Richardson to position his guns at Blackburn's Ford. At approximately 5.15am Richardson fires the first shots of the day, his artillery raining cannon fire down on the enemy positions across the water, some of which fly far enough to smash down close to where General Beauregard is eating his breakfast.

02 SHERMAN TAKES THE INITIATIVE

As the numerically superior Unionists press their advance on the Confederate left flank in the hope of routing the enemy before its reinforcements arrive, Colonel William Sherman orders his men to cross an unguarded part of the creek and hit the Confederate right flank, catching their opponents off guard. Colonel Nathan 'Shanks' Evans of the Confederates, having previously rushed to hold off the Unionist thrust before Sherman's intervention, now finds himself withdrawing with his men to the slopes of Matthews Hill.

03 CONFEDERATE COLLAPSE

Despite fighting tenaciously, the Confederate line begins to crumble under intense pressure from the surprise Unionist thrust against its right flank. A chaotic retreat to Henry House Hill ensues at about 11.30am.

04 STAND AND FIGHT

Fortunately for Evans and his fellow commanders, help arrives in the form of Captain John D Imboden's artillery battery, which unleashes a hail of fire on the pursuing Unionists for long enough to enable the Confederates to establish a defensive line on Henry House Hill. A potential rout has been averted.

10 FLEE FOR YOUR LIVES

Having begun their retreat in a relatively calm manner, the Unionists instantly panic when a blast of artillery overturns a wagon rolling among them. Intermingled with terrified civilians who had come to witness the spectacle of a crushing Confederate defeat, the soldiers of the North scramble back to the Unionist capital at Washington, DC, having been thrashed.

Map: Nicholas Forder

Commanding general of the United States Army, General Winfield Scott, developed the so-called Anaconda Plan to defeat the South

THE PLAN FOR VICTORY

Northern strategy rested upon the economic strangulation of the Confederacy by coastal naval blockade and the conquest of the Mississippi River

WORDS **MARC DESANTIS**

In April 1861, with the slave states of the Confederacy breaking away from the Union and a civil war dawning, President Abraham Lincoln proclaimed a naval blockade of the Southern coastline from the Potomac River in Virginia all the way around Florida to the mouth of the Rio Grande in south Texas. The foundational Union strategy for encompassing the defeat of the Confederacy was developed by the United States Army's commanding general, 74-year-old General-in-Chief Winfield Scott.

Scott's first need was to formulate a coherent plan of action against the South. An initial war plan was drawn up by 34-year-old General George McClellan and sent to Scott in late April 1861. This envisioned a short war brought to a victorious conclusion by the advance of two separate Union armies, each of which would steamroll their way through different parts of the South, crushing any Confederate opposition along the way.

Scott disliked much about the McClellan plan, seeing it as overly optimistic. He modified it, adding his own ideas to it, and presented the much-transformed plan to President Lincoln on 2 May 1861. In Scott's own words, the Confederates would be surrounded by a "cordon of posts on the Mississippi to its mouth from the junction with the Ohio [River], and by blockading ships of war on the seaboard."

Scott himself warned that the "greatest obstacle in the way of this plan – the great danger now pressing upon us – the impatience of our patriotic and loyal Union friends." There were incessant demands for "instant and vigorous action, regardless, I fear, of consequences," a worried Scott wrote. Scott also disliked the idea of an invasion of the South, and held that such an attack, if it occurred, would actually severely hinder a settlement of the secession crisis, not make such a thing more likely.

Scott's plan was endlessly examined by Northern newspapers, and it was dubbed the 'Anaconda' plan after the South American constrictor snake that kills its prey by suffocating it slowly. A printmaker in Cincinnati, Ohio, produced a map of the Confederacy being grappled by a giant snake, and entitled the work 'Scott's Great Snake.' Generally, more conservative Northerners approved of the Anaconda Plan, but radical newspapers typically did not, with one predicting that pro-Union Southerners would "be crushed out… long before the anaconda has got the whole country enveloped in its coils". Another paper urged immediate action. "Forward to Richmond! Forward to Richmond!" it insisted.

Pressure on the Union to act quickly was therefore intense. William Tecumseh Sherman, who would later go on to hold an exalted rank in the United States Army, had spoken with General Scott and was sure of his superior's judgment. "Genl. Scott knows what he is about," Sherman believed, but he also worried that with "so many pushing him that he says he may be beaten, by Genl. Impatience". Unlike many others in the North, Scott believed that the war would be a lengthy one.

The elements of Anaconda

Scott kept much of the Anaconda Plan, beyond its broadest outline, to himself. No less than Abraham Lincoln would say that "Scott will not let us outsiders know anything of his plans." Scott explained his strategy in broad strokes to Lincoln that May. It contained four primary elements. First, the United States Navy would blockade the Confederate coast, as the president had ordered the previous month. This would act to sever all links between the South and the outside world. Scott understood that the South obtained a significant portion of its income from the export of cotton and tobacco. Quashing their shipment overseas would necessarily impair the Confederacy's ability to either pay for or import weapons and other military supplies.

Second, the western rebel states of Louisiana, Arkansas, and Texas would be cut off from the eastern Confederate states by the capture of the full length of the Mississippi River. Third, the Confederate armies in Virginia would

"SCOTT DISLIKED THE IDEA OF AN INVASION OF THE SOUTH AND HELD THAT SUCH AN ATTACK, IF IT OCCURRED, WOULD ACTUALLY SEVERELY HINDER A SETTLEMENT OF THE SUCCESSION CRISIS"

Image: Alamy

The Union naval blockade of the Confederacy prevented the import of Southern cotton to Britain, which had harmful effects on Britain's textile industry

be subjected to unrelenting pressure. Lastly, the United States Navy would act in concert with the United States Army to move troops about and support them ashore with naval artillery fire.

Scott did not foresee big battles against Confederate armies, though in the actual course of the war these would occur on many occasions. Scott's goal was to crush the rebels economically. "We rely greatly on the sure operation of a complete blockade of the Atlantic and Gulf ports," he wrote. In conjunction with the blockade, Union forces would make a "powerful movement down the Mississippi to the ocean." The Confederate states would thereby be encircled and loss of life, in Scott's mind, would be kept to a minimum.

"SCOTT DID NOT FORSEE BIG BATTLES AGAINST CONFEDERATE ARMIES, THOUGH THESE WOULD OCCUR ON MANY OCCASIONS"

The blockade

Once the goal of the blockade had become fixed, there remained the practical problem of how to put it into practice. Ironically, the US Navy had a better understanding of the coasts of Mexico and Africa, having operated off of them in earlier years, than it had of the coasts of the United States. US Secretary of the Navy Gideon Welles convened the Commission of Conference, also known as the Blockade Board, to compile whatever information could be found in the United States governmental archives about the Southern shores. The Blockade Board

Running the Blockade

SWIFT CONFEDERATE BLOCKADE RUNNERS BRAVED THE UNION BLOCKADE TO OBTAIN GOODS FROM THE OUTSIDE WORLD

Southerners did not sit idly by while the Union blockade strangled their economy and hindered their war effort. They employed fast ships to run the blockade to carry on trade with the outside world. In the early days of the blockade, before the Union cordon tightened to suffocating levels, blockade runners could reap fantastic profits of over 700 percent on a single voyage.

A typical rebel blockade runner was a steam-driven, screw or sidewheel-propelled vessel. They would bear no masts, and would often be painted grey to better hide in the grim vastness of the ocean. Cargoes originating in neutral nations such as Britain would be deposited in neutral ports closer to the Confederacy, such as could be found in Cuba, Bermuda, and the Bahamas, to make picking them up and taking them back easier. While in port taking on their cargoes, the blockade runners were off-limits to Union attack, but once they left and were in international waters they were under constant threat from US warships.

CSS Florida ran the Union blockade twice and was a scourge of Union shipping for nearly two years

Not every blockade runner hauled supplies though; some were outfitted as commerce raiders. One notorious blockade runner was the CSS Florida. The 700-ton vessel had been built at Confederate behest in Liverpool and then steamed to the Bahamas, under the name of Oreto, where it obtained guns and ammunition that had been shipped separately from Britain. In August 1862, its British colors were taken down to be replaced by those of the Confederacy. Renamed Florida, it was tasked with roaming the high seas, hunting down Union merchantmen.

It would, however, first need to find more sailors. Yellow fever had decimated the crew and Florida's captain, Lieutenant John Newland Maffitt, had himself fallen ill. To find refuge before every last man aboard perished, Maffitt made a daring daylight run into the Confederate port of Mobile, Alabama. Despite being hit several times by Union blockading ships, Florida made it into harbor safely on 3 September 1862, much to the embarrassment of the United States Navy.

After fitting out and taking on more sailors, Florida departed Mobile in January 1863, once again successfully running the Union blockade. Over the next two years, Florida would help decimate the United States merchantmen before being rammed and sunk by a Union ship.

Blockade runners were not as effective as they might have been. The Confederate government failed to bring the runners under central direction, leaving the organization to private citizens. Blockade runners therefore tended to carry cargoes that would fetch the highest prices, not those the Confederate war effort required most produced seven reports on the nature of the Confederate coastline over the summer and autumn of 1861. These reports were thereafter incorporated into the overall Anaconda strategy.

Among the recommendations made by the Blockade Board was the need to capture naval bases between Hampton Roads, Virginia, and Key West, Florida. Union blockading forces would benefit from having stations where they could take on coal – the fuel of steam warships – and make repairs. The blockade itself would also be enhanced by the acquisition of these additional bases, and help prove to the outside world that the United States maintained full control of its coastline. European attitudes toward the rebellion was of great importance to the Lincoln administration and no one wanted to see the Confederacy win diplomatic recognition as an independent state.

The Blockade Board also suggested that two separate squadrons should be organized on the Atlantic seaboard depending on the nature of the coasts they would have to guard, with the dividing line between their area of operations being set along the state border between North and South Carolina. The Blockade Board stated that the Hatteras Inlet, an ingress/egress point for Southern blockade runners, should be captured. The Board also said that the Gulf of Mexico coast should be better guarded. The United States maintained but a single base along that vast stretch of shoreline, at Key West, and this was far distant from the major Confederate ports at Mobile, Alabama, and New Orleans, Louisiana. A base nearer to both should be occupied, the Board held, and recommended that Ship Island, which lay off the Mississippi coast between the two ports, be taken.

Though the blockade would never, and could never, be airtight, its imposition did have a serious and rapid effect on the South and its ability to prosecute the war against the North. Ammunition stocks began to dwindle soon after the blockade was established.

***Above** SS Banshee, a steampowered sidewheeler Confederate blockade runner*

Down the Mississippi

The Mississippi River, in the Western Theater, was another crucial component of the Anaconda Plan. General Scott had called for a step-by-step movement down it until Union armies held the whole of the river from the Ohio River in the north all the way to its outlet at the Gulf of Mexico. Not only would this cause the western Confederate states to be separated from their eastern Confederate brethren, but possession of the entire run of the river would allow Northern farmers upriver to use the enormous, watery highway to ship their produce to distant markets.

The Union's task of securing the Mississippi was made more difficult by the inescapable need to clear out every last Confederate stronghold from the banks of the river. A single rebel artillery position of steam warship haven could deny Union movement along the river to the Gulf. Such positions could also act as crossing points for the Confederate. There was

The Anaconda Plan as depicted by a Northern artist in 1861

Image: Alamy, Wikipedia Commons / Public Domain

United States Navy Flag Officer David Glasgow Farragut captured the Mississippi port of New Orleans in April 1862

therefore no viable alternative to total Union control of the river, and its conquest of the stretch from Cairo, Illinois, south to New Orleans dominated Union operations in the Western Theater during the early years of the war.

Eventually, after the expenditure of much blood and treasure, the length of the Mississippi was brought under Union control. A major step in the Northern conquest of the waterway came in April 1862 with the capture of the exit to the Gulf of Mexico. A Union fleet under the command of Flag Officer David Glasgow Farragut braved the fire of two forts commanding the river's mouth, defeated a rebel fleet stationed there, and advanced upriver in order to seize New Orleans.

The exit of the Mississippi was now in Union hands, but the entire stretch did not come under Northern control until the fall of Vicksburg in July 1863. Vicksburg commanded the river from an extremely powerful position on heights overlooking the water, but in an extended campaign, General Ulysses S Grant brought the city under siege and forced its surrender.

Diplomacy and Union victory

The American Civil War was as much a diplomatic struggle as it was a military conflict. The United States government strove to prevent the Confederate States of America from securing diplomatic recognition by foreign governments, and thus prevent the possibility of them giving substantial military aid to the South. However, one episode occurring in late 1861, when the Civil War was only a few months old, combined the awful possibility of foreign recognition of the Confederacy with war against another major power. Jefferson Davis, the president of the Confederate States of America, had sent two men, James Mason and John Slidell, to be the South's commissioners in Europe. High on their agenda of business was the desire to have Britain bring an end to the Union's blockade of Southern ports. The inability of the South to export its cotton, particularly to the huge market that was Britain, was crippling its ability to earn money needed to pay for the war. But that wasn't all – it was also having deleterious effects on the British textile industry.

John Slidell, the second of the Confederate commissioners removed from the RMS Trent in November 1862

Mason and Slidell were traveling across the Atlantic Ocean aboard RMS Trent, a British mail steamer, not far from Cuba, when it was boarded by USS San Jacinto, a United States warship under the command of Captain Charles Wilkes. Wilkes made Mason and Slidell his prisoners, justifying their removal from a neutral ship on the creative grounds that they were both living dispatches, and as such, could be seized as 'contraband of war.'

Under international law, however, Wilkes' search of a neutral vessel and the seizure of the commissioners were clear violations. The seizure ignited a firestorm of protest in Britain, engendering some heated talk of war. This would naturally have been disastrous for the North, and an utterly unexpected, but welcome, boon to the South.

The United States had been placed in severe diplomatic peril by the unsanctioned act of a single naval captain. Complicating the Lincoln administration's response was Wilkes' subsequent popularity. The seizure of Mason and Slidell from the Trent was gratifying to many Northerners, who wanted the rebellion to be stamped out, and Wilkes was applauded by many citizens who considered him to be a hero. The *New York Times* even said that the captain deserved a medal.

Southerners, in contrast, were happy to hear the news, but only because they thought that

THE LAIRD RAMS

HOW A CONFEDERATE QUEST TO BUILD STEAMPOWERED IRONCLAD 'RAMS' IN LIVERPOOL WAS FOILED

Matters would trouble Anglo-American relations over the course of the war. The Union blockade was curtailing the shipment of Southern cotton to Britain and contributing to unemployment among textile factory workers there. With the Confederacy unable to build warships of its own, it looked abroad to find firms to construct ships for it. Britain, with its massive and modern shipbuilding industry, was an obvious place to seek out builders. Southern purchasing agent James Bulloch contracted with the Liverpool firm of Laird & Co to build two steampowered, ironclad rams – ships with bows strengthened to deliver devastating ramming attacks – for the Confederate fleet.

However, it did not take very long for the American ambassador to Britain, Charles Francis Adams, the son and grandson of prior US presidents, to learn of the Confederate order, and he quickly made his protest known to the British government that their construction was a violation of Britain's neutral status. On 5 September 1862, Adams made it clear that, should the British government fail to act, there would be war between the United States and Britain. Matters had changed since late 1861 when the Lincoln administration had backed down in the wake of the Trent affair. The Union fleet was now much more powerful, and Britain's merchant marine would have been subject to attack if war should come. Canada was of course still extremely vulnerable to an American invasion. On 8 September, the British government ordered Laird to cease all construction work on the rams.

In June 1863, the tireless Bulloch found a straw buyer for the rams, in this case the Khedive of Egypt, with loans provided by a pair of French banks. The rams were then to be steamed out to sea and handed over to Confederate sailors. The watchful Adams learned of the subterfuge and squelched the plan with another timely protest to the British government. The two rams were impounded in October 1863, and by 1864 were taken into service by the Royal Navy, after the French banks were appropriately compensated.

Charles Francis Adams prevented the South from taking possession of the Laird rams

The fall of Vicksburg was a crowning achievement of the Anaconda Plan

James Mason, one of the Confederate commissioners seized from the RMS Trent in November 1862

it would sour Anglo-American relations, and thereby bring benefit to the Southern cause. Jefferson Davis had no doubt that the removal of the commissioners was an insult to Britain. "These gentlemen were as much under the jurisdiction of the British government upon that ship and beneath its flag as if they had been on its soil," he told the Confederate Congress.

Many in Britain agreed with Davis, believing that Wilkes' action had been an insult. The British cabinet, when composing its message to Washington concerning the incident, was in a quandary as to how to respond to the provocation. If they responded too forcefully, Lincoln would have no room in which to back down gracefully and save face. If its response were to be too soft, then the United States would not get the proper impression as to how angry the British government was at the boarding of the Trent and the seizure of the Confederate commissioners.

Above all else, the British cabinet wanted an apology for the stopping of a British ship on the high seas and the removal of Mason and Slidell. The apology was to be delivered within seven days of the receipt of the letter, or there would be war between Britain and the United

A Laird ram, after it had been seized by the British government and commissioned by the Royal Navy as HMS Wivern

Image: Alamy, Getty, Wikipedia Commons / Public Domain

States. The task of writing the letter was given to Lord John Russell, Britain's foreign secretary. Russell's letter pleased no one, and the cabinet then decided that two separate letters should be sent to Washington. One would express disapproval for the boarding of the Trent, while the other would demand an apology and threaten war if it was not forthcoming.

Crisis averted

The British cabinet could not come to agreement on either of the two letters, which though still in unfinished form, were sent to Queen Victoria and also to Prince Albert, who was stricken with typhoid fever and near to death. Albert's influence was to ameliorate the harshness of the planned letters. The prince advised that they include the expressed hope that Wilkes had not acted under orders from the United States government, thereby giving the Lincoln administration some chance with which to save face.

Russell made it clear to the British ambassador in the United States, Lord Richard Lyons, that the prisoners would have to be released. Nothing, not even an apology for their seizure, would suffice if this one condition was not met.

The possibility of war between Britain and the United States loomed as the British cabinet awaited a response. The prospect of war was not a happy one. There was real fear that the US Army might invade Canada should war erupt. Some 11,000 British troops were sent to Canada in December 1861.

Likewise, the United States could ill-afford having another war. The war scare had made it impossible for the US government to sell bonds to pay for the current war with the South. Further, the Royal Navy was the most powerful fleet in the world. If war came, it would quickly bring about an end to the blockade, and the secession of the South would succeed.

President Lincoln saw the folly of war with the United Kingdom, and his secretary of state, William Seward, composed a letter in answer to that of Britain. The response was delivered to Lyons on 27 December 1861. Seward placed the blame for the Trent affair squarely on Wilkes, saying that the captain had erred in not seeking out a prize court to adjudicate the seizure. Mason and Slidell were released, and on 1 January 1862, they sailed to Britain aboard a Royal Navy warship.

A costly and unnecessary war had been averted because Lincoln, showing true strategic sense, had grasped that the true aim of the war, the re-incorporation of the rebellious Southern states, would be better served by remaining at peace with the United Kingdom. ★

Union Major General Ulysses S Grant captured the Confederate stronghold of Vicksburg in July 1863

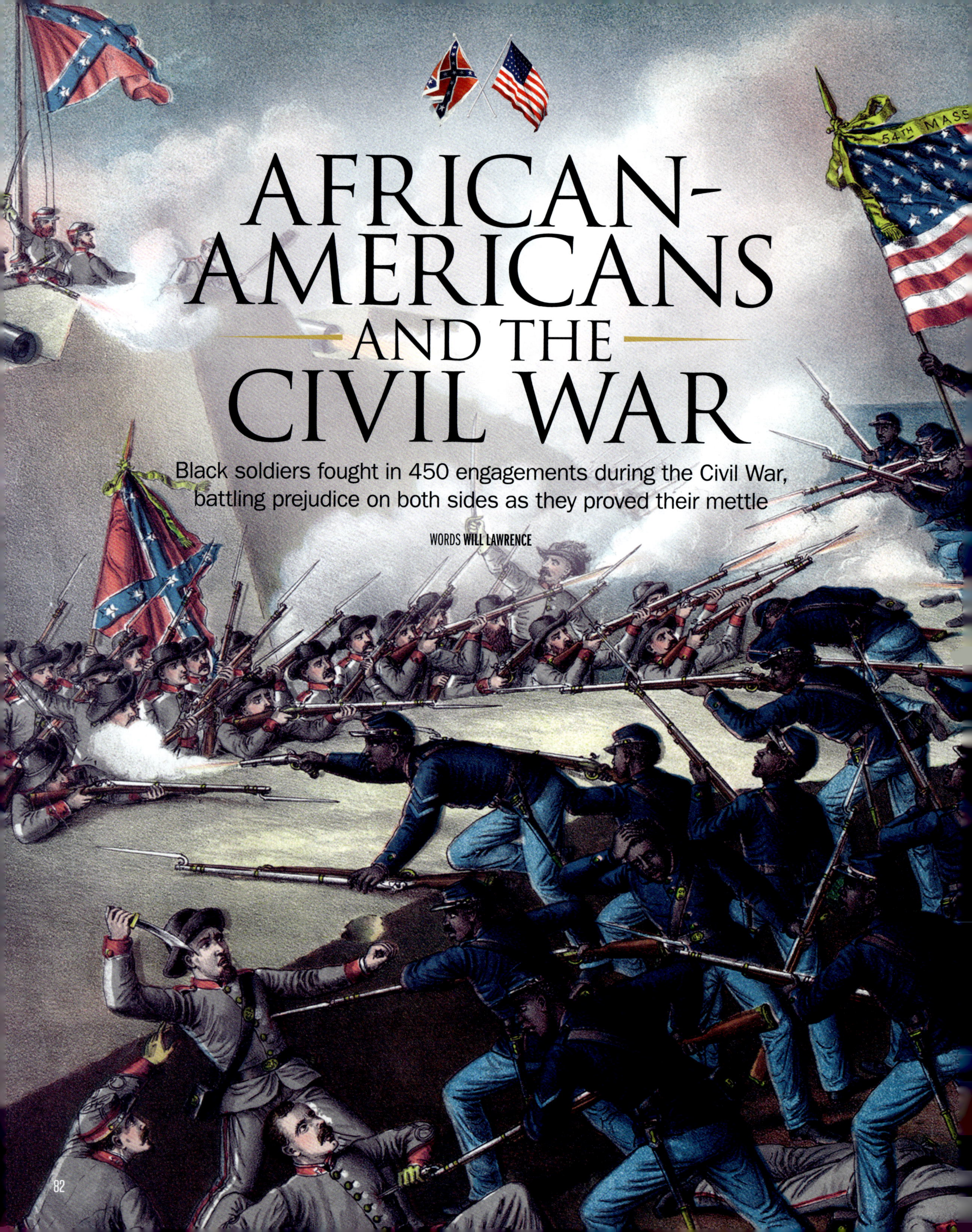

AFRICAN-AMERICANS AND THE CIVIL WAR

Black soldiers fought in 450 engagements during the Civil War, battling prejudice on both sides as they proved their mettle

WORDS **WILL LAWRENCE**

The Union attack on Fort Wagner in July 1863, led by the 54th Massachusetts Volunteer Infantry, one of the first major American military units made up of African-American soldiers

The band of the Union Army's 107th US Colored Infantry, Arlington, Virginia, in 1865

It was the Union navy that showed the way. From the outset of the war, the naval authorities had welcomed men of all colors and creeds, who tended to serve primarily as cooks and stewards, firefighters and haulers of coal. But that was not the limit of their efforts. In 1861, the USS Minnesota appointed a group of contraband slaves to serve as a gun crew, while in May 1862 a South Carolina slave by the name of Robert Smalls took charge of a dispatch boat in Charleston Harbor and ran it out to the Union's blockading fleet. He was eventually appointed a pilot in the US Navy.

At that time, however, Pilot Robert Smalls could not serve in the army. The notion of black troops fighting the South on land had been mooted since the outbreak of hostilities. After all, as one Civil War historian notes, "Armed blacks were truly the bête noir of Southern nightmares." Yet most considered the conflict to be a 'white man's war', and the war department refused to consider the enlistment of any black troops, even though they marched in their hundreds to Union recruitment offices, eager to volunteer, once war was declared.

Black troops had fought in the Revolution, plus the War of 1812, but prejudice was still rife across America. Black fighters had been banned from state militias since 1792, and the regular army had never permitted their inclusion. Those that had fought in earlier conflicts were irregulars. All across the Northern states, black people were still regarded with suspicion and contempt, especially among the poorer classes with whom they competed for work.

Proving their worth

Lincoln's Emancipation Proclamation of 1 January 1863, which authorized the arming of freed slaves, was unpopular on both sides. The vast majority of Northern troops believed they were fighting for the continuation of the Union, not the emancipation of Southern slaves. Even Lincoln's proclamation imagined a limited role for black troops: "To garrison forts, positions, stations, and other places." Indeed, in the words of a leading war historian, "One of the first battles these black troops had to fight was for a chance to prove themselves in combat."

And yet prove themselves they did. Even before Lincoln's proclamation, five regiments of free black soldiers were organized in Louisiana, Kansas, and South Carolina, with the latter, the 1st South Carolina Volunteers, officially authorized by the War Department. The Kansans saw action in a Missouri skirmish during October 1862, and ten of them fell as the first black combat casualties of the war.

In January 1863, the 1st South Carolina Volunteers saw action during a raid along St Mary's river between Florida and Georgia, prompting their commander, Colonel Higginson, to write, "No officer in this regiment now doubts that the key to the successful prosecution of the war lies in the unlimited employment of black troops." The pilot of one of the ships employed in the raid was Robert Smalls.

Lincoln's thoughts on the use of black soldiers stiffened as the year progressed and as early as March 1863 he was writing that the sight of "50,000 armed and drilled black soldiers on the banks of the Mississippi would end the rebellion at once".

Certainly, when called upon to fight their first major engagement, black soldiers more than proved their worth. The action unfolded at Port Hudson on the morning of 27 May 1863, with two Union regiments of black fighters from Louisiana overcoming their inexperience to mount three charges on Confederate lines. They suffered terribly – 37 dead and 155 wounded – but earned their laurels.

They fared even better at the nearby engagement at Milliken's Bend. Here Texan

"THE WAR DEPARTMENT INITIALLY REFUSED TO CONSIDER BLACK TROOPS, EVEN THOUGH THEY MARCHED TO UNION RECRUITMENT OFFICES IN THEIR HUNDREDS, EAGER TO VOLUNTEER"

regiments set upon three black regiments raised by General Lorenzo Thomas, a great proponent of black recruitment. The 9th and 11th Louisiana Infantry and the 1st Mississippi fought bravely with their outdated muskets and, supported by Union gunboats, pushed the Confederates back.

Assistant Secretary of War Charles A Dana was impressed by what he saw, writing, "The bravery of the blacks… completely revolutionized the sentiment of the army with regard to employment of negro troops." A Confederate lady, meanwhile, could not believe her ears. Texans whipped by "a mongrel crew of white and black Yankees", she wrote. "There must be some mistake."

Assault on Fort Wagner

There was no mistake. Black troops would continue to serve with distinction throughout the war, following up Milliken's Bend with a further show of valor at Fort Wagner a few weeks later. The Confederacy had built up huge earthworks and the Union's 54th Massachusetts Infantry, described by one historian as "the North's showcase black regiment", were chosen to storm the defenses.

The attack began on the evening of 18 July. The defenders held their fire until the Unionists had drawn close before unleashing a succession of volleys that tore into the attacking troops. The 54th suffered the heaviest casualties, losing almost half of its number, including its abolitionist leader, Colonel Robert Shaw, who was shot in the heart.

RALLY! RALLY! RALLY!
TO MEN OF COLOR!
AUTHORITY HAS BEEN RECEIVED TO RAISE
A REGIMENT
OF
MEN OF COLOR
FOR 100 DAYS
Rally, Men of Color, at Once for Your Country
COL. TAGGART
$50 CITY BOUNTY
Will be Paid each Man. Come, then, to Head-quarters.

Above A recruiting poster for the Union Army printed in Philadelphia c.1863

Black Troops & the Confederacy

Surprisingly, the first black troops to shoulder arms had volunteered for the Confederacy…

Louisiana was the one Southern state with something approaching a free black population and in May 1861 a group banded together to form a volunteer militia unit, calling themselves the Regiment of Free Men of Color. The volunteers wanted to express their devotion to, and willingness to serve, their state.

However, while the state governor announced his gratitude by appointing a white colonel to command them, they were not officially recognized by the Confederate government, and had to supply their own weapons and uniforms. There is no evidence that the regiment ever actually fired in anger upon Union troops.

The regiment was disbanded and reformed several times before being disbanded for good by General John L Lewis of the Louisiana Militia on 25 April 1862, as federal ships arrived opposite the city.

Elsewhere, slaves were employed by the Confederacy as a labor force, with plantation owners offered remuneration for any that were drafted into work gangs. Though this proved highly unpopular – slaves were a valuable commodity – many slaves were recruited. Many deserted and, as contraband of war, the Union troops felt no obligation to return them to their owners.

As defeat loomed, the Confederacy debated the enlistment of slaves with General Robert E Lee eventually adding his considerable voice to the argument, agreeing that the only way of finding the manpower to sustain the war was to enlist black soldiers. By March of 1865, the Confederate Congress decreed that owners make 25 percent of their slaves available for military service. Two companies of black soldiers were mustered but the final Union victory rescued them from combat.

The Regiment of Free Men of Color were at their post when federal ships arrived opposite New Orleans, 25 April 1862

The heroic assault on Fort Wagner encouraged more African-Americans to enlist in the Union Army

The 54th held Wagner's parapet for an hour in the darkness before a Confederate counter-attack pushed them back. So ferociously had they fought, however, that *Atlantic Monthly* declared that Fort Wagner was for "the colored race as Bunker Hill had been for 90 years to the white Yankees".

Here, the 54th's Sergeant William H Carney won the first Medal of Honor ever granted to a black soldier. When the Unionists asked for the return of Shaw's body, however, the Confederates replied that they had thrown him in a pit, unmarked, with his troops. The rebels despised the officers as much as they did their black troops. Shaw's father later said that he was proud for his son to lie in rest with such gallant troops.

This regiment, despite losses pushing 300 killed, captured, or wounded, were subsequently brought into a small army of white and black troops, under the command of General Quincy Gillmore, which was charged with retaking Florida. They were defeated at Olustee, with Confederates showing little mercy to the black troops. The medical officer of the 8th US Colored Troops saved many men by prioritizing black troops over white for battlefield evacuation, knowing that the white troops would fare better in captivity.

Captured black troops also suffered at Confederate hands in the wake of their defeat at Fort Pillow by General Nathan Bedford Forrest,

Black Union soldiers convalescing at Aitken's Landing, James River, Virginia, in 1864

whose troops shot a host of black prisoners, as well as some white. It became known as the Fort Pillow Massacre. The Union went after Forrest but suffered another defeat, the heaviest in the Western Theater, when a force half the size of the Union's 8,000 men won a victory at Brice's Cross Roads on 10 June 1864. Again, black troops suffered heavy losses, though few blamed the soldiery. This was a failure of general-ship.

Poor leadership also undermined the efforts of black troops in what many regard as their most celebrated action of the war, the Battle of the Crater, a move that in its conception was a masterstroke, in its execution a disaster. As part of the 1864 Siege of Petersburg, Union troops improvised and executed a daring explosion in the Confederate defenses on 30 July, blowing open a large gap in their line.

Leading the way

At first, troops from the black Ninth Corps were chosen to lead the charge into the gap, but General Grant then approved a white unit to act as the vanguard. This division was underprepared and faltered. By the time the black troops initially chosen entered the fray, the Confederates had launched a sizeable counter-attack and claimed the lives of 3,500 Ninth Corps soldiers. The black soldiers again fought valiantly in defeat and seven received the Medal of Honor.

Though this engagement was a disaster, the Union and its black troops were eventually able to take Petersburg and they occupied Charleston, too, in February 1865. Their greatest glory came a few months later when soldiers from the 9th Regiment US Colored Troops led the march into Richmond, the rebel capital, in early April. In the following month, the 62nd US Colored Troops fought the final battle of the war, at Palmito Ranch, Texas. By 1865, the Union army was almost ten percent black, though the units remained almost entirely segregated with white officers continuing to command black troops. Among 166 black regiments, fewer than 100 featured black officers, none of whom ranked above captain. In all, nearly 180,000 fought for the Union army and though they did not engage in many of the greatest battles – most of which unfolded before their enlistment – in the words of one leading historian, "Psychologically, the commitment of black soldiers enormously enhanced the Northern war effort." ★

Two black soldiers poised at a 'picket post' at Dutch Gap, Virginia, c.1865

BATTLE OF NEW ORLEANS

With the secession of the Southern states from the Union in 1861, General Winfield Scott put forth the 'Anaconda Plan' calling for a total blockade and encirclement of the South, including the Mississippi River

WORDS **MARC DESANTIS**

Stretching some 2,320 miles north to south, both sides of the American Civil War recognized the Mississippi's strategic importance. If the North could gain control of the river, it would sever the rebellious western states of Texas, Louisiana and Arkansas from the their eastern brethren. Accomplishing this goal was no easy thing: Union naval forces on the river at the outbreak of the war were next to nothing. Further, the entire length of the river would have to be taken in order to open it to the Union, deny passage to the Confederates, and enforce an effective blockade. The war for the Mississippi river would be one of not just riverine naval forces but also of fortifications and gun batteries situated on its banks.

A Union river naval force needed to be either built from scratch or converted from existing ships. US Secretary of the Navy Gideon Welles approved the formation of a gunboat force to fight for control of the river. As an inland waterway, the US Army claimed jurisdiction over the Mississippi and the many other rivers that fed into it, but the navy sent experienced officers to command the boats and whip them into fighting shape.

The weakest point of the Union naval blockade lay at the Mississippi's mouth as it empties into the Gulf of Mexico. The area was cut by so many waterways that guarding it was next to impossible, and so any blockade of it was bound to be porous – it was a matter of geography. At New Orleans, the river split into four separate channels, spreading out some 30 miles from one side to the other once it reached Gulf waters. It was also well-protected. Some 15 miles up from the Gulf entrance the channels converged to form a junction called the Head of Passes. Here, the rebels had their main defensive fortifications: Fort Jackson, on the western bank, and Fort St Philip, positioned on the eastern bank.

The Confederates would not simply allow the Federals to take control of the river without a fight, and they started building their own river fleet. An early Union attempt to cut traffic through the river by taking its blockading squadron inside the river

The Union screw sloop USS Hartford, lead ship of her class, battles her way past Fort Jackson as it presses up the Mississippi River, 24 April 1862

Flag Officer David Glasgow Farragut was overall commander of the Union fleet that attacked and captured New Orleans

mouth up to the Head of Passes was thwarted when, on 12 October 1861, the converted ironclad ram CSS Manassas appeared, rising only three feet above the water and armed with a 32-pound gun and a wicked array of below-the-waterline iron spikes. It looked like a floating cigar. Manassas rammed into the screw sloop USS Richmond, splintering its hull. Richmond grounded, along with one of its companions, the sailing sloop USS Vincennes. Its mission accomplished, Manassas withdrew, leaving the humiliated Federals alone to refloat their stranded warships. The Manassas's escapade was reported with delight by the press in New Orleans, while the bumbling US Navy was ridiculed by their Northern counterparts.

Despite New Orleans' strategic location, Jefferson Davis, president of the Confederacy, had not seen fit to do much to defend the city itself, thinking that Forts Jackson and St Philip just below it would be more than sufficient to turn back any Federal attempt to move upriver. The bulk of the city's defenses were instead oriented to the north – the direction in which any Union offensive was expected to come, leaving it vulnerable to an attack from the south. While Forts Jackson and St Philip were themselves substantial, if a Union fleet could actually find a way past them, New Orleans would be unable to repel a Federal assault.

Only by holding New Orleans could Southern commercial traffic be stopped with any certainty. Union strategists had been encouraged in their belief that the city was vulnerable to a naval assault. Earlier operations by the US Navy had demonstrated that ships could overcome land fortifications. In August 1861 a US Navy flotilla had bombarded Forts Clark and Hatteras at the Hatteras Inlet on the coast of North Carolina into submission. In November 1861 US Navy ships had forced the surrender of Forts Walker and Beauregard protecting Port Royal, South Carolina, leading to the fall of that city.

The Northern plan for seizing New Orleans was the making of 48-year-old Commander David Dixon Porter of the US Navy. He had spent much of 1861 in command of ships struggling

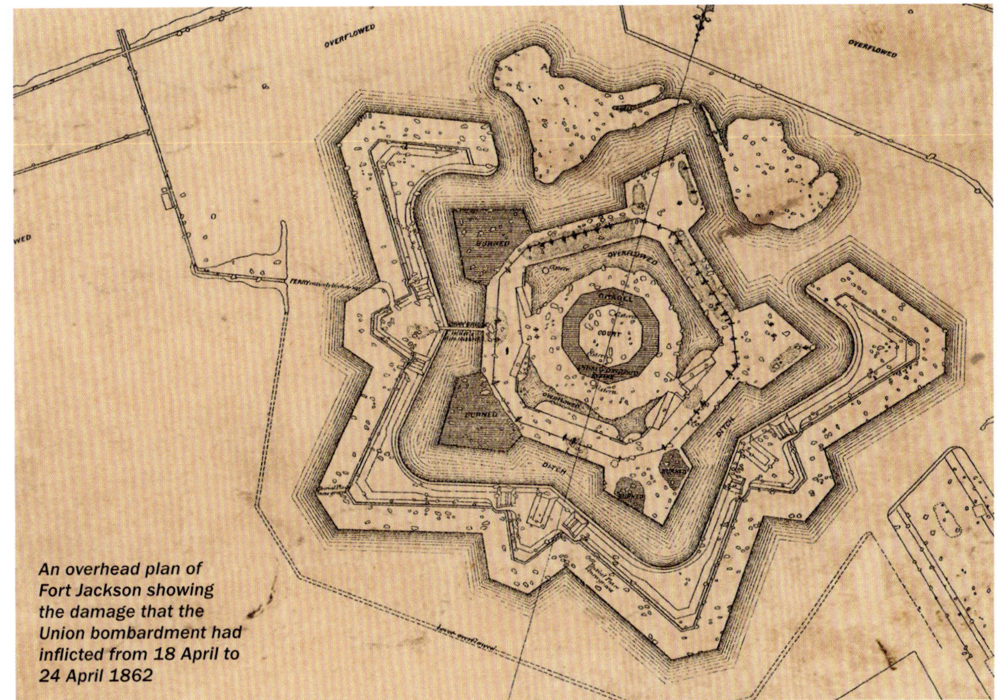
An overhead plan of Fort Jackson showing the damage that the Union bombardment had inflicted from 18 April to 24 April 1862

The deck of Farragut's flagship USS Hartford. The capture of New Orleans was a great achievement in Farragut's career, which until that moment had been solid if somewhat undistinguished

to maintain the blockade of the southern end of the Mississippi. Though nothing in concrete terms had been achieved, Porter had learned much about the river through his talks with local fishermen and his own nocturnal exploratory forays upriver. The information led him to believe that New Orleans could fall to a determined Union naval assault.

Returning to Washington, DC, in November 1861, Porter disclosed his plan to a pair of United States senators, whose influence soon brought him before Secretary Welles, the Union General-in-Chief George B McClellan, and President Abraham Lincoln himself.

Porter's plan called for a bombardment of Forts Jackson and St Philip by a flotilla of 21 schooners carrying 13-inch mortars – which could loft explosive shells on high trajectories – to be accompanied by other warships that would then make the run past the smothered forts to head up to New Orleans. The ensuing occupation of the city would be undertaken by a large body of soldiers from the US Army.

Enter David Farragut

With the plan of attack against New Orleans settled, the matter of who would lead the expedition now loomed. Porter was himself too junior to assume overall leadership of the expedition but would be given command of the mortar flotilla. He suggested his own foster-brother, Flag Officer David Glasgow Farragut, for the command. The now 60-year-old Farragut had been adopted by Porter's father and had, at the age of ten, served as a midshipman during the War of 1812. Since then he'd had a good if somewhat unspectacular career. Though a Southerner, he had scorned the secession and had remained loyal to the United States. Porter was instructed by Secretary Welles to sound out Farragut's opinion as to whether New Orleans might fall to the proposed naval assault coming from the Gulf of Mexico. Farragut thought the attack could work and was ready to lead it himself. He was soon given command of the expedition.

The Union's Gulf Blockading Squadron was cut in two. The East Gulf Blockading Squadron took oversight of the coastline stretching from Cape Canaveral, round the southern tip of Florida, and up to St Andrew Bay. From St Andrew westward to the mouth of the Rio Grande in Texas, Farragut, aboard his flagship, the screw (meaning steam-powered) sloop USS Hartford, would have the command of the West Gulf Blockading Squadron. To keep the true target of his operation secret, rumors were deliberately put out that it was headed for Texas, or to Mobile, Alabama.

Fire from Fort Jackson strikes the gunboat Iroquois, causing devastation to the crew. Despite the mortar attacks on the forts, they were still a threat to the Union ships

Confederate disorder

The Confederate defense of New Orleans was poorly prepared to meet the coming Union attack. The city itself was held by Major General Mansfield Lovell, but its more distant defenses, such as Forts Jackson and St Philip, were under the command of another officer, Major General Johnson Kelly Duncan. Lovell thought that the Confederate government was ill-informed about the "real situation at New Orleans" and anticipated a disaster should a Northern blow fall. He was not being dramatic. The 'fleet' tasked with guarding New Orleans was organizationally unsound. Control of the ships around the city, which taken as a group were theoretically formidable, was split between three separate entities. The ironclads CSS Manassas and CSS Louisiana, along with the steam gunboats CSS Jackson and CSS McRae, and a few tugboats, were in the hands of the Confederate Navy. However, Governor Moore and General Quitman, both cottonclad rams, were part of the Louisiana State Navy. Six further vessels – Defiance, Warrior, Resolute, General Breckenridge, General Lovell and Stonewall Jackson – were held by the Confederate Army's River Defense Fleet.

Neither of the latter two forces would accept orders from the Confederate Navy, thereby immeasurably complicating the issue of operational control of the naval units that would have to resist Farragut's attack. The widely held expectation among the Confederate forces that they had most to fear from a descent from the north by Federal river forces did not help them to prepare for the Union's assault from the south either.

On to New Orleans

Farragut arrived at Ship Island in the Gulf of Mexico, the jump-off point for the operation, on 20 February, where he linked up with 18,000 US Army soldiers under the command of Major General Benjamin F Butler. These were the troops that would be tasked with seizing the city. Farragut's fleet was substantial. In addition to Hartford, he had its sister ships USS Brooklyn, USS Pensacola, and USS Richmond. These were joined by the steam frigate USS Colorado, the steam corvettes USS Iroquois and USS Oneida, the ancient sidewheeler frigate USS Mississippi, and the converted packet steamer USS Varuna. Supplementing these larger units were 11 steam gunboats and a congeries of auxiliary vessels. He was met by Porter with his mortar boat flotilla at Ship Island in early March.

News now came to Farragut that Forts Henry and Donelson were in Union hands, and that Union river gunboats had advanced south down to Island No 10. He also knew that the Southerners were building two big ironclads, Louisiana and Mississippi, on the river and that, when completed, they would be deadly to the wooden ships in his own fleet. It would be better to move before they were operational, and he decided to take his ships into the river.

Beginning on 7 March, simply getting the ships over the shallows proved a laborious chore. Tugs were needed to pull many of them over the submerged sandbars in the passes that had silted up higher due to the reduction of river traffic that followed the coming of the war. The mortar ships and gunboats got through the Pass à l'Outre without too much fuss, but the bigger ships could not manage it. Farragut tried instead the South West Pass. Hartford, Brooklyn, and Richmond made it over relatively easily. USS Pensacola and USS Mississippi eventually were able to cross, but only after a struggle lasting 11 days. The giant frigate USS Colorado drew so much water that it could not be yanked across, no matter how much weight was removed from it. Farragut took with him all of her guns and its better sailors and stationed it outside the South West Pass as a reserve ship. The fleet was not fully across until 8 April.

On 13 April the tug Sachem moved north to reconnoitre Confederate positions, returning with precise ranges for Porter and his mortar boats. It was time for the bombardment to begin. The mortar schooners, led by Porter in Harriet Lane, pushed up the 20 miles from the Head of Passes to the forts. Starting on 18 April, the mortars began lobbing shells against Fort Jackson and Fort St Philip, with

"LOVELL THOUGHT THAT THE CONFEDERATE GOVERNMENT WAS ILL-INFORMED ABOUT THE 'REAL SITUATION AT NEW ORLEANS' AND ANTICIPATED A DISASTER SHOULD A NORTHERN BLOW FALL"

each vessel hurling a 13-inch shell aloft every ten minutes. Their aim was largely accurate, thanks to the skill of the mortar-men and the information provided by Sachem. The forts returned fire ineffectually. The Union bombardment continued for ten hours, at the end of which Fort Jackson was ablaze. The pummeling ceased with the coming of night, and then resumed the next morning, but at a reduced rate of one shell every 30 minutes. Porter's ammunition stocks had begun to run low, and he now understood that his original estimate, which had called for 48 hours to reduce both forts, had been wildly optimistic.

Ready for battle

In preparation for the general assault, Farragut had every bit of superfluous equipment removed from his ships. Even their masts were reduced so that they could carry only the most limited of sail. His crews daubed their ships' sides with mud to make them less visible in the hours of darkness and their decks were painted white to make their weapons easier to see at night. About the midships they hung heavy anchor chains as a kind of rudimentary 'chain mail' armor to protect the boilers behind them. "The day is at hand," Farragut told his men drily, "when you will be called upon to meet the enemy in the worst form of our profession."

The Confederates were of course certain that Farragut was on his way and had hastily improved their defenses. Across the Mississippi they had chained eight dismasted schooner hulks in a row. On the shore they had readied fire rafts to be let loose downstream at the oncoming Federals.

Ships had also arrived to join the fight. CSS Manassas had come, along with the cottonclad ram CSS Stonewall Jackson. The long-awaited ironclad Louisiana also made its appearance, having been towed to a position just to the north of Fort St Philip, outside of the range of Union mortar ships. But it was a paper tiger really, with non-functional engines and guns that were not fully operational.

The night hours were enlivened by the release of the fire rafts. Flames leapt skyward as the rafts, piled with flammable materials, drifted downriver. Farragut, however, had anticipated their use, and they were easily caught by his numerous auxiliary boats and redirected to the river's banks, where they consumed themselves without effect.

But here remained the obstacle of the hulk line across the river. These were hacked apart by a daring team of Union seamen in three gunboats while under heavy enemy fire. With the line severed, the Confederates towed Louisiana further downstream, anchoring it closer to Fort

Warships of the American Civil War

From cottonclad rams and timber sidewheelers to ironclad gunboats

The American Civil War saw the naval forces of both North and South deploy a plethora of ships and boats of all types, and the New Orleans campaign of April 1862 saw virtually all such vessels plying the waters of the Mississippi River and the Gulf of Mexico. Though most ocean-going wooden warships still carried sails, large numbers of frigates and sloops were now also equipped with steam engines and driven through the waves by screw propellers. Sails were employed when cruising, and the steam engines were turned on when battle was in the offing. In addition to the guns sited to fire broadsides, some newer warships were fitted with a pair of large, muzzle-loading 'pivot' guns that could be turned to fire to both port and starboard as required.

With the coming of war, the strategic importance of the Mississippi was immediately apparent, and both sides scrambled to procure warships to contest the control of the vast inland waterway. The earliest efforts of the Union resulted in the so-called 'timberclads', steam-powered sidewheeler gunboats armored with thick lengths of timber. The first of these were the Lexington, Tyler, and Conestoga. Armament varied from four 32-pound cannons in Conestoga to one 32-pounder and six eight-inch smoothbore cannons in Tyler to two 30-pounders and four eight-inch smoothbores in Lexington.

A step up from the timberclads were the 'tinclads'. These Union gunboats were armored in thin sheets of tin. Converted from flat-bottomed riverboats, their shallow drafts would allow them to patrol the maze of waterways that radiated over several hundred miles from the Mississippi. Most tinclads were rather small, displacing under 200 tons, and were armed with whatever ordnance could be obtained. Most were pushed through the water by stern-mounted paddle wheels. Tinclads were typically not given names but instead received individual identification numbers.

Among Confederate forces, another type of gunboat that saw service was the 'cottonclad'. As the name suggests, these vessels were given protection in the form of cotton bales that had been inserted between their outer superstructure and a false inner bulkhead. The result was a form of composite enamoring. With their bows reinforced, these small and fast steamers made for effective rams.

Ramming as a viable naval tactic had reappeared in the 19th century, having fallen into disuse in most modern navies for a long time. The wind had always been too fickle to make rams effective, but the advent of steam power brought ramming back into favor. Unfettered from reliance on the wind, Union rams were converted from riverboats. Their wooden bows were strongly reinforced, as were their hulls, so as to better absorb the tremendous impact of a ramming strike. Armaments on such ships were very limited – perhaps just one or two guns were mounted. Major vessels included the Union's sidewheelers Queen of the West and Switzerland. Their relatively high speed – around 12 knots – made their ramming attacks formidable.

Ironclads – driven by steam, covered in iron plates, and perhaps the iconic vessels of the war – were employed both at sea and on the Mississippi. Famous ironclads included the USS Monitor and the CSS Virginia, the former USS Merrimack, which dueled to a standstill at Hampton Roads in 1862. Ironclads were also used on the river itself, with many being converted from existing river craft, while others were purpose-built. The low and squat boats of the North's City class were nicknamed 'Pook's Turtles' after their designer. The cannon-armed vessels were 175 feet long, 51 feet wide, and were covered in 2.5-inch thick iron plates, but drew only six feet of water, making them usable in the shallows of the Mississippi and its tributaries.

The waters between Forts Jackson (left) and St Philip (right) were ablaze with burning ships in the early morning hours of 24 April 1862

Technological Advances

ADVANCES TO CANNONS, SHIPS, AND MUNITIONS CHANGED THE BALANCE OF POWER

The fall of the Hatteras and Port Royal forts to solely naval elements had been made much easier by several technical developments earlier in the century. In the days of sail, the advantage in any contest between a ship and a land fort had been with the guns ashore. A sailing man o'war would have been compelled by its reliance on wind for movement to remain in place to duel with a fort's guns, since maneuvering while under sail and having to contend with shifts in the wind, currents, and changes in tide, all while shooting at the shore, was very tricky. Staying put was also risky, as the wooden ship became increasingly vulnerable to being hit the longer it was there and the shore gunners had found the range. A steam-powered vessel, in contrast, could cruise by the enemy fort at a distance of more than one mile, firing as it did so, exit the range of enemy shore guns, and then turn around to have another go. As constantly moving targets, the steam ships were hard for Confederate shore gunners to accurately attack.

The size of shipborne artillery had also increased, as had its range. Most prominent among these were the Dahlgren guns - enormous smoothbore pieces with extra reinforcement around the chamber to enable them to withstand the pressure of powerful charges. Artillery had become more accurate too. Parrot guns were rifled cannons able to hurl a projectile over longer distances and with better accuracy than a smoothbore gun. The key was the rifling. These were grooves cut inside the barrel of the gun that imparted a spin to the fleeing projectile that made it fly further as well as truer.

There was another advance besides. Once these projectiles had hit their targets, they were more lethal because of the incorporation of explosive charges that detonated when they struck home. Old-style cannonballs used by warships in the age of sail were solid, and when they smashed into earthen defenses would typically be absorbed without much trouble. Exploding shells, on the other hand, could tear apart such defenses. Altogether, steam engines, bigger, more accurate guns, and exploding shells made a naval force a much more formidable opponent for land fortifications.

"AS MOVING TARGETS, THE STEAM SHIPS WERE HARD FOR SHORE GUNNERS TO ACCURATELY ATTACK"

A 13-inch mortar of the type used by Commander David Porter's mortar ships to bombard the Confederate forts

St Philip. It was still wholly unfit for real combat, and it was to be used only as a floating battery. This decision to hold it back upstream was not welcomed by all. The forts' commander, General Duncan, asked the Confederate Navy commander, John K Mitchell, to move Louisiana even further south, past the forts to the now-tattered hulk line, where he thought it would be of more use. Mitchell, however, declined, on the grounds that if he did so, no further work could be carried out on the ship.

This was not the only example of friction in the Confederate defenses. Even at this late hour, the Confederate Army's River Defense Fleet still steadfastly refused to accept orders from Mitchell, who had now taken command of the Louisiana State Navy ships in addition to those of the Confederate Navy. The army rivermen would fight, but only at their own direction, and they turned down a request to bring their cottonclad rams down to the hulk line to do battle where they were sorely needed.

The battering from the mortar boats continued for several more days, with no sign that Fort Jackson was ready to capitulate. Farragut decided that he would have to chance a run past the forts even though they had not been put out of action. At 2.00am on the morning of 24 April, the mortar barrage slackened and a pair of red lanterns on USS Hartford's mast gleamed, indicating that the Union fleet was to steam onward. The vanguard, Red division, under Captain Theodorus Bailey in the gunboat Cayuga and comprised of Pensacola, Mississippi, Oneida, Varuna, Katahdin, Kineo, and Wissahickon, led the slow advance in the Stygian darkness. Behind them came the Blue division of Hartford, Brooklyn, and Richmond. Farragut was high above in his flagship's rigging, getting a better look of the unfolding night scene, all the while shouting orders to his sailors below. He came down, after being begged to do so, only just in time to avoid being hit by a Confederate shell. Taking up the rear, in the third division under Chief of Staff Henry Bell, were Iroquois and five gunboats.

The battle intensifies

Ahead, Cayuga was struck all along its length by shells from Fort St Philip. It pushed on to engage Confederate warships, set afire an enemy vessel and forced it ashore. Cayuga's companions Oneida and Varuna moved forward. An enemy ship crossed Oneida's bow, and with every ounce of speed it could muster, Oneida rammed it, afterwards firing its guns at any enemy in range.

Varuna, on its own, took out four Confederate ships, and was then engaged by the cottonclad Governor Moore of the Louisiana State Navy. Governor Moore approached Varuna

Union ships risk the fire of the Confederate forts as they move upriver

from behind and both ships let loose with a hellstorm of fire. The Confederate ram came so close to Varuna that it could not depress its bow gun enough to fire at the Union craft. Frustrated and desperate, its commander, Lieutenant Beverly Kennon, ordered his gun to fire through his own ship's hull at Varuna.

Governor Moore next rammed Varuna, and then once again for good measure. Coming up, CSS Stonewall Jackson also rammed Varuna. When Stonewall Jackson backed off to make another ramming attack, Varuna used the breathing space to fill its tormentor with five eight-inch shells, and this pounding forced the Confederate ship ashore in flames. But Varuna was by now also sinking, and its captain brought it to the safety of the riverbank. Governor Moore, in the meantime, was so badly damaged by the fire from other Union warships that it too was forced ashore, and Kennon set Governor Moore ablaze to keep it out of the enemy's hands.

Elsewhere, Pensacola had gotten lost in the darkness and had come perilously close to Fort St Philip before veering off to the western side of the river. The elderly USS Mississippi was behind it, sidewheels pounding. Off the port bow appeared a low silhouette, shaped like a cigar. It was the infamous ram CSS Manassas, under Lieutenant Alexander Warley, come to do battle for the passage of the river. He rammed Mississippi, but only inflicted a glancing hit, which nonetheless managed to tear a gaping hole in the old sidewheeler. The Union ship shuddered and began to list, but then quickly righted itself. Manassas headed off to find another victim.

Back with the Blue division, the screw sloop Brooklyn had become entangled in the broken remnants of the hulk line. Brooklyn finally extricated itself, but only after having taken heavy fire from the forts. Once past Fort St Philip, Brooklyn met another enemy. Manassas had reappeared, firing its single cannon at Brooklyn and then ramming the Union ship. With its gun ruined in the collision, Warley backed up the Manassas for another strike, but his first attack had done less damage than hoped. The chains hung over the side of Brooklyn had protected it, and it steamed onwards, leaving Manassas in its wake.

Aboard Hartford, Farragut struggled to guide his ships past the forts, but he could see very little in the death shroud of smoke that hung over the battle. At around 4.15am, a Confederate tug, Mosher, had nudged a fire raft against Hartford's portside hull. Hartford's guns annihilated the impudent little boat, but the screw sloop was now itself aflame. Fire parties worked furiously to fight the blaze, and the flagship continued to move ahead. Farragut noticed that Confederate fire had begun to lessen. Hartford was, at last, past the forts, but was not altogether safe. Lieutenant Warley in Manassas had found them. The vengeful steam frigate Mississippi, which had also made it past the forts, was looking for a rematch, but its captain felt the need to ask for permission to attack. Farragut, once again aloft in the rigging of Hartford, shouted the order himself through a trumpet. "Run down the ram!"

Mississippi fired its guns twice at Manassas, which had been so damaged in its earlier battles that it could hardly keep up the fight. Warley grounded his ship on the riverbank, got his crew off, and set his stricken ship alight, even as the pursuing Mississippi continued to rake its hull with grapeshot.

Almost all of Farragut's ships managed to find a way past the forts, which quit their own firing at about 5.30am. His fleet arrived at the defenseless New Orleans the next day, on 25 April. The forts held out for another two days, under bombardment by the mortar ships, until they too surrendered on 27 April. By 1 May, Butler's US Army troops had come up and had begun the occupation of the city. Commander Mitchell set CSS Louisiana alight and cast it adrift, with five tons of powder aboard, allowing it to float down the river, drifting past where General Duncan was right then signing surrender terms with Porter. The half-built ironclad, so unfulfilled in its potential – much like the entirety of the Confederate defense of New Orleans – blew up.

Aftermath

One historian has gone so far as to say that the fall of New Orleans was "the night the war was lost". Even if that summary is a bit of an exaggeration, the capture of the South's biggest port was surely an awful loss to the Southern cause, as the flow of traffic out of the river was now completely in Northern hands. The capture of Vicksburg the next year, in July 1863, was the culminating act in the Union's seizure of full control over the Mississippi, and with it, the Confederacy had effectively been cut in half. ★

BATTLE OF NEW ORLEANS

18-24 APRIL 1862

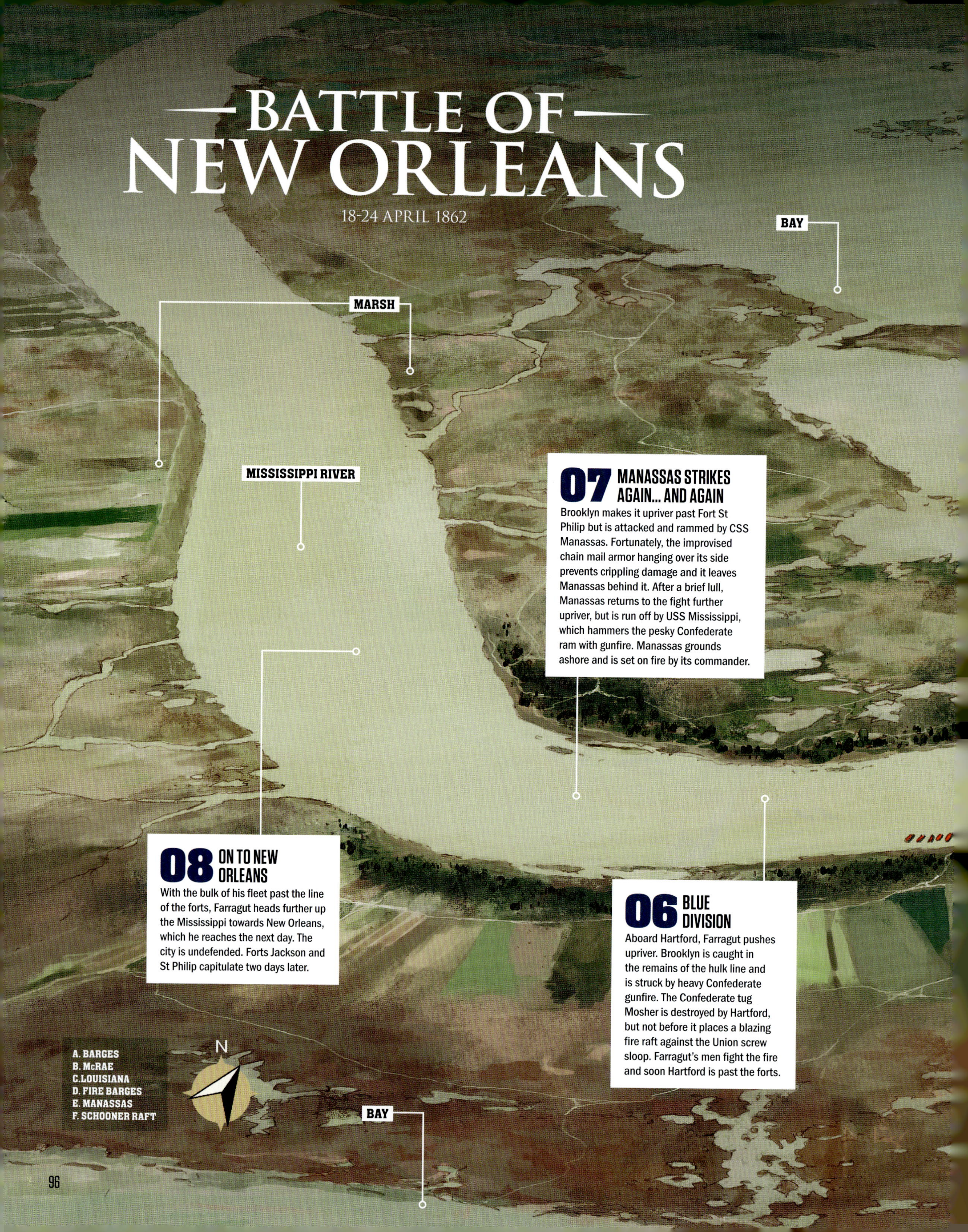

BAY

MARSH

MISSISSIPPI RIVER

06 BLUE DIVISION

Aboard Hartford, Farragut pushes upriver. Brooklyn is caught in the remains of the hulk line and is struck by heavy Confederate gunfire. The Confederate tug Mosher is destroyed by Hartford, but not before it places a blazing fire raft against the Union screw sloop. Farragut's men fight the fire and soon Hartford is past the forts.

07 MANASSAS STRIKES AGAIN… AND AGAIN

Brooklyn makes it upriver past Fort St Philip but is attacked and rammed by CSS Manassas. Fortunately, the improvised chain mail armor hanging over its side prevents crippling damage and it leaves Manassas behind it. After a brief lull, Manassas returns to the fight further upriver, but is run off by USS Mississippi, which hammers the pesky Confederate ram with gunfire. Manassas grounds ashore and is set on fire by its commander.

08 ON TO NEW ORLEANS

With the bulk of his fleet past the line of the forts, Farragut heads further up the Mississippi towards New Orleans, which he reaches the next day. The city is undefended. Forts Jackson and St Philip capitulate two days later.

A. BARGES
B. McRAE
C.LOUISIANA
D. FIRE BARGES
E. MANASSAS
F. SCHOONER RAFT

BAY

04 HULK LINE

Across the broad Mississippi the Confederate defenders have chained together eight dismasted schooner hulks to prevent an easy sortie upriver by the Union fleet. Before Farragut orders his advance, a team of Federal seamen goes forward, under cover of night, and hacks apart the chains that bind the ships together. Fire rafts are launched by the Confederates at night but they prove to be mere nuisances to the well-prepared Federals.

05 RED DIVISION

Farragut signals a general advance by the ships in his fleet. Cayuga takes the lead and is hit hard. Pensacola veers off course. Oneida rams an enemy ship and then takes up position, firing at targets of opportunity. Varuna knocks out four Confederate ships before it is rammed by Governor Moore. It duels furiously with Governor Moore, is rammed by CSS Stonewall Jackson, and then reduces Jackson to a flaming wreck with cannon fire. Both Varuna and Governor Moore are forced ashore by sustained battle damage. USS Mississippi is rammed by CSS Manassas.

01 FORT JACKSON AND FORT ST PHILIP

Neither Jackson nor St Philip can be considered modern forts. Fort Jackson has been sinking into the mud of the Mississippi Delta for some time and is perennially flooded, requiring constant pumping to keep its magazines dry. St Philip is no better, being an elderly fort originally of Spanish construction. Its guns are unprotected and vulnerable to the plunging fire of Union mortar bombs. The bulk of the guns in both forts are also outdated, being old-fashioned 32 pounders with short ranges.

03 THE REBEL NAVY WAITS

Union fleet commander David Glasgow Farragut realizes that he can't wait for the mortar ships to force the surrender of the forts and decides he must run the gauntlet past them so that he may continue on to New Orleans. Waiting for him, just upriver of the forts, is a disorganized but dangerous collection of Confederate warships, including Manassas, Stonewall Jackson and the incomplete ironclad, Louisiana.

02 BOMBARDMENT BEGINS

21 mortar schooners under Commander David Dixon Porter begin the bombardment of Fort Jackson. They pound the fort with close to 3,000 13-inch shells on the first day alone, and continue the barrage for the next few nights. Though much damage is done, Fort Jackson does not succumb.

This romanticized image of the Battle of Antietam depicts the fighting along the creek at Burnside Bridge

ANTIETAM: THE BLOODIEST DAY

Robert E Lee's first invasion of the North ended with a bloody strategic defeat on the banks of a previously obscure creek in western Maryland

WORDS **MIKE HASKEW**

Image: Getty

The summer of 1862 was a season of great promise for the Confederacy. Virginia was virtually free of Union soldiers for the first time since hostilities had been declared. On the battlefield, Generals Robert E Lee and Thomas J 'Stonewall' Jackson had inflicted an embarrassing defeat on the Union Army of Virginia, under General John Pope, at the Battle of Second Bull Run in August. General George B McClellan's ambitious Peninsula Campaign against the Confederate capital at Richmond, Virginia, had been thwarted the previous spring.

The Confederate cause was ascendant, and for Lee, already gaining a reputation as an audacious field commander, the time was appropriate for bold offensive action. A strike by the vaunted Confederate Army of Northern Virginia into Northern territory, although fraught with risk, might pay immeasurable dividends if a substantial military victory could be won there. Marching through Maryland, Lee's mighty host might rally the people of that border state to the Confederate flag, resulting in new recruits for his ranks and supplies for his always-famished and ill-clad soldiers. The farmers of Virginia could bring in their harvest in peace while his troops also sustained themselves with the produce of Northern farms previously untouched by war. Most significantly, European powers might grant long-awaited diplomatic recognition to the Confederacy. Recognition from Great Britain and other European nations meant the possibility of negotiated peace, perhaps economic and military aid, or even armed intervention on the Confederate side.

Lee's Maryland Campaign

Envisioning a momentous grand strategy, Lee wrote to Confederate President Jefferson Davis, "The present seems the most propitious time since the beginning of the war for the Confederate Army to enter Maryland [...] we cannot afford to be idle." Lee's army, 55,000 strong and organized in two wings under Jackson and General James Longstreet, splashed across the Potomac River from Virginia on 4-7 September 1862.

Meanwhile, in Washington, DC, President Abraham Lincoln needed a battlefield victory to legitimize the issuance of the Emancipation Proclamation, a document that would ostensibly free all slaves held in territory in rebellion against the United States, transforming the Civil War from a struggle only to maintain the Union into a crusade for human rights and the end of slavery. Lincoln had lost confidence in McClellan after the Peninsula failure. He had transferred much of McClellan's troop strength to General Pope and the Army of Virginia. But with Pope's stinging defeat at Second Bull Run, Lincoln swallowed his pride, calling upon McClellan once again – this time to consolidate the Union forces, protect Washington, DC, and destroy Lee's army.

Lincoln understood that McClellan was painfully cautious. However, he was immensely popular with the troops and a superb organizer. On 4 September, just two days after resuming overall command, McClellan received word that the Army of Northern Virginia was moving. The ranks of the Army of the Potomac swelled to nearly 90,000 men, and McClellan was adroit in assimilating reassigned soldiers. However, he was true to form in other ways as well. Relying on spurious intelligence reports that the Confederate invaders numbered nearly 200,000, he pursued Lee at a ponderously slow pace. The Army of the Potomac broke camp at Rockville, Maryland, on the afternoon of the 4th

The Dead Of Antietam

A SERIES OF PHOTOGRAPHS TAKEN IN THE AFTERMATH OF THE BATTLE OF ANTIETAM ELECTRIFIED THE AMERICAN PUBLIC WITH WAR'S HORROR

Within hours of the conclusion of the Battle of Antietam, two photographers, Alexander Gardner and James Gibson, employed by famed entrepreneur Matthew Brady, were at work. Photography was in its infancy, but the photographic record these men produced after the Battle of Antietam shocked the American public.

Gardner and Gibson exposed 70 plates within five days of the battle. It was the first time that photographers had recorded fresh scenes of carnage. Stark, haunting images of bodies mangled by artillery shells, shot to death, their sightless eyes staring and limbs contorted, were published at Brady's New York City studio in October, and New Yorkers flocked to gaze at the gruesome face of war.

A *New York Times* editorial at the end of the month observed, "The living that throng Broadway care little perhaps for the Dead of Antietam, but we fancy they would jostle less carelessly down the great thoroughfare, saunter less at their ease, were a few dripping bodies, fresh from the field, laid along the pavement... As it is, the dead of the battle-field come up to us very rarely, even in dreams. We see the list in the morning paper at breakfast, but dismiss its recollection with the coffee... We recognize the battle-field as a reality, but it stands as a remote one...Mr. BRADY has done something to bring home to us the terrible reality and earnestness of war. If he has not brought bodies and laid them in our dooryards and along our streets, he has done something very like it...."

"STARK, HAUNTING IMAGES OF BODIES MANGLED BY ARTILLERY SHELLS, SHOT TO DEATH, WERE PUBLISHED IN NEW YORK"

In one of Alexander Gardner's death studies, the bodies of Confederate soldiers lie along a rail fence on the Hagerstown Turnpike

Confederate soldiers cross the Potomac River prior to the Battle of Antietam

and reached the town of Frederick on the 12th, five days after the Army of Northern Virginia had passed through.

Although Lee knew McClellan well, accurately assessing his timid tendencies, the Confederate commander's Maryland Campaign was troubled from the start. When Lee's army marched into Frederick, the townspeople stayed in their homes. Shops were locked up tight. An appeal to the citizenry of Maryland left them unmoved. Still, he pressed on. When the 12,000-man garrison at the Federal arsenal at Harpers Ferry and the 2,500 Union troops at Martinsburg did not abandon their positions immediately, to secure his supply lines through the Shenandoah Valley at Winchester, Virginia, Lee was compelled to divide his army, sending Jackson to deal with the threat. Lee continued northward with Longstreet, hoping the army could concentrate at Hagerstown, Maryland, by 12 September. From there, the Confederates could move into Pennsylvania, burn the great railroad bridge across the Susquehanna River, possibly occupy the state capital at Harrisburg, and then threaten Philadelphia, Baltimore, or even Washington, DC.

But Lee fretted as precious time slipped away. He knew that McClellan, slow as he was, might catch the divided Confederate forces and overwhelm each in detail. Therefore, against superior Union strength, he exchanged blood for time, contesting the Union transit of the passes in South Mountain on 14 September. Believing the campaign had come to naught, he reluctantly ordered a general withdrawal across the Potomac to safety in Virginia. Within hours of the order, though, his hopes were buoyed by word from Jackson that the fall of Harpers Ferry was imminent. Countermanding the retirement order, Lee rode with Longstreet to Antietam Creek, a tributary of the Potomac near the town of Sharpsburg, Maryland. He surveyed the ground and issued new orders for his scattered forces to concentrate along a low ridgeline east of town. "We will make our stand on these hills," he concluded.

Meanwhile, McClellan had frittered away an intelligence coup that could have brought on Lee's demise and possibly ended the Civil War. On 13 September, he received a captured document. An Indiana soldier, lounging in the grass in a meadow that had recently been the bivouac site of General DH Hill's division, came across several cigars rolled up in a piece of paper. He took the cigars and read the scrawled page with disbelief. Soon enough, Lee's Special Order No 191, detailing the complex Confederate plan, made its way up the Union chain of command. McClellan rejoiced and exclaimed, "Now I know what to do!" He crowed to his friend General John Gibbon, commander of the 4th Brigade in General Joseph Hooker's I Corps, "Here is a paper with which, if I cannot whip Bobbie Lee, I will be willing to go home."

***Above** There were approximately 23,000 casualties during the Battle of Antietam*

But McClellan failed to press his numerical advantage at South Mountain, and Jackson would soon be on the march from Harpers Ferry. Instead, McClellan was content to concentrate 75,000 troops to fight Lee on his enemy's chosen ground along Antietam Creek.

On the morning of 15 September, Lee remained in a precarious position but still thought he might salvage a battlefield victory. He expected McClellan's deliberate approach to work in his favor. With the fall of Harpers Ferry, the bulk of Jackson's command was rapidly covering the 17 miles to Sharpsburg. General AP Hill's Light Division stayed at the arsenal, paroling prisoners and securing captured supplies before racing toward the Antietam.

Lee deployed his forces skillfully with General JEB Stuart's cavalry screening his left flank,

Despite losing faith in him, Lincoln called on McClellan to lead the Union forces against General Lee due to his popularity with the troops and excellent organization

which was secured by the division of General John Bell Hood at the edge of a thick forest locally known as the West Woods and on open ground around a whitewashed house of worship belonging to the German Baptist Brethren, commonly called the Dunkers because of their ritual of baptism by immersion. Within hours, the diminutive Dunker Church would become the scene of horrific fighting. Here, in the center, Lee deployed DH Hill's division across the Boonesborough Pike and into the natural defensive trench of the Sunken Road that would soon be known the world over as 'Bloody Lane'. Lee's line terminated in the south, at the lowest of three stone bridges across the creek, five brigades of General DR Jones's division covering a mile of ground.

On the afternoon of 15 September, McClellan's forces began filtering into the vicinity. Union strength grew rapidly, but he declined to attack Lee. Instead, McClellan spent hours positioning his troops with the idea that Generals Hooker and Joseph KF Mansfield would attack Lee's left flank with the I and XII Corps respectively, while the IX Corps, under General Ambrose Burnside, would assault the Confederate right. If either met with success, the II and VI Corps, commanded by Generals Edwin V Sumner and William B Franklin respectively, would exploit the gain. General Fitz John Porter's V Corps in the Union center was also positioned for support.

Bloody battlefield

By the evening of the 16th, shots were exchanged as Hooker maneuvered into position to attack with first light. At the same time, three divisions of Jackson's command came tramping onto the field, improving Lee's odds a bit. As his soldiers were arriving, Jackson rode up to Lee and Longstreet about noon, and the three men watched thousands of Union troops crowding into position across Antietam Creek.

At dawn, Hooker's corps advanced down the Hagerstown Turnpike as the opposing artillery dueled, opening the action on the bloodiest single day of combat in American history. To reach the chosen objective, the Union soldiers were required to cross a cornfield belonging to a local farmer named David Miller. The stalks were head-high, ready for harvest. This field became the focus of savage fighting on the morning of 17 September. Afterward, it was simply known as 'The Cornfield.'

Hooker noticed Confederate soldiers moving among the stalks and ordered an artillery battery to open fire. He was shaken with the carnage: "In the time I am writing every stalk of corn in the northern and greater part of the field was cut as closely as could have been done with a knife, and the slain lay in rows precisely as they stood in their ranks a few moments before. It was never my fortune to witness a more bloody, dismal battlefield."

The engagement on the Confederate left lasted about three hours as control of the Cornfield changed hands 15 times. During the night, Hood's men had been relieved by two brigades under General Alexander Lawton. As his line wavered, Lawton requested help. Hood's men, most of them from Texas, were cooking breakfast – their first hot meal in days. They threw away coffee and biscuits, stuffing bacon into their mouths, and charged. Their anger boiling over, the Texans slammed into Hooker's troops and threw them back 400 yards, essentially to their starting point. However, the exuberant Confederates became overextended, and the 1st Texas Infantry Regiment suffered 186 killed or wounded in half an hour, a casualty rate of 82 percent, the highest of any regiment, Union or Confederate, in the entire war. Hood was appalled at the losses, and when another officer asked where his division was located, the general replied, "Dead on the field."

General Mansfield soon led an attack in support of Hooker, pressing toward the Dunker Church and further along the Hagerstown Turnpike, but Mansfield fell, and Confederate artillery smashed the assault. As General Sumner led two divisions in support, Jackson sprang a trap. One Union division strayed off course, and the other was caught in a murderous crossfire, half its 5,000 men shot down in only 20 minutes in the vicinity of the West Woods.

Burnside's Bridge

By 10am, the situation on the Confederate left was stalemated, and the action shifted to the center. New York and Massachusetts troops of the Union Irish Brigade assaulted the North Carolina and Alabama men holding the Sunken Road, and casualties were heavy on both sides until two New York regiments worked their way around the right flank and poured devastating fire down the length of Bloody Lane. Confederate bodies were heaped atop one another, and a misunderstood command caused the defenders to fall back 600 yards. McClellan had ample reserves but did not commit more troops to the breach. He actually ordered a halt and consolidation of the new Union position, allowing another opportunity to slip away.

General Longstreet personally helped to steady the Confederate center, and again the fighting shifted southward.

From morning until mid-afternoon, General Burnside was obsessed with crossing the lower stone bridge, which from 17 September 1862 forward would bear his name as Burnside Bridge. Even after some Union troops forded Antietam Creek a mile away, he persisted. Four hundred Georgia and South Carolina troops under General Robert Toombs occupied the bluffs above the bridge and repulsed repeated attempts to take the span. Finally, two regiments of New York and Pennsylvania troops, who were promised the return of their whiskey ration that had been taken away for disciplinary purposes if they gained the west bank, charged under a hail of fire. They drove the defenders back, expecting to begin working their way up the bluffs.

Burnside was now in position to crush Lee's right flank, from which he had pulled reinforcements all day to shore up his threatened center and left. But the IX Corps commander wasted two hours before starting toward Sharpsburg. He got going around 3pm with the thinly stretched Confederates fighting all the way. Sluggishly, Burnside's troops drove to within half a mile of Sharpsburg, but just as Lee's position neared collapse AP Hill's Light Division came rolling down the dirt road from Harpers Ferry and smashed into Burnside, halting the Union drive and taking

MIRACULOUS SURVIVAL AT ANTIETAM

JOHN B GORDON WAS WOUNDED REPEATEDLY AT THE BATTLE OF ANTIETAM BUT LIVED TO TELL THE TALE

The colonel commanding the 6th Alabama Infantry Regiment was in the maelstrom at the Sunken Road on 17 September 1862. Future General John B Gordon ordered his men to wait until the enemy was 30 steps away. He yelled "Fire!" and the line erupted. "My rifles flamed and roared in the Federals' faces…" he wrote years later.

But if Gordon's men had sown the wind, their commander endured the whirlwind. Already surviving a wound suffered at Malvern Hill earlier that spring, Gordon was near death by afternoon. The first wound was through the right calf, and the second tore into the same leg. A third bullet ripped into his left arm. The fourth struck his shoulder. Incredibly, he remained on his feet. Then, his fifth wound of the day nearly took his life. The missile struck his right cheek, shattering his jaw. Gordon fell face down on the ground, bleeding profusely. He remembered later that only a bullet hole in his hat that allowed drainage kept him from drowning in his own blood.

When he regained consciousness, Gordon crawled some distance before being loaded on a stretcher and taken to a field hospital. He defied the odds, his wife at his side keeping an infection at bay with iodine and feeding him broth. Ten months after his grievous wounds, Gordon returned to service. He participated in several later engagements, was wounded at least two more times, and eventually led troops in the last battle of the Army of Northern Virginia at Appomattox Court House in 1865.

General John B Gordon survived the Civil War and went on to a political career, later serving as Governor of Georgia

After Antietam, President Abraham Lincoln meets with General George B McClellan at the headquarters of the Army of the Potomac

the last bit of fight out of McClellan. Hill's march had been virtually non-stop. Some men had fallen out of the ranks, overcome by the heat and the pace of the advance. But those who reached the field, though exhausted, went into action immediately.

Aftermath

The Battle of Antietam, a bloody tactical draw, ended with darkness. A staggering 23,000 dead and wounded lay strewn across the landscape, at least 12,000 Union and nearly 11,000 Confederate. Lee was in no position to assume the offensive but stood his ground the entire next day. McClellan declined to renew the struggle, allowing Lee to then withdraw across the Potomac unmolested.

Despite the cost, Antietam was enough to validate Lincoln's issuance of the Emancipation Proclamation, effective 1 January 1863.

For the Confederate cause, the Maryland Campaign was a major setback. With the withdrawal following the Battle of Antietam, the state of Maryland remained in the Union, while the possibility of European recognition faded with the prospect of the Emancipation Proclamation. Britain had abolished slavery years earlier. Lee would continue to lead the Army of Northern Virginia, and great triumphs lay in its future; however, never again were the prospects for ultimate victory as bright as they had been in the summer of 1862. A year later, Lee would invade the North once more, but by this time Stonewall Jackson was dead, and the road led to Gettysburg. ★

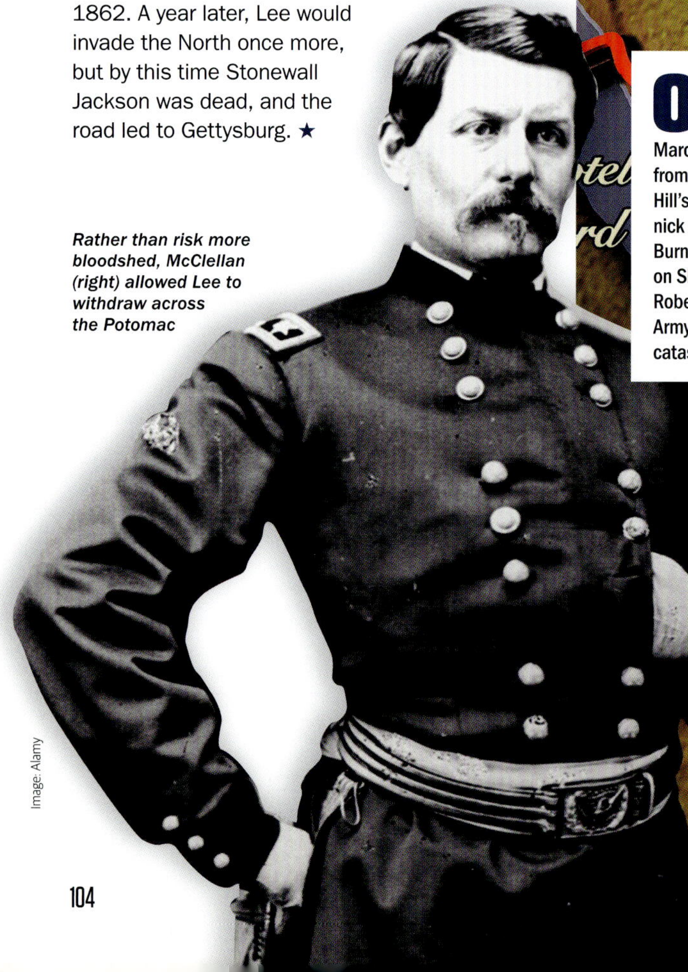

Rather than risk more bloodshed, McClellan (right) allowed Lee to withdraw across the Potomac

Image: Alamy

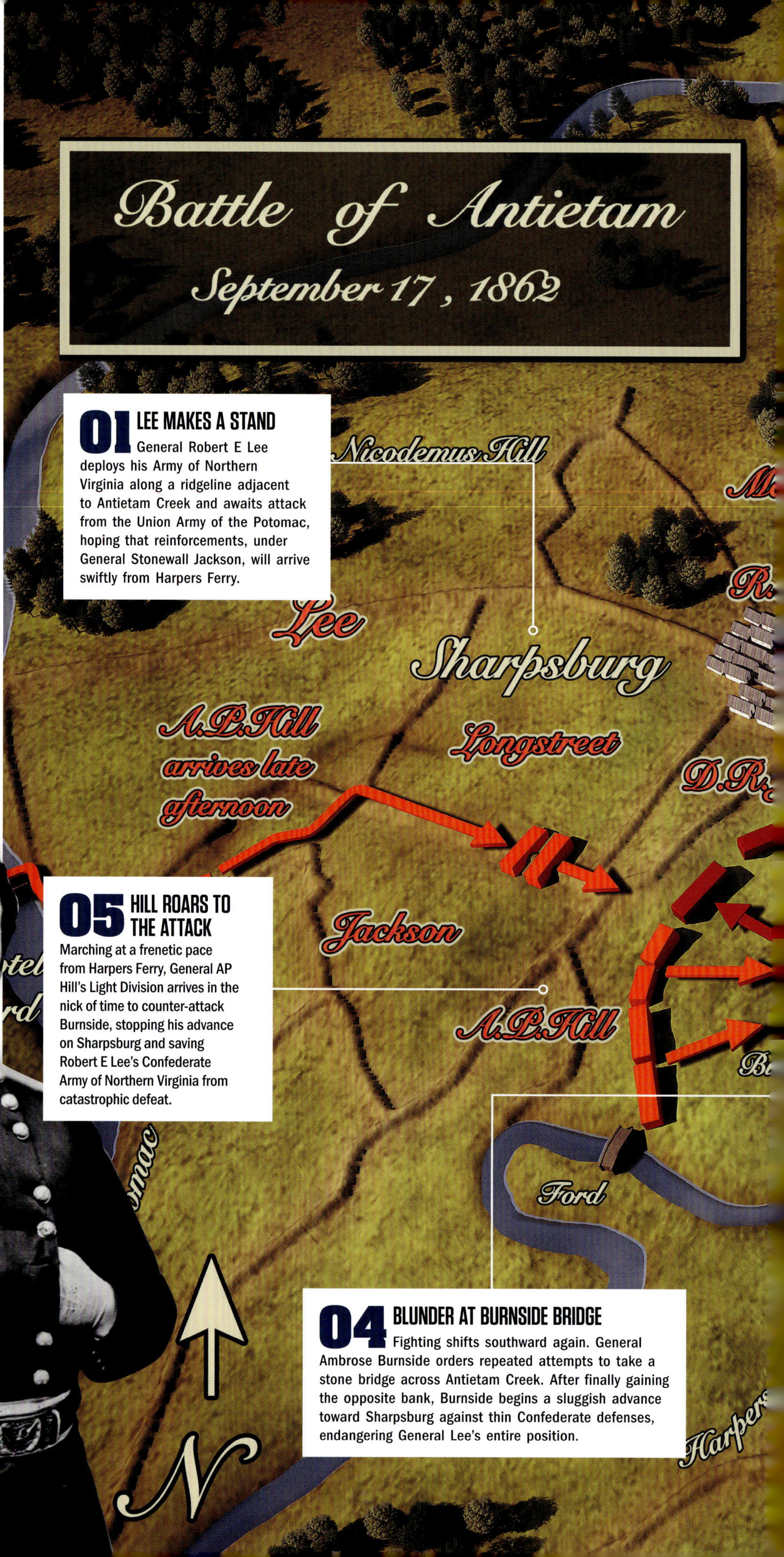

Battle of Antietam

September 17, 1862

01 LEE MAKES A STAND
General Robert E Lee deploys his Army of Northern Virginia along a ridgeline adjacent to Antietam Creek and awaits attack from the Union Army of the Potomac, hoping that reinforcements, under General Stonewall Jackson, will arrive swiftly from Harpers Ferry.

05 HILL ROARS TO THE ATTACK
Marching at a frenetic pace from Harpers Ferry, General AP Hill's Light Division arrives in the nick of time to counter-attack Burnside, stopping his advance on Sharpsburg and saving Robert E Lee's Confederate Army of Northern Virginia from catastrophic defeat.

04 BLUNDER AT BURNSIDE BRIDGE
Fighting shifts southward again. General Ambrose Burnside orders repeated attempts to take a stone bridge across Antietam Creek. After finally gaining the opposite bank, Burnside begins a sluggish advance toward Sharpsburg against thin Confederate defenses, endangering General Lee's entire position.

02 FIGHTING RAGES IN THE CORNFIELD

Early in the morning, a 24-acre cornfield becomes the center of the storm on the Confederate left as combat ebbs and flows. Fighting also swirls around the nearby Dunker Church and the West Woods, but neither side gains the upper hand. Though much damage is done, Fort Jackson does not succumb.

03 SLAUGHTER AT THE SUNKEN ROAD

The fighting shifts to the center, where repeated Union attacks against the Sunken Road, later known as 'Bloody Lane', are repulsed. Finally, Union troops flank the defenders, turning the position into a deathtrap. No reinforcements appear to exploit a Confederate withdrawal.

Image Source: Wikipedia Commons / Public Domain

FREDERICKSBURG

The Confederate invasion of the north had been repulsed in Maryland by the Army of the Potomac. President Abraham Lincoln now urged his military to seize the initiative and crush the Confederates in the east and capture their capital Richmond. It would culminate in another catastrophic defeat

WORDS **IAIN MACGREGOR**

Artist Carl Rochling's depiction of the battle, which was a disaster for the Union forces

Image: Alamy

By early November 1862, anxious that his administration was rapidly losing public support in the north, an impatient President Abraham Lincoln had grown weary of the Army of the Potomac's popular commander – Major General George B McClellan – and installed his subordinate and close friend Major General Ambrose Burnside as his reluctant successor. Though a capable corps-level commander, Burnside himself admitted he was not capable of commanding an army in the field. The daunting figure of General Robert E Lee and his victorious Army of Northern Virginia only added to his lack of confidence. Yet Burnside was damned if he would step aside to allow his fellow corps commander, and political intriguer, Brigadier General Joe Hooker, to be given the promotion instead. Against his better judgment, Burnside acquiesced to Lincoln's request.

Burnside's ambitious plan to defeat Lee would commence with a rapid advance south to Fredericksburg, situated on the Rappahannock River, where they would seize the town and then march on to the Confederate capital at Richmond in order to overwhelm the city. This would give them the strategic advantage, forcing off-balance Lee's intended defensive plan and compelling the Confederates to fight on ground of the Union's choosing. For once, thought Burnside,

Major General Edwin V Sumner commanded the Union's Grand Right Division in the battle

Battle of Fredericksburg
December 13, 1862

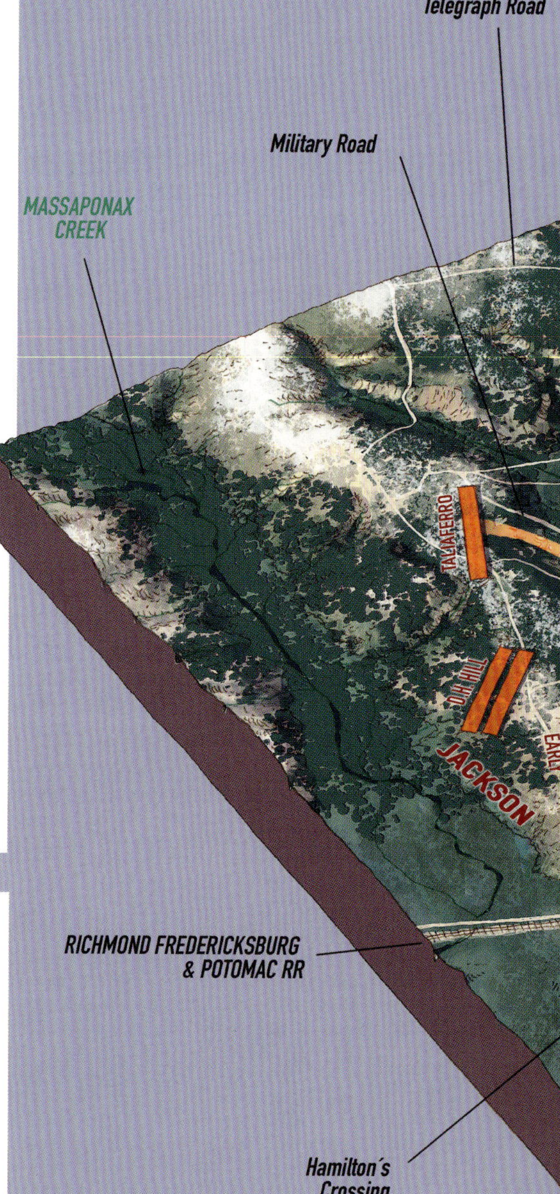

01 MEADE'S DIVISION FORGES AHEAD TOWARDS PROSPECT HILL

By 9.00am, with the battlefield shrouded in low-lying mist, restricting visibility for both sides, Franklin has missed the opportunity to launch his attack at dawn. Burnside's instructions to use "a division at least" to carry the rebel position will limit Franklin's ability to fight. Despite this, a cautious commander, he follows his instructions and only sends in Major General George G Meade's 3,800-strong Third Division to assault Jackson's position, supported by Brigadier John Gibbons' Second Division (to his right) and Brigadier Doubleday's First Division to his left.

02 THE GALLANT PELHAM'S ARTILLERY DUEL

Major John Pelham, commanding the horse artillery of Major General JEB Stuart's Cavalry Division, is granted permission to place two cannons ahead of Jackson's defensive lines and spends the next hour harassing Meade's movements. Lee, watching the action from Prospect Hill, remarks: "It is glorious to see such courage in one so young." Upon his retreat back to Confederate lines, a fierce artillery duel breaks out for the next hour.

03 JACKSON'S LINES ARE THREATENED

Meade orders a bayonet charge through a triangular-shaped marshy wood. Discovering it undefended by Jackson's troops, his men surge through a large gap, catching resting Confederates commanded by Brigadier Maxcy Gregg by surprise. Gregg is mortally wounded as he tries to rally his retreating men. The Pennsylvanians surge through the wood and deep into Jackson's interior before he brings up significant reinforcements to engage in hand-to-hand fighting.

04 MEADE RETREATS

Despite a frantic defense of the ground his men had won, Meade's requests to Franklin for aid are seemingly ignored as Gibbon's division also comes under intense counter-attack from Jackson's lines. By that afternoon, with his men running low on ammunition and with increasing Southern attacks on all sides, Meade orders a fighting retreat towards Franklin's main positions a mile away. Over 20,000 fresh troops remain by their bridgehead as Franklin seeks to ensure its safety. Meade's unit suffers over 40 percent casualties: 179 killed, 1,082 wounded and 509 missing.

05 THE FIRST ASSAULT ON MARYE'S HEIGHTS BEGINS

At 12pm Sumner's first assault goes in. Brigadier General William H French's Third Division, II Corps, marches towards the stone wall occupied by Cobb's Georgians and 24th North Carolina. Massed four deep, they offer a ceaseless line of rifle fire as rebel artillery pours down from above. By the end his unit has suffered 1,153 killed, wounded or missing.

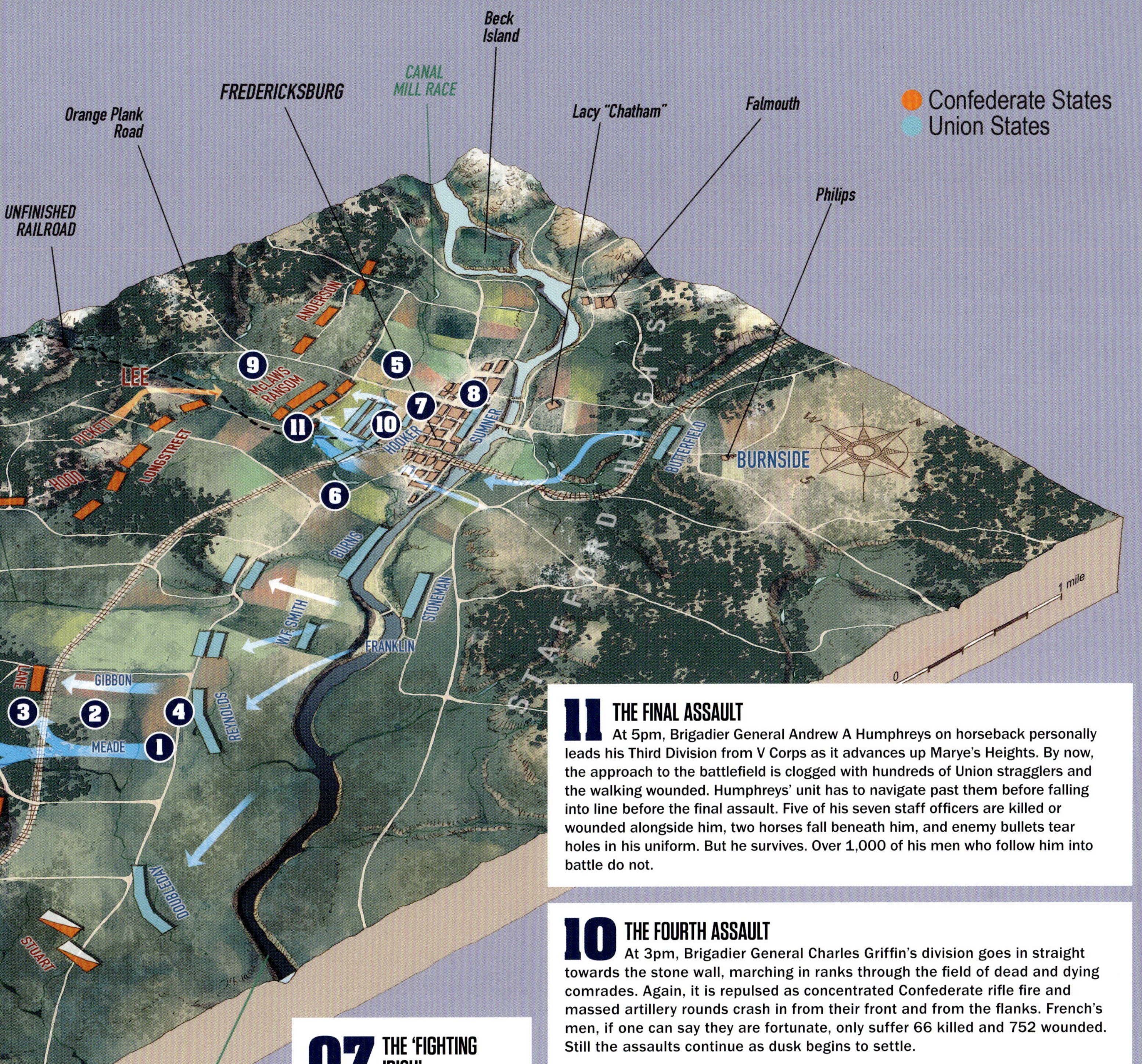

11 THE FINAL ASSAULT

At 5pm, Brigadier General Andrew A Humphreys on horseback personally leads his Third Division from V Corps as it advances up Marye's Heights. By now, the approach to the battlefield is clogged with hundreds of Union stragglers and the walking wounded. Humphreys' unit has to navigate past them before falling into line before the final assault. Five of his seven staff officers are killed or wounded alongside him, two horses fall beneath him, and enemy bullets tear holes in his uniform. But he survives. Over 1,000 of his men who follow him into battle do not.

10 THE FOURTH ASSAULT

At 3pm, Brigadier General Charles Griffin's division goes in straight towards the stone wall, marching in ranks through the field of dead and dying comrades. Again, it is repulsed as concentrated Confederate rifle fire and massed artillery rounds crash in from their front and from the flanks. French's men, if one can say they are fortunate, only suffer 66 killed and 752 wounded. Still the assaults continue as dusk begins to settle.

09 A PAUSE IN THE FIGHTING

So far, Burnside's plan is failing. He has lost over 5,000 men before the wall. While both sides pause, Longstreet reinforces the Georgians at the wall with more ammunition. Hooker makes his way to Burnside's headquarters to demand an end to the assault on Marye's Heights. He is ignored.

08 THE THIRD ASSAULT

At 2pm, Sumner tries something different. He orders two different units to attack the stone wall at the same time from different directions. Oliver O Howard's brigades are next in line for the assault, where they originally intend to sweep around to attack the Confederate left. But with Hancock's division destroyed, Howard's men instead quick-time over the field of casualties towards the center, with the support of Brigadier Samuel Sturgis's division. Again, it is met with devastating firepower from behind the stone wall. Not one Union man gets to within 20 paces before falling.

07 THE 'FIGHTING IRISH'

From within Hancock's division, General Meagher's Irish Brigade, comprising of men from the 116th Pennsylvania, 28th Massachusetts, 63rd, 69th, and 88th New York storm forward into another hail of shrapnel and bullets. Many of Cobb's Georgia Brigade are of Irish descent, but they still offer a hot reception to their brethren. Of the 1,200 men Meagher takes into battle, 545 are killed, wounded or missing. Overall, Hancock's division has suffered 2,032 casualties.

06 THE SECOND WAVE ATTACKS

At 1pm, Brigadier General Hancock's division is ordered into action. Colonel Zook's brigade leading the first charge, the survivors managing to get within 25 paces of the wall before falling back with heavy losses.

Map illustration: Rocío Espín Piñar

The stone wall at Marye's Heights was the scene of carnage

Brigadier General Joseph Hooker (seated second from right) with some of his officers

Lee would finally get a taste of the deadly medicine his troops had meted out to him a few months prior at Antietam. But the fair weather of Maryland in September was a memory now, as troops on both sides sought to survive the campaign in rapidly deteriorating winter conditions. Freezing rain made roads hazardous to navigate for armies marching to battle and for wagon trains to supply them. Fredericksburg's key transportation rail hub, and access to river traffic towards Richmond, was vital for Burnside's plan to work. Speed was essential. It would force Lee to attack on ground that favored Burnside, and with his forces well prepared to inflict savage losses his Army of the Potomac would then victoriously march on Richmond.

Lincoln readily endorsed the plan, unaware of the infighting within the Army of the Potomac's leadership. Although now over 140,000-strong and reorganized into three Grand Divisions, Burnside oversaw a team of commanders who loathed, or at best lacked confidence in, their appointed leader. In addition, the new commander was acutely aware the rank and file had worshipped his predecessor. As the Union offensive commenced, the poor state of the roads led to a breakdown in communication and supply chains between his army on the move and the War Department back in Washington. The delays would prove both calamitous for his plans and deadly for his troops.

Burnside sets his plans

The Army of the Potomac moved toward Fredericksburg from its base near Falmouth on 17 November, but the few hundred rebels occupying the town had already destroyed the bridges across the fast-flowing Rappahannock River. When Burnside arrived, he was aghast to discover the pontoons to ford the treacherous river that he had requested from the War Department, and the engineers who would assemble them, were nowhere to be seen. The pontoons were a remarkable invention: 40-foot wooden barges lashed together with rope before a matted road was laid over them to create a makeshift bridge. Somewhere in between Burnside's headquarters and Washington his request had been delayed. It would derail his whole strategy.

Major General Edwin V Sumner, commander of Burnside's Grand Right Division, was anxious

"WE COULD HAVE HAD THE HILLS ON THE OTHER SIDE OF THE RIVER WITHOUT THE COST OF 50 MEN. NOW IT WILL COST AT LEAST 10,000, IF NOT MORE!"

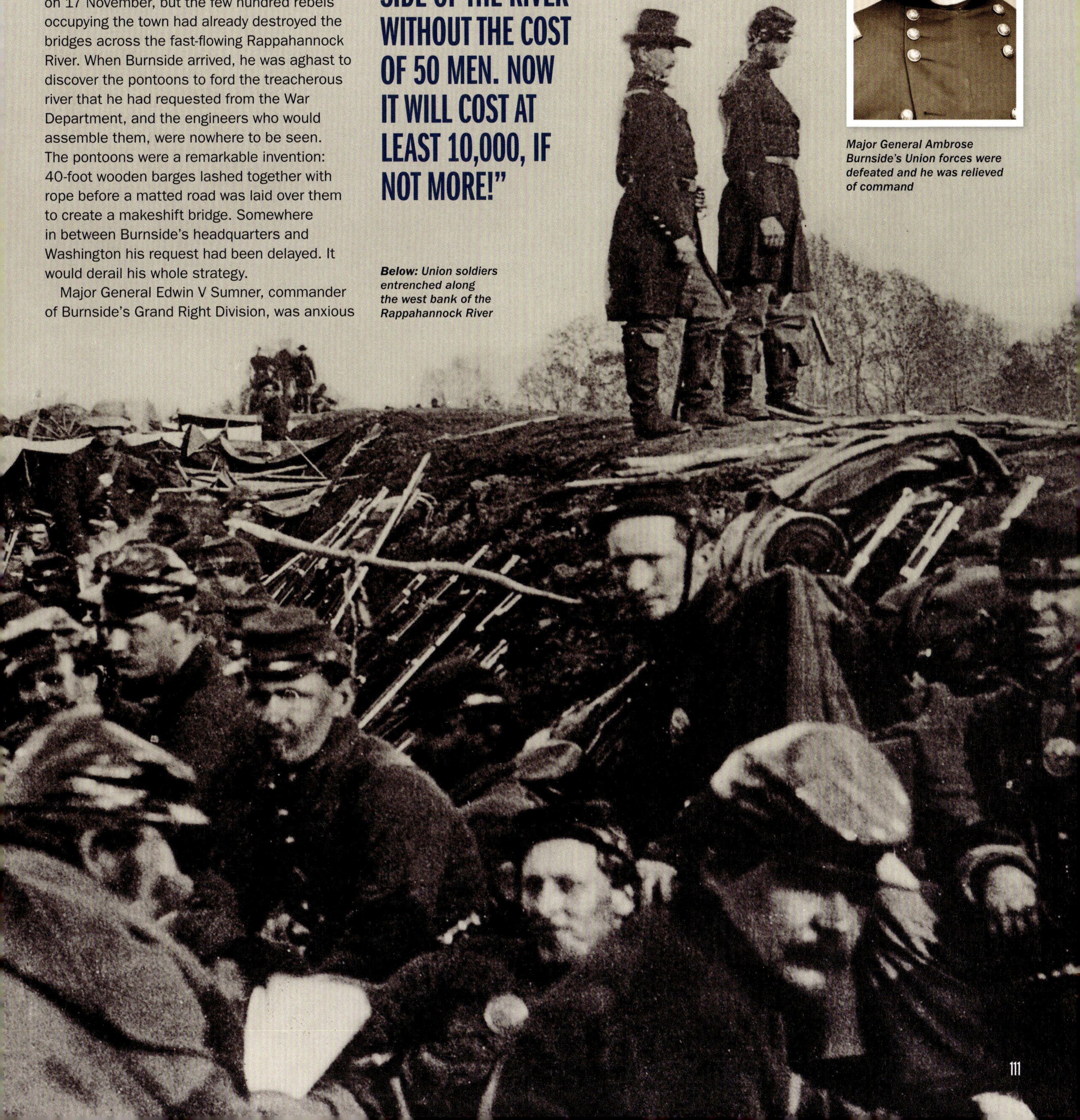

Below: *Union soldiers entrenched along the west bank of the Rappahannock River*

Major General Ambrose Burnside's Union forces were defeated and he was relieved of command

Images: Alamy, Getty

to get across to take the town and occupy the heights beyond, which he could see were lightly defended. However, fearful that they might be stranded across a flooded barrier, Burnside's natural inclination to deliberate failed any such initiative. He instead ordered a halt and demanded his boats and pontoons be made ready as soon as possible. A few days dragged to two weeks, and by the end of the month the element of surprise had evaporated. Lee had rushed up two corps totalling 79,000 men, commanded by Generals James Longstreet and Thomas 'Stonewall' Jackson.

Across the Rappahannock

Burnside's army could only watch as the enemy across the river now constructed a seven-mile-long series of defensive works in the hills behind Fredericksburg, ready and well positioned to await an expected Union assault. Lee himself was sure no Union commander would be foolish enough to attempt such a move. Recording in his personal diary of his growing frustration at how badly the outcome now looked for the Union forces, Colonel Samuel K Zook, commander of the 57th New York Infantry, knew the fate that now awaited his men: "If we had had the pontoons promised when we arrived here, we could have had the hills on the other side of the river without the cost of 50 men. Now it will cost at least 10,000, if not more!"

Survivors bury the dead in the aftermath of the vicious battle

He was right to be fearful. The Confederate forces had established formidable lines of defenses above and below the city, as well as the commanding Marye's Heights 1,800 feet to the west of the town, where Lee's troops and artillery had an excellent field of fire. Should the enemy get across a canal and into the main field to then attack the position they would be sitting ducks for a fusillade of rifle and cannon. Lee's commanders were confident in their defenses, internal lines of supply and communication. Any breaks in their lines could be reinforced quickly. Even if Burnside did intend carrying the ridge of Marye's Heights, they would first need to take positions protected by a four-foot-high stone wall a few hundred yards in front, which lined an old sunken farm road. Behind this natural barrier, four lines of infantry belonging to Brigadier General Thomas R Cobb's

Union troops battled to build their pontoons and gain a foothold across the river

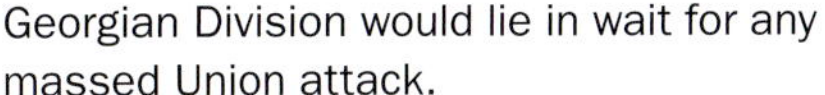

Burnside (right) was a capable corps-level commander but doubted his ability to lead an army in the field

Confederate troops in Fredericksburg after their victory

Georgian Division would lie in wait for any massed Union attack.

As both sides watched one another across the Rappahannock, whereas Lee was content to sit and wait for the next move by the Army of the Potomac, Burnside was inundated with pressure from Washington to move to take the Confederate position. On 12 December, while Confederate sharpshooters hiding in the town tried to pick off Union engineers constructing the pontoon bridges, Burnside ordered a lengthy artillery bombardment to suppress them. It would be the largest artillery bombardment of the war so far. From Stafford Heights where Burnside's headquarters were situated, overlooking the river from the Union positions, 150 artillery pieces fired over 8,000 projectiles into the town. After the barrage, remarkably, Confederate troops still continued to fire upon Union bridge builders from amid the ruins.

Burnside called for volunteers to undertake the very first amphibious infantry assault of the war, to clear the town. Union troops established a bridgehead and slowly pushed back the Confederates through its streets, despite never being trained for urban combat. By 4.30pm Lee's pickets had retired back to the heights as Union massed columns started crossing for the main attack the next day. In the lull, many Union troops looted and vandalized what was left of the town, causing widespread damage.

The carnage begins

The Army of the Potomac attacked on the morning of 13 December as the freezing fog was lifting off the Rappahannock. The previous day, Burnside had mapped out to his commanders his strategy of a two-pronged assault. To many of them gathered in his headquarters, this planned offensive seemed overambitious, to others, foolhardy. Burnside was asking his men to advance up steep ground: on the far left of the Union line, Major General William B Franklin's Left Grand Division (some 65,000 men) would lead the main attack, on Prospect Hill, only 65 feet in height, to capture the positions occupied by Stonewall Jackson's 36,000 2nd Corps. With the Confederates preoccupied on their right flank, General Sumner's Right Grand Division (37,500 men) would then assault Marye's Heights to tie down Longstreet's 38,000-strong 1st Corps, and eventually link with Franklin on the high ground. Joe Hooker's Grand Center Division (47,000 men) would maintain a defense of the center and provide reinforcements to Sumner and Franklin where necessary.

Ultimately, Burnside believed he could sweep up Lee's whole position above the town. Despite fierce arguments from his subordinate commanders, he waived away their concerns. A brigade at a time, Sumner's units now began their funereal march across the pontoon bridges and through the ruins of the town to line up for the coming assault of Marye's Heights. To the south of Stafford Heights, facing Prospect Hill, Franklin established three more pontoon bridges across the Rappahannock to get his own units in place for the expected early morning attack.

However, Burnside's lack of clear orders to Franklin, combined with the latter's inherent distrust of his commander's ability, led to confusion, valuable time lost, and a missed opportunity. Dawn had come and gone, and with it the element of surprise, by the time Franklin received his orders at 7.30am. Burnside wanted his powerful wing of over 60,000 men to carry Prospect Hill with a "division at least". Instead of a massed infantry assault that might well have overwhelmed Jackson's positions, Franklin followed his order to the letter and sent in just one Pennsylvanian division, commanded by Brigadier General George Meade, comprising just over 3,800 men. Meade had to take a position occupied by almost ten-times that number of Confederates, supported by entrenched artillery.

Despite this, the Pennsylvanians acquitted themselves, overcoming murderous Confederate artillery fire as they marched up the elevation, to by chance discover a weak link in Jackson's defenses through a marshy wood, where inexplicably the rebel commander had failed to man a 1,800-foot line. Meade's opportunist surge into the gap almost caused the rebel line to break, as the survivors of the initial charge crested the hill and caused Jackson to summon heavy reinforcements.

A sustained Confederate counter-attack stemmed the tide and drove Meade's men

"THEY GOT TO WITHIN 25 PACES OF THE STONE WALL BEFORE THEY WERE DRIVEN BACK BY A TEMPEST OF REBEL FIRE"

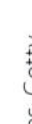

back through ground that would be ominously titled the 'Slaughter Pen'. Without the promised reinforcements from Franklin, who was more concerned to protect his lines of retreat across the river, Meade was forced to retire by that afternoon with losses to his division of over 40 percent. Further to the north the fighting would be relentless and far more brutal for other Union divisions.

Fateful advance

By late morning, Burnside, beset with anxiety at Franklin's failure, directed a main thrust towards Marye's Heights. Sumner was ordered to send "a division or more" to seize the high ground. Sumner's brigades would march out from the relative safety offered by Fredericksburg, navigate a valley bisected by a water-filled canal ditch, and reform their lines before ascending an open slope of 1,200 feet to reach the base of the heights.

Lee had been concerned as to the strength of Sumner's units that would assault Longstreet's position. But with his artillery bedded in to a strong defensive position, many cannons sighted down onto the plain instead of being hidden behind the hill. With such firepower at his disposal, and his lines of infantry massed behind the stone wall at the base of Marye's Heights, protected by the sunken road, Longstreet oozed confidence.

"General… if you put every man now on the other side of the Potomac in that field to approach me… and give me plenty of ammunition, I will kill them all before they reach my line," he assured Lee.

His men would prove as good as his word. At noon, the first of several divisions, a brigade at a time, went in, each to face intense artillery fire as they double-timed in rank up to the Confederate positions: across the canal, stumbling over wooden fences, and reassembling in their two lines of battle to continue their assault. All while under relentless Confederate artillery fire. As each brigade marched valiantly in line towards Longstreet's positions, it melted before the firestorm meted out by Confederate riflemen behind the stone wall. It was as brave as it was pitiless.

Throughout the afternoon and towards sunset, Sumner sent in his men 14 times. The most gallant charge of the day was made by the Irish Brigade led by General Thomas Meagher, green sprigs of boxwood in their kepis. They got to within 25 paces of the stone wall before they were driven back by a tempest of rebel fire from the 24th Georgia (also an Irish formation), who cheered their countrymen's heroism as they fell back.

Witnessing the carnage from the rear, Major General Hooker rode to Burnside's headquarters above Stafford Heights to demand a halt in the attack. Suspicious of his subordinate's motives, and knowing Washington expected victory, Burnside ordered the attack to continue until the heights were taken.

By the evening, as the light started to fade and all assaults had been repulsed, the route up to Marye's Heights was littered with the dead and dying – almost 9,000 men. Fredericksburg was still under Confederate artillery fire as Lee continued to hold his positions. Jackson had managed a break in his lines effectively, and Longstreet had kept his word. Not one Union soldier had penetrated his lines that afternoon. Two-thirds of Union casualties that day lay before the stone wall.

"THE ROUTE UP TO MARYE'S HEIGHTS WAS LITTERED WITH THE DEAD AND DYING – ALMOST 9,000 MEN"

Aftermath

Distraught at how his plans had unraveled so calamitously, Burnside resolved to personally lead the next day's attacks in atonement for the disaster. Thankfully for the officers and men of his old corps, he was talked down by his subordinates. His own misgivings of his unsuitability to command an army had come to pass. Leading yet more men to destruction against Lee's defenses would not change the overall strategic outcome, and he knew it. He ordered a withdrawal back across the Rappahannock.

After the battle, the Union dead and dying carpeted the field below Marye's Heights. The survivors lay in freezing temperatures upon the hard ground next to the corpses of their comrades. The sound of Confederate snipers shattering the cries and moans of the wounded. One Confederate, Sergeant Richard Kirkland, would earn the title of the 'Angel of Marye's Heights' as he displayed immense courage in going out into no man's land to give water and comfort to the Union wounded who had been marooned under fire for over 24 hours.

On 15 December, much to his frustration, Lee was convinced no further Union assault was coming. He had hoped to finish the job. Burnside's army had instead retreated back across the river under cover of darkness with

Burnside's plan was to take Fredericksburg (seen here just before the war) then march on to the Confederate capital at Richmond

the pontoons muffled to soften the noise of men and horses. Confederate skirmishes discovered the enemy's giant encampment in and around Fredericksburg deserted the next day.

Southern newspapers claimed a great victory, Lee's casualties of 5,377 (with 595 dead) were light compared with the Union figure of 12,653 (1,284 killed). But although he had achieved a stunning victory, strategically Lee was aware it did not achieve his goal of destroying the Army of the Potomac. He knew a fresh, newly equipped opponent would come again into Virginia. Sooner or later, he feared, they would find the right man to lead it.

Burnside was determined to remove the stain of bloody, ignoble defeat and sought to continue his offensive towards Richmond, despite the worsening weather. It was doomed to failure as the winter rains continued; his wagon trains and artillery became stuck in the mud, and his senior commanders plotted his downfall – weary of his inept leadership. He was relieved of command on 25 January 1863 as Lincoln took on the chin the political backlash from his opponents in Washington and continued to look for a Union general who could deliver him victory. ★

Both sides suffered heavy losses during the Battle of Fredericksburg

STATE OF PLAY 1863-1864

An arduous struggle against tenacious Confederate opposition finds the Union forces ascendant on all fronts

During the difficult years of 1863 and 1864, the Confederacy's fortunes of war reached high tide and then began slowly, agonizingly to recede. On 1 January 1863, President Abraham Lincoln issued the Emancipation Proclamation, transforming the Civil War from a struggle to save the Union into a crusade for human rights.

Building on previous successes, General Ulysses S Grant took command of Union armies in the West and began a difficult campaign to capture Vicksburg on the Mississippi River. By spring, however, the Union Army of the Potomac, under General Joseph Hooker, was defeated by Robert E Lee's Confederate Army of Northern Virginia at Chancellorsville. The cost was high, as General Stonewall Jackson was mortally wounded by friendly fire.

Lee's army invaded the North a second time but found frustration and defeat in the Battle of Gettysburg on 1-3 July 1863. The Confederacy's conduct of the war became decidedly defensive. In the West, Grant took Vicksburg on 4 July, and the Battle of Chickamauga resulted in a Union rout in September. But the Confederates, under General Braxton Bragg, could not maintain the siege of Chattanooga. Grant raised the siege, leading to General William T Sherman's Atlanta Campaign and the March to the Sea.

Grant pursued Lee during the Overland Campaign in the spring of 1864, fighting pitched battles at the Wilderness, Spotsylvania Court House, and Cold Harbor, finally besieging the Confederates at Petersburg. Sherman captured Atlanta in September and began his epic march of death and destruction. His army occupied Savannah in December. ★

Confederate General Thomas J 'Stonewall' Jackson died after he was mortally wounded by friendly fire at the Battle of Chancellorsville

Images: Getty, Alamy, Wiki

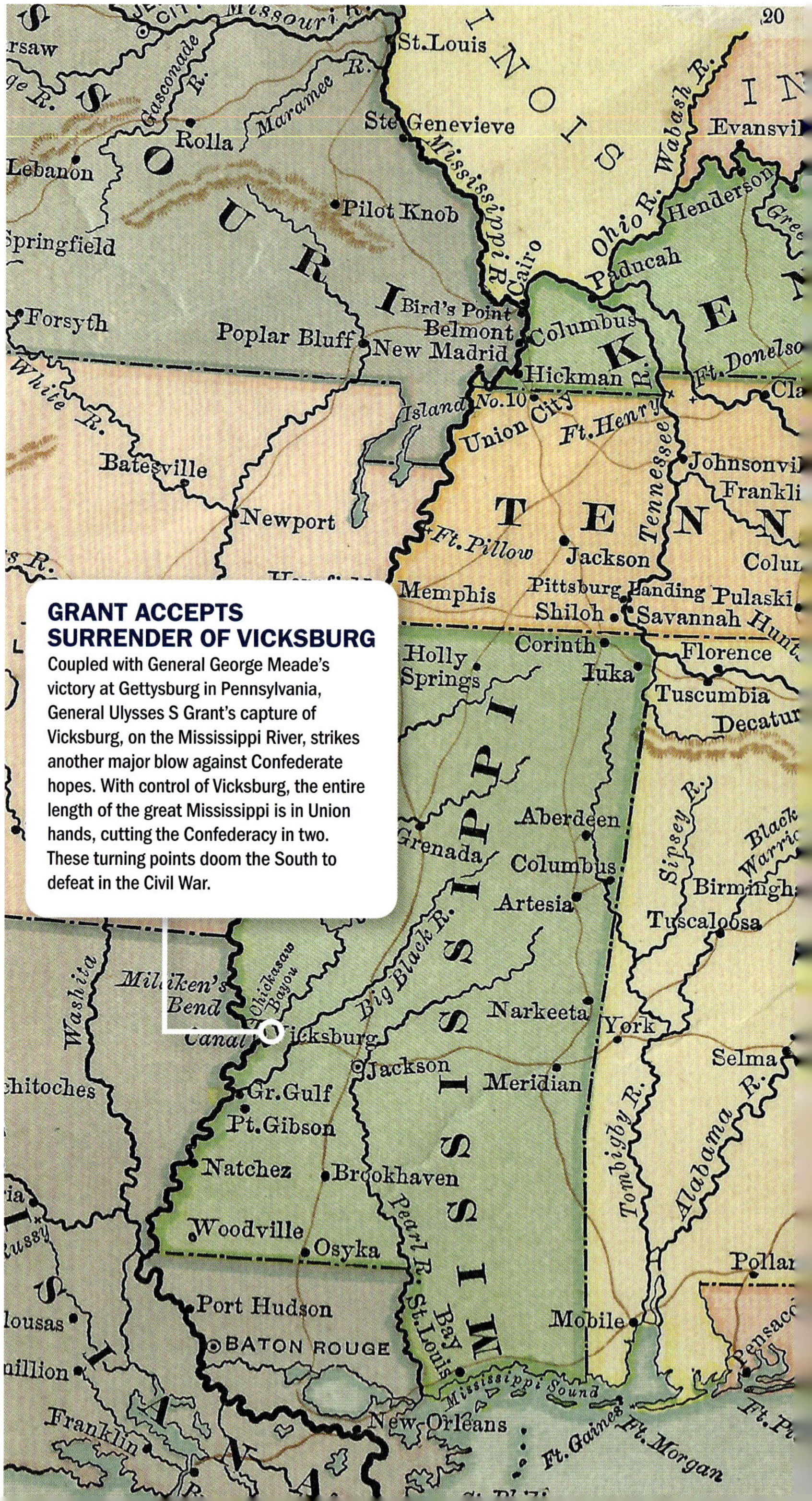

GRANT ACCEPTS SURRENDER OF VICKSBURG

Coupled with General George Meade's victory at Gettysburg in Pennsylvania, General Ulysses S Grant's capture of Vicksburg, on the Mississippi River, strikes another major blow against Confederate hopes. With control of Vicksburg, the entire length of the great Mississippi is in Union hands, cutting the Confederacy in two. These turning points doom the South to defeat in the Civil War.

***Right:** A campaign poster touts the successful Republican ticket of Abraham Lincoln and vice presidential candidate Andrew Johnson in 1864*

***Left:** Union General Ulysses S Grant (left) negotiates the surrender of Vicksburg with Confederate General John Pemberton*

LEE'S MASTERSTROKE AT CHANCELLORSVILLE

On 1-4 May 1863, the Battle of Chancellorsville, Lee's most brilliant tactical success of the war, results in a tremendous victory as the Confederate commander divides his forces and Stonewall Jackson executes a stealthy flanking march. Union General Joseph Hooker's offensive is stymied, and the Confederate Army of Northern Virginia seizes the initiative. However, Jackson is mortally wounded by friendly fire and dies days later.

DECISIVE SIEGE OF PETERSBURG

In mid-June 1864, Grant's Overland Campaign ends, and the lengthy siege of Petersburg, a rail center a few miles south of the Confederate capital of Virginia, begins. Periodically, Grant tries to cut the rail lifelines extending southward and forces Confederate General Robert E Lee to stretch his defensive lines more thinly. The siege drags on but leads to victory the following spring.

LINCOLN WINS PIVOTAL REELECTION

Facing Democratic nominee George B McClellan, his former Army of the Potomac commander, Abraham Lincoln wins the presidential election of 1864 on the strength of 55% of the popular vote and 212 of 233 votes in the electoral college. Battlefield successes are crucial in Lincoln's victory. He also wins the majority of votes cast by soldiers in the field.

THE COMING OF CONSCRIPTION

On 3 March 1863, the US Congress authorizes a draft but simultaneously votes to allow those who can afford to pay $300 to hire a proxy to serve in their place. Although the measures augment the ranks of the Union armies, they incite anger among the poor, common people, leading to protests and bloody, violent draft riots in New York City.

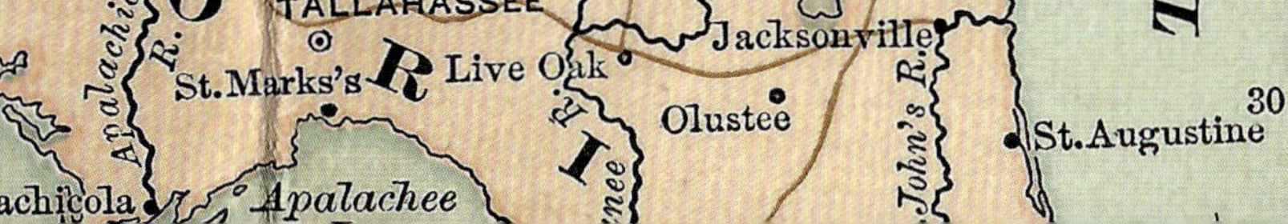

THENCEFORTH AND FOREVER FREE

The Emancipation Proclamation joined the end of slavery with preservation of the Union as President Lincoln's ultimate goals in the Civil War

WORDS **MIKE HASKEW**

Cabinet members cluster around President Lincoln in this painting depicting the first reading of the Emancipation Proclamation

President Abraham Lincoln is known to history as the 'Great Emancipator'. Personally, Lincoln was appalled by the institution of involuntary servitude. However, he was also a pragmatic politician.

With the outbreak of the Civil War, the foremost objective of the Lincoln administration and the armies that mobilized to quell the rebellion was the preservation of the Union. Lincoln was obliged to delicately balance the perspectives and political influence of both the Republican and Democratic political parties in government. Obviously, the early advocacy of a slavery-ending policy would jeopardize the loyalty of the 'Border States,' Delaware, Maryland, Kentucky, Missouri, and later West Virginia, where slavery was common but the governments had declined to leave the Union. Further, the Constitution allowed slavery to continue in areas where it was the will of the people. Yet, as a Republican, Lincoln was the leader and policy-shaper of the party that sought an end to the "peculiar institution."

Lincoln's dilemma

In August 1862, Lincoln wrote to Horace Greeley, editor of the *New York Tribune*: "If I could save the Union without freeing any slave I would do it, and if I could save it by freeing all the slaves I would do it; and if I could save it by freeing some and leaving others alone I would also do that." As he wrote to Greeley, a draft of the Emancipation Proclamation, a transformative document, was in his desk drawer at the White House.

***Above** The text of Lincoln's Emancipation Proclamation*

Image: Alamy

The progress of the Civil War dictated Lincoln's walk along the political tightrope. As Union armies operated in the South, slaves fled plantations and sought sanctuary within their lines. At first, it was a trickle of humanity, then a flood. At first, Union officers either accepted the 'runaways' or returned them to their owners who asserted loyalty to the United States. They were, according to the law, property. However, the situation changed as it became evident that some slaves were being used to support the Confederate war effort. In that manner, they were contraband of war, subject to forfeiture or seizure. Congress passed two confiscation acts and a militia act that bolstered this position, even authorizing the employment of freed slaves as soldiers of the US Army. Also, logically, a war against a slaveholding rebellion was a war against slavery itself, the underpinning of the Confederate economy.

By mid-1862, it had become apparent that Lincoln had to act against slavery or potentially lose the support of the majority of his own party. His response was bold and far-reaching, an Emancipation Proclamation that freed the slaves in territories then in rebellion against the United States. It did not free slaves in the Border States or in certain areas, such as the state of Tennessee, where the Union army had already established a provisional government and it was not considered actively in rebellion.

Secretary of State William H Seward and the rest of Lincoln's cabinet agreed with the language of the Emancipation Proclamation, but Seward persuaded the president to withhold its issuance until a significant victory would further legitimize it. After the fateful Battle of Antietam, Lincoln did issue the Emancipation Proclamation effective 1 January 1863. In the process, the politically astute Lincoln successfully linked the end of slavery and the proclamation to the preservation of the Union – both turned out to be necessary steps to ensure victory.

A black man reads a newspaper bringing word of the Emancipation Proclamation and its implications for the future of slavery

A moral victory

The Emancipation Proclamation weakened the Confederate war effort substantially as a source of labor continued to ebb and by the end of the war 180,000 free blacks had joined the US Army. The possibility of interference from European nations, where slavery had long been outlawed, was virtually eliminated. The text asserts that the Emancipation Proclamation was an "...act of justice, warranted by the Constitution, upon military necessity..."

Subsequently, the eradication of slavery became a Union war objective. Historians argue as to whether the Emancipation Proclamation actually freed any slaves. Regardless, its transcendent implications were clear. Lincoln had seized the moral high ground, managed to maintain the support of his political base, defused the objections of opponents, and transformed the conflict into a crusade for freedom and human rights.

In January 1865, Congress passed the 13th Amendment to the Constitution abolishing slavery, and in December two-thirds of the states ratified the amendment. Slavery was dead in the United States of America. ★

***Below** While visiting the former Confederate capital of Richmond, Virginia, President Lincoln addresses a crowd of free blacks*

This illustration from Harper's Weekly *depicts a new reality for freed blacks. It appeared in print in 1865*

THE TIMELESS GETTYSBURG ADDRESS

PRESIDENT LINCOLN ELOQUENTLY DESCRIBED THE CAUSE OF FREEDOM AND SANCTIFIED THE SACRIFICE OF THOSE WHO DIED FOR IT

The Battle of Gettysburg, like so many others in the terrible Civil War, had left thousands dead in its wake. By the fall of 1863, an effort to permanently inter the Union soldiers who had made the ultimate sacrifice there was well underway, and the time came for the dedication of the new national cemetery. President Abraham Lincoln was invited to attend and deliver a few "appropriate remarks."

In that era, such an event was indeed a spectacle, and speeches were often lengthy. At the Gettysburg dedication, the featured speaker was Senator Edward Everett of Massachusetts, known far and wide for his captivating oratory skills. Lincoln traveled to Gettysburg by train, and on 19 November 1863, a crowd gathered. Everett delivered a two-hour discourse on the momentous battle, and it was well received. The Baltimore Glee Club rose and sang *Consecration Chant*. Then, President Lincoln moved to the speakers' post and delivered a 272-word, ten-sentence commentary that required scarcely two minutes to complete. Polite applause greeted its end, and Lincoln remarked, "That plough didn't scour!" believing he had failed to deliver the resonating words that were worthy of the occasion.

He was wrong. The Gettysburg Address stands today as one of the most revered documents in American history. In clarity and brevity, it has few, if any equals. Everett freely acknowledged the triumph telling Lincoln, "I should be glad, if I could flatter myself that I came as near to the central idea of the occasion, in two hours, as you did in two minutes."

***Above** One of two confirmed photographs of Lincoln at Gettysburg shows the president seated, bareheaded, near the center of the image.*

CHANCELLORSVILLE

The rejuvenated Union Army of the Potomac was crushed in the dense woods of Northern Virginia as the brilliance of Robert E Lee delivered the 'perfect victory' for the Confederacy... but at a cost

WORDS **IAIN MACGREGOR**

By the spring of 1863, the American Civil War in the Eastern Theater of Northern Virginia was in stalemate. Both sides had been busy rebuilding their forces in winter quarters since the bloodletting at the Battle of Fredericksburg the previous December. Since the beginning of the war itself, President Abraham Lincoln had been searching for a general who could effectively lead the enormous resources Washington would place under his command in terms of men and materiel. The industrial North had the resources to conduct and win a strategic war against the weaker agricultural-based Southern rebel states, but what it repeatedly failed to do was defeat Robert E Lee's Army of Northern Virginia.

The Battle of Fredericksburg in December 1862 had been a bloody calamity for the North, with thousands needlessly killed as Union divisions marched up to entrenched Confederate positions above the Virginian town on Marye's Heights only to be mercilessly cut down by massed musketry and cannon. Yet Lee's victory had not been turned into a strategic success and his exhausted forces failed to follow up with their own counter-attack to finish off the enemy. Both sides now settled for a winter truce.

Union troops pictured loading cannons before the Battle of Chancellorsville

The Army of the Potomac had survived, but yet again was given a new commander. The hapless Ambrose Burnside, who had overseen the carnage, was replaced as he suggested his next move that spring of 1863 would follow the exact strategy that had brought disaster on the slopes of Marye's Heights. Two of his own corps commanders with political connections lobbied Washington for change. Aware of a lack of enthusiasm for his leadership, Burnside's offer of resignation was readily accepted by Lincoln, who now installed one of the more outspoken officers who had lobbied against him – Major General Joseph Hooker.

Already a veteran of the battles of Bull Run, Antietam and Fredericksburg, Hooker believed he had the strategic nous to beat Lee's army and the resources to make it happen. It was here that alarm bells should have rung in the White House. Lincoln had given command of the Army of the Potomac to Hooker with the clear instructions for him to defeat Lee and protect Washington, but now looked on as that spring Hooker developed a plan to invade Virginia and capture Richmond, believing that would culminate in Lee being forced to give battle on Hooker's terms. Though a good organizer of commands – Hooker restructured the Army of the Potomac along the corps system that would remain throughout the war – events would prove he had been promoted above his ability as a frontline army commander.

Background

The fallout from Fredericksburg had forced Lincoln to quickly install yet another new commander of the Army of the Potomac in order to bring defeat upon the seemingly unbeatable Army of Northern Virginia. 'Fighting Joe' Hooker from Massachusetts, 48, was a hard-drinking, womanizing general who had already been involved in many of the Army of the Potomac's defeats the previous year. Though severely bloodied at Fredericksburg, Hooker would still command a formidable force of 130,000 men, now encamped at Falmouth, Virginia, as they were resupplied. By April, he had successfully reorganized the unwieldy Grand Division structure to a more sensible corps formation, with an independent cavalry wing. Just as significantly, he improved his men's morale, having them adopt specific insignia for their units, improving supplies, implementing more drilling and reinvigorating the Army of the Potomac esprit de corps.

"HOOKER WAS A HARD-DRINKING, WOMANIZING GENERAL WHO'D ALREADY BEEN INVOLVED IN MANY PREVIOUS DEFEATS"

He realized that to bring Lee to battle on ground of his choosing he must first threaten the Confederate capital, Richmond. On 27 April, 10,000 Union horse crossed the Rappahannock River upstream, then swung around Lee's rear and attacked his supply lines. At the same time another corps crossed downstream, while three more corps

of infantry crossed the Rappahannock and Rapidan rivers and marched as planned toward the hamlet of Chancellorsville to the west – a large brick mansion, sited at a crossroads in a clearing. By 1 May, Hooker had over 70,000 troops situated around Chancellorsville awaiting what he was sure would either be a doomed Confederate frontal assault, or their withdrawal.

Lee had uncharacteristically been taken by surprise, but realizing the enemy troops at Chancellorsville were the immediate threat he gambled and divided his smaller force to attack a portion of the Union army before it had time to gather itself. Leaving a much smaller force of 11,000 men still situated above Fredericksburg to hold in place Union forces, Lee was strengthened by Major General 'Stonewall' Jackson's corps and thus marched to Chancellorsville with at least 40,000 troops – still far fewer than the bulk of Union troops awaiting them.

The battle begins

The battle began mid-morning on 1 May as Hooker's columns advanced to capture a strategic crossroads, unaware that Stonewall Jackson's forces were there too. The fighting was fairly even, yet Hooker became anxious. The realization that his enemy had not retreated from such superior forces and instead wished to fight had spoiled his strategy and shaken his confidence. Against the wishes of his corps commanders, he ordered Union troops back behind their original fortifications, not only giving up valuable high ground but also handing the

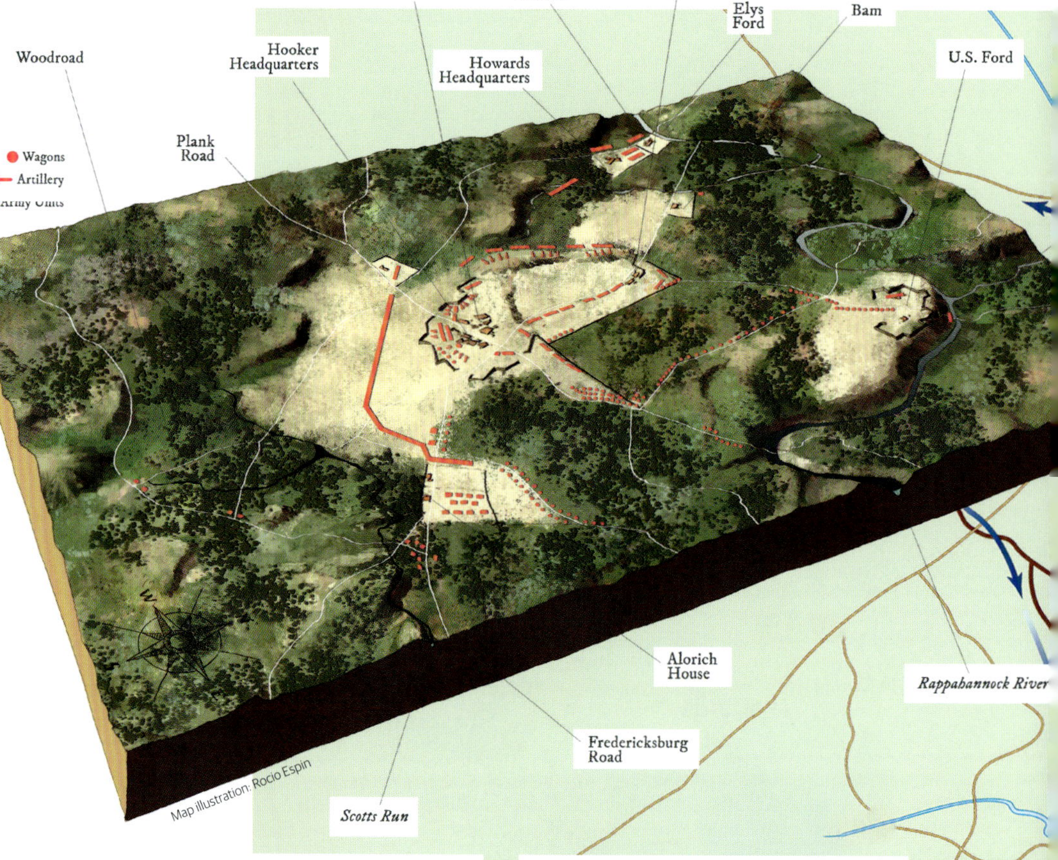

Map illustration: Rocio Espin

01 THE UNION OFFENSIVE TO DESTROY LEE

Major General Joseph Hooker implements a new offensive that he believes will encircle General Robert E Lee's flanks around Fredericksburg and force him to retreat, giving the Union the opportunity to beat him on their own terms.

02 HOOKER LOSES HIS NERVE

On first contact with Lee's forces on crossroads within the Wilderness, Hooker's confidence evaporates. Against the wishes of his subordinates, he orders his army back to defensive positions around Chancellorsville on 1 May.

03 LEE DIVIDES HIS COMMAND

That evening, Lee meets with Thomas 'Stonewall' Jackson at a bivouac in the dense woodlands around Chancellorsville to review reconnaissance reports. Scouts report Hooker has overextended his line and can be flanked. The Confederate commanders plan an audacious assault on the furthermost Union point – XI Corps.

04 THE WEAKNESS OF XI CORPS

Major General Oliver O Howard fails to follow Hooker's orders for his men to dig in and construct fortifications. Jackson's forces are in place by late afternoon along the unprotected flank of XI Corps. Despite reports coming into Hooker's HQ of sightings of Jackson's troops, the Union commander thinks Lee is retreating. XI Corps fate is sealed as Jackson attacks.

05 RALLYING THE MEN

Thousands of terrified Union troops pour into and past Howard's headquarters. Realizing the unfolding disaster, he holds aloft the corps colors and gallops his horse into the hordes of fleeing troops to rally them. It only buys the collapsing Union line 30 minutes, but as the daylight ebbs it proves crucial to averting complete annihilation.

A contemporary map of the battlefield depicting each side's movements on 2 and 3 May

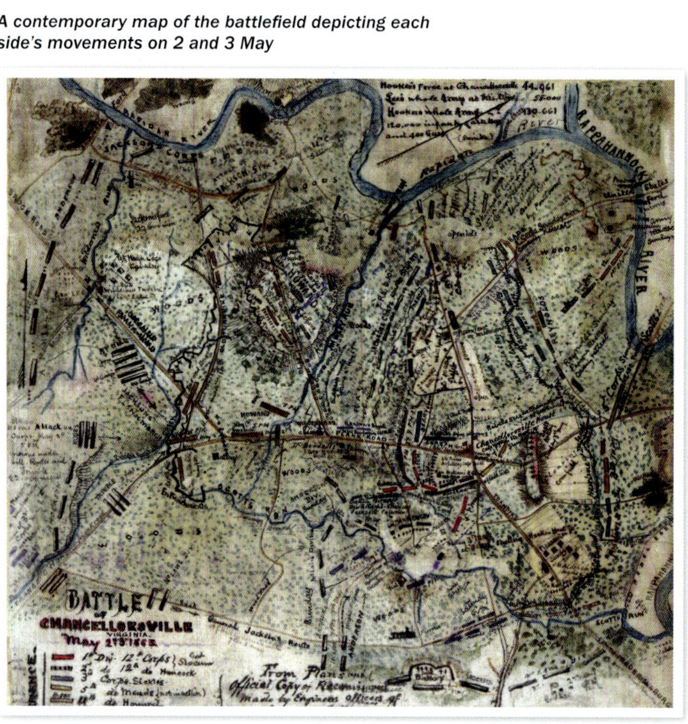

Image: Alamy

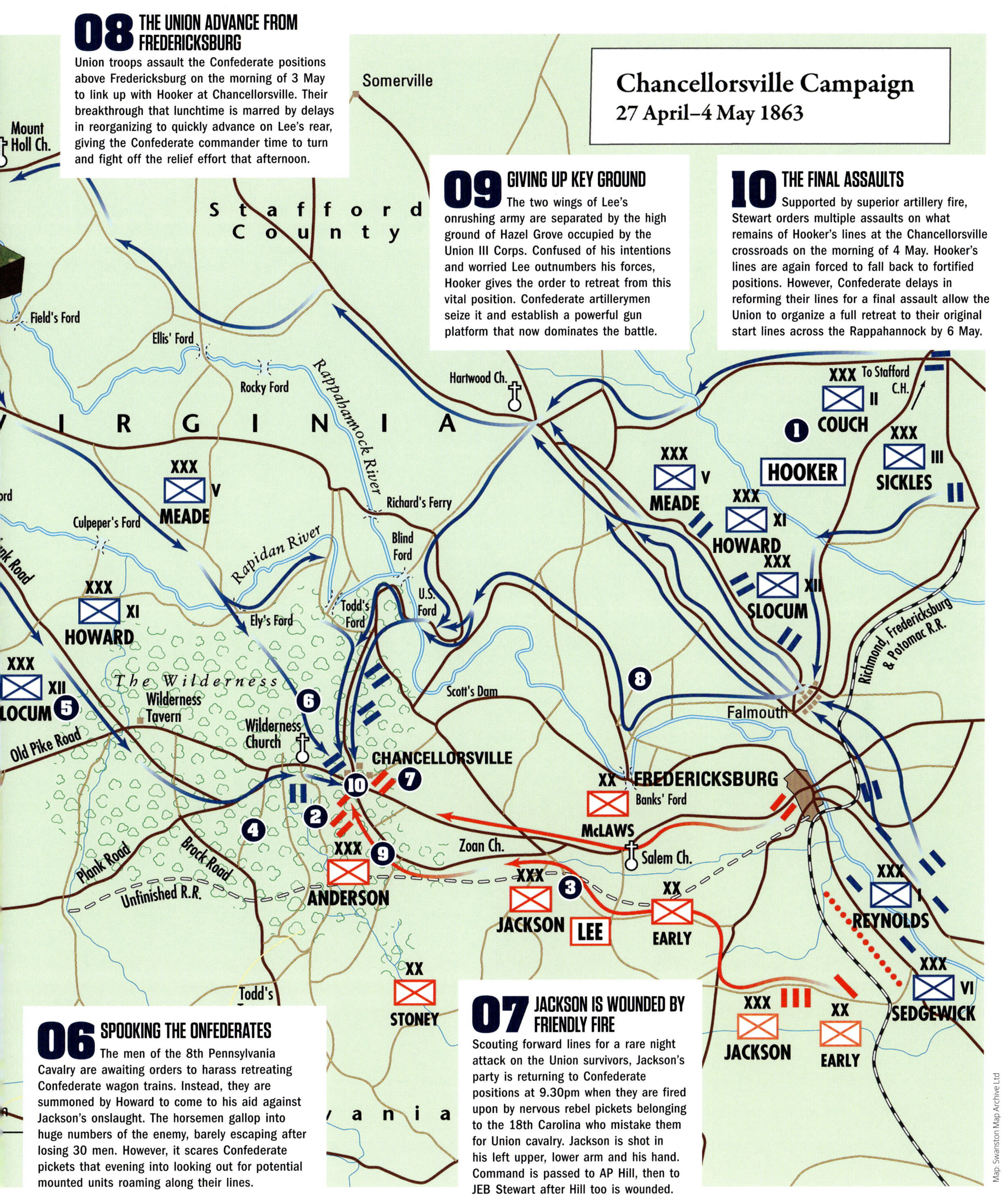

08 THE UNION ADVANCE FROM FREDERICKSBURG

Union troops assault the Confederate positions above Fredericksburg on the morning of 3 May to link up with Hooker at Chancellorsville. Their breakthrough that lunchtime is marred by delays in reorganizing to quickly advance on Lee's rear, giving the Confederate commander time to turn and fight off the relief effort that afternoon.

09 GIVING UP KEY GROUND

The two wings of Lee's onrushing army are separated by the high ground of Hazel Grove occupied by the Union III Corps. Confused of his intentions and worried Lee outnumbers his forces, Hooker gives the order to retreat from this vital position. Confederate artillerymen seize it and establish a powerful gun platform that now dominates the battle.

10 THE FINAL ASSAULTS

Supported by superior artillery fire, Stewart orders multiple assaults on what remains of Hooker's lines at the Chancellorsville crossroads on the morning of 4 May. Hooker's lines are again forced to fall back to fortified positions. However, Confederate delays in reforming their lines for a final assault allow the Union to organize a full retreat to their original start lines across the Rappahannock by 6 May.

06 SPOOKING THE ONFEDERATES

The men of the 8th Pennsylvania Cavalry are awaiting orders to harass retreating Confederate wagon trains. Instead, they are summoned by Howard to come to his aid against Jackson's onslaught. The horsemen gallop into huge numbers of the enemy, barely escaping after losing 30 men. However, it scares Confederate pickets that evening into looking out for potential mounted units roaming along their lines.

07 JACKSON IS WOUNDED BY FRIENDLY FIRE

Scouting forward lines for a rare night attack on the Union survivors, Jackson's party is returning to Confederate positions at 9.30pm when they are fired upon by nervous rebel pickets belonging to the 18th Carolina who mistake them for Union cavalry. Jackson is shot in his left upper, lower arm and his hand. Command is passed to AP Hill, then to JEB Stewart after Hill too is wounded.

initiative back to Lee. The Union army was now stretched out for several miles, anchored on the left flank by the Rappahannock River to the east, with strong fortifications in the center; right on the farthest point, surrounded by thick woods, was XI Corps led by Major General Oliver Howard. Such was Howard's belief in his natural defenses that he'd shied away from Hooker's general order for all corps commanders to construct fortifications; it would be his downfall.

That night, Lee and Jackson sat in conference debating an audacious idea. Lee would again divide his forces in the face of superior numbers and have Jackson take his 2nd Corps of 28,000 men through the back roads of the Wilderness – a wide area of dense shrubs and trees – to position himself at the flank of XI Corps, while Lee held at bay the bulk of Hooker's army facing him. Using a local guide, Jackson's men set out at 4am, reaching their destination by 5pm.

Jackson's men hit XI Corps like a sledgehammer, enveloping the startled Union troops as Hooker's whole line retreated before his eyes. Darkness saved a total Union collapse, as both sides halted and dug in where they stood. Jackson and his staff ventured ahead of the Confederate line to assess if a night-time attack could work. As they returned, rebel pickets, tired and anxious from the day's fighting, mistook them in the dark for Union cavalry reported to be in the vicinity. The trigger-happy Confederate sentries opened fire, killing two of the general's staff and wounding Jackson himself. Though a tragic loss, the enemy still needed to

***Left:** Major General Joseph Hooker led the Army of the Potomac but was a poor frontline commander*

"THE TRIGGER-HAPPY CONFEDERATE SENTRIES OPENED FIRE, KILLING TWO OF THE GENERAL'S STAFF AND WOUNDING JACKSON HIMSELF"

be finished off the next day and his corps would be led by Major General JEB Stuart.

Generals Lee and Stuart now needed to eliminate Hooker's III Corps, which stood between them, if they were to bring both halves of the Confederate Army together and drive the remaining Federals from the battlefield. The daring marches of the previous days now gave way to a series of bloody encounters in the dense undergrowth and woods as both sides slugged it out throughout the morning of 3 May. Again, Hooker's timidity resurfaced as he gave up a key elevated position at Hazel Grove, allowing the Confederates to take it and establish a formidable gun park which would dominate the rest of that day's fighting. That morning Jackson's old corps crashed into the center of the Union positions, bringing calamity to Hooker's forces. Fearing for the overall

A depction of 'Stonewall' Jackson's wounding during the battle, which in fact occurred at night

Union artillery at Chancellorsville, by photographer AJ Russell

Left: *Wounded soldiers from the Union Army recuperate after their defeat at Chancellorsville*

"ONCE AGAIN, A SUPERIOR UNION ARMY HAD BEEN OUT-GENERALED INTO ABJECT DEFEAT"

Above: This contemporary wood engraving of the battle has the description "repulse of Jackson's men at Hazel Grove, by artillery under General Pleasonton"

position, Hooker ordered Major General John Sedgwick's VI Corps of 22,000 men to come to his aid. Sedgwick successfully advanced up Marye's Heights at the Second Battle of Fredericksburg and marched west to Chancellorsville – unaware Hooker's position was about to cave in.

Though wary of this new threat coming from fresh Union forces advancing from Fredericksburg, Lee remained calm and, turning away from Hooker, divided his army a third time to meet Sedgwick head on. The Union VI Corps was held at a crossroads at Salem Church, and then driven back. A rattled Hooker refused to come to Sedgwick's aid to coordinate a counter-attack that might have at the last moment turned the battle in the Union's favor.

Unsupported, Sedgwick was forced to retreat eastwards to protect the Union flank and support Hooker's order for the bulk of his army to undertake a rapid withdrawal back to the safety of the Rappahannock River. With Union troops disappearing westwards, both of Lee's wings finally met in the clearing of the Chancellorsville mansion. It was a crushing Union defeat as Lee surveyed his weary and bloodied troops raising their rifles in triumph, their yelling echoing through the woods. Once again, a superior Union army had been out-generaled into abject defeat.

Aftermath

Lee's comprehensive victory would later be described as the 'perfect battle', but the cost to the South was enormous in terms of casualties that they could ill afford and the mortal wounding of their legendary general Stonewall Jackson.

Of the 133,000 Union troops that Hooker had taken into the campaign, he had suffered 17,197 casualties with 1,606 killed, including three divisional commanders – more than had been lost at the disaster at Fredericksburg the previous December. The news caused shock and disbelief in Washington, with President Lincoln lamenting to his staff: "My God, my God, what will the country say?"

For the South, despite the elation of Lee's superb victory, it had come at a terrible price. The Army of Northern Virginia's losses amounted to 13,303 (a staggering 22 percent of Lee's command), more than the bloodletting his army had suffered at Antietam in September 1862 when he had invaded the North. Compounding these figures would be the shocking news a few days later on 10 May that Stonewall Jackson, despite a successful amputation of his wounded arm, had then succumbed to infection. A crestfallen Lee bemoaned to staff: "He may have lost his left arm, but I have lost my right." The loss to the command structure of the Army of Northern Virginia going forward, and to the morale of the Confederacy, was incalculable.

For both sides, the outcome of Battle of Chancellorsville brought into sharp focus what they needed to achieve in 1863. Lee was despondent. Despite this famous victory, his losses and his failure to finish off Hooker's beleaguered and confused army convinced him that only taking the war to the Union once again might bring about a strategic victory. Lee would convince the South's leadership that they should focus all their energies on the Eastern Theater, to the detriment of those Confederate forces defending vital western interests on the Mississippi. For the Union, President Lincoln once again began the desperate search for a commander who could successfully use the North's superior strength in numbers and materiel to bring him victory. A feeling of a coming reckoning pervaded Washington circles as many saw the summer campaign season as pivotal to the outcome of the war. ★

Left: This painting shows the last meeting between Stonewall Jackson (left) and Robert E Lee. Jackson was mortally wounded during the battle by friendly fire

LEE'S FATEFUL MARCH NORTH

Believing victory lay with a successful offensive in the North, Robert E Lee led the Confederate Army of Northern Virginia in a second, climactic invasion

WORDS **MIKE HASKEW**

In the spring of 1863, General Robert E Lee and his Confederate Army of Northern Virginia stood victorious after a shattering defeat of the Union Army of the Potomac, under General Joseph Hooker, at Chancellorsville.

The victory at Chancellorsville is remembered as Lee's tactical masterpiece, but it was also costly. General Thomas J 'Stonewall' Jackson, his most capable subordinate, was mortally wounded by friendly fire and died a few days after the battle.

Prior to Chancellorsville, Lee had already contemplated the future. The Army of Northern Virginia had maintained a generally defensive posture since its first invasion of the North had been turned back at Antietam the previous September. Still, he knew the war could not be won defensively. Provisions were scarce, and the combat efficiency of his army would eventually melt away.

Moving north

Despite the loss of Jackson, the time had come again to invade Northern territory. Lee's objectives were similar to those of his 1862 Maryland Campaign. With a major victory on Northern soil, the Confederates might threaten Baltimore, Maryland, Pennsylvania's capital of Harrisburg, or even Washington, DC. The Democratic Party's peace faction in the US government, and possibly delegations from Great Britain and France, might urge an end to the war on terms favorable to the South. Lee's hungry army could forage off the Pennsylvania countryside, and Virginia would benefit from a respite of hostilities. Of greater urgency, the fortunes of war had turned against the Confederacy in the West, where Vicksburg, Mississippi, was besieged by Union forces. An offensive into Pennsylvania might draw Union troops away from the imperiled Western Theater.

In 1863, Confederate General Robert E Lee chose to invade the North a second time, leading to the Battle of Gettysburg

An image from Harper's Weekly *magazine shows a group of black Americans being driven south by Rebel officers*

In mid-May, Lee traveled to the Confederate capital at Richmond, Virginia, to confer with President Jefferson Davis and other government officials. Leveraging his immense prestige, he won approval for a second invasion of the North. Tremendous risk remained. Much of Lee's movement would be dictated by the response of the Union army. He would also need to allow columns to disperse across the Pennsylvania countryside to forage while remaining close enough to concentrate rapidly when a decisive engagement developed.

Lee's advance

Lee's troop strength approached 75,000 men. Prior to launching his offensive, he reorganized the Army of Northern Virginia into three elements, General James Longstreet, his 'Old Warhorse', commanded I Corps. General Richard S Ewell, was given II Corps, comprised mainly of Jackson's old command, and General AP Hill was placed in command of the newly established III Corps. Hooker remained in command of the Army of the Potomac, more than 100,000 strong, but had lost the confidence of President Abraham Lincoln, who wished to avoid the turmoil of relieving another general and waited for circumstances that would induce Hooker to resign.

On 3 June, Lee ordered an advance from Fredericksburg, Virginia, toward Culpeper. From there, his army would move into the Shenandoah Valley, its progress screened by the Blue Ridge Mountains, eventually crossing into Maryland and Pennsylvania and entering the fertile Cumberland Valley. Lee's advance would

Lee And Stuart

THE RELATIONSHIP BETWEEN GENERAL ROBERT E LEE AND HIS CAVALRY COMMANDER, GENERAL JEB STUART, GREW FOR OVER A DECADE

When General JEB Stuart arrived at the headquarters of the Army of Northern Virginia on the field at Gettysburg, General Robert E Lee is said to have greeted the dashing cavalier with a cold, "Ah, General Stuart, you are here at last!" While there were no witnesses to the exchange on the afternoon of 2 July 1863, there is no doubt that Lee believed he had been ill-served with Stuart's adventurous raid that had deprived the Confederate army of its eyes for more than a week.

It may have been the first rift in a relationship that began in 1852, when then-Colonel Lee was appointed superintendent of the US Military Academy at West Point and Stuart was a cadet there. In 1859, Lee, with Stuart as his aide-de-camp, commanded the Marines and Maryland militia that captured John Brown, the abolitionist attempting to incite a slave insurrection with the seizure of the Federal arsenal at Harpers Ferry.

During the Civil War, Stuart's stature as a brilliant cavalry commander grew along with his reputation as a bon vivant, who enjoyed dancing and ostentatious uniforms. On two occasions prior to the fateful Gettysburg campaign, he had ridden around the main Union army, raising havoc and providing valuable intelligence. After Gettysburg, Lee created a cavalry corps, naming Stuart its commander, but declined to pursue a promotion for Stuart to lieutenant general, perhaps as a reprimand. Nevertheless, any fracture in the relationship healed, and when Lee learned of Stuart's death in May 1864, he lamented, "I can hardly think of him without weeping."

General JEB Stuart, the dashing Confederate cavalry commander, often wore a hat decorated with an ostrich plume

be covered by veteran cavalry under flamboyant General James Ewell Brown 'JEB' Stuart, the epitome of the dashing cavalier.

As early as 27 May, Hooker had received reports that the Confederates would soon be on the march. A week later, he dispatched a strong force of cavalry and infantry under General Alfred Pleasonton to destroy Stuart's cavalry concentrated around Culpeper. On 9 June, the largest cavalry engagement of the Civil War, the Battle of Brandy Station, took place. Until Brandy Station, the Confederate cavalry had reigned supreme. All that changed in a single day.

Stuart was taken by surprise, and a pitched battle ensued, pistols firing and sabers slashing. While Union flank attacks stretched the defenders, counter-attacks slowed the momentum of the initial assault. The fighting raged for 14 hours, but the Confederates forced a Union retirement, claiming a tactical victory. However, Stuart's embarrassment with being caught off guard would lead to a costly attempt to redeem himself. Union losses amounted to 935 killed, wounded and captured, while the Confederates lost 525 cavalrymen that day.

Penetrating into Pennsylvania

The day after Brandy Station, Lee sent Ewell's corps streaming across the Blue Ridge toward Winchester, Virginia. Ewell took the city, capturing more than 3,300 of its 5,000-man Union garrison. On 19 June, Longstreet was in the Shenandoah, slowed while assisting Stuart in fending off Union cavalry in the Blue Ridge gaps. Hill's corps followed Longstreet.

Still smarting from Brandy Station, Stuart proposed a bold, harassing ride around Hooker's army to wreak havoc and disrupt the pursuit of the invading Confederate army. Lee depended on the cavalry to act as the 'eyes' of his army, and accurate knowledge of the Union army's movements was essential to the success of the campaign. On 22 June, he authorized Stuart's movement only if Hooker's army remained stationary, south of the Potomac River, admonishing, "[…] judge whether you can pass around their army without hindrance, doing all the damage you can, and cross the river east of the mountains […] after crossing the river, you must move on and feel the right of Ewell's troops."

Stuart discounted the full meaning of Lee's order, and on the morning of the 25th took his cavalry eastward and out of communication with Lee for eight days. During that time, Lee had no idea of the whereabouts of the Army of the Potomac. In reality, Hooker had moved his army into northern Virginia, roughly 20 miles southwest of Washington, DC. His cavalry reports confirmed that Lee's army was strung out for miles in the Shenandoah and marching northward.

The Confederate vanguard crossed the Potomac River, and General Robert Rodes' division of Ewell's corps reached Chambersburg, 20 miles into Pennsylvania on 19 June. Lee advised Ewell to turn and capture Harrisburg if circumstances were favorable. Ewell ordered

Union troops occupy the town of Carlisle, Pennsylvania, as the Army of the Potomac concentrates at Gettysburg

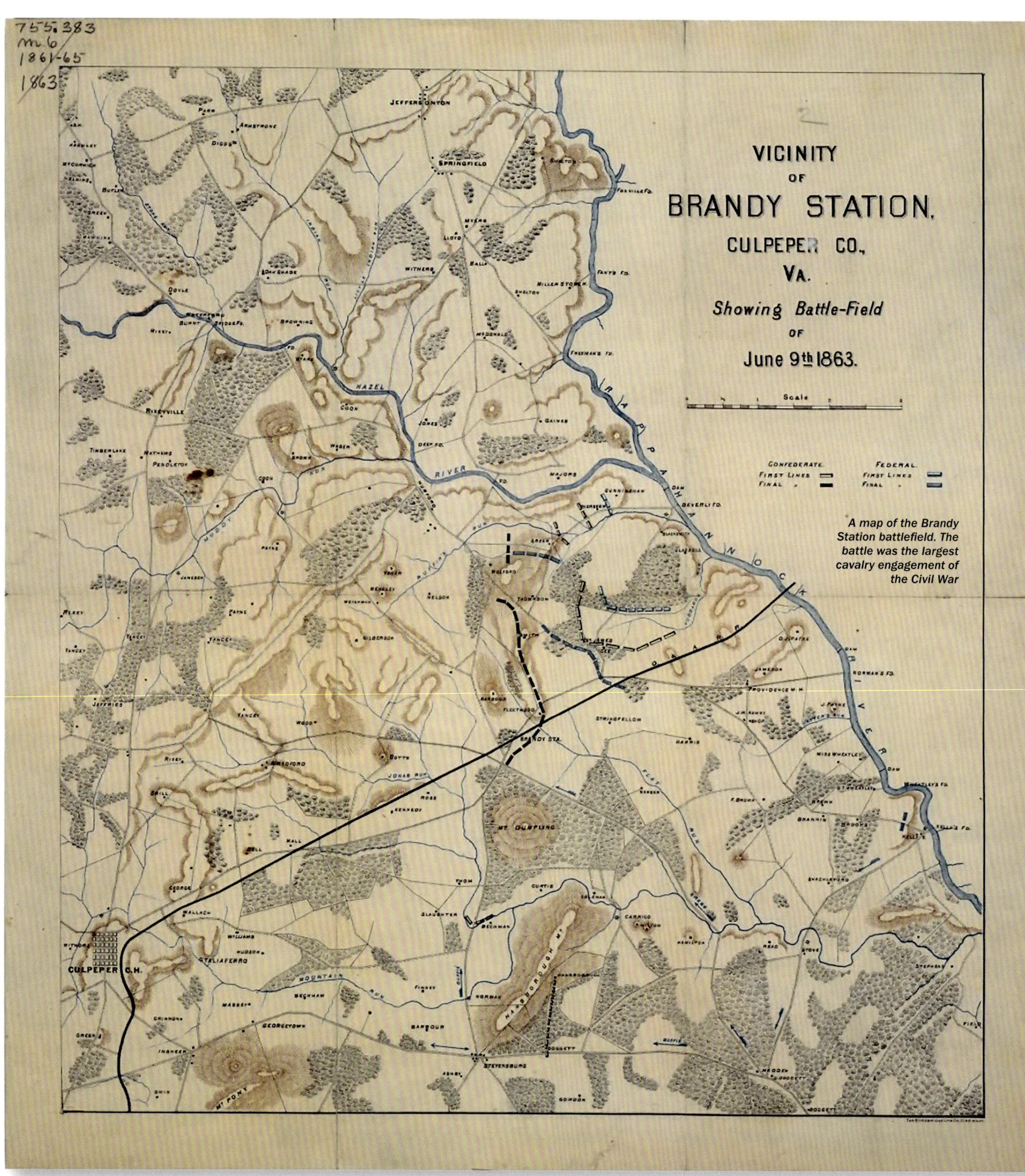

A map of the Brandy Station battlefield. The battle was the largest cavalry engagement of the Civil War

Citizens working on defensive fortifications near Harrisburg, Pennsylvania

Generals Rodes and Edward Johnson to Carlisle, Pennsylvania, toward Harrisburg, while General Jubal Early's division was directed to Wrightsville on the Susquehanna River. Lee's army eventually stretched a length of 72 miles across southern Pennsylvania. Although some brief clashes had occurred, he still had no concrete information on the dispositions of the Army of the Potomac.

Early's division reached the town of Gettysburg on the afternoon of 26 June, and the Confederate general demanded $10,000 worth of provisions. When the townspeople replied that they could not comply, the Confederates conducted a brief search for hidden produce. Early was impatient to move on, but he noticed that a shoe factory was nearby. Many Confederate soldiers had marched into Pennsylvania barefoot, so Early scrawled a note to AP Hill that III Corps soldiers might find shoes there. A day later, Early marched into the town of York, Pennsylvania. The head of his column, under General John B Gordon, moved on toward Wrightsville only to find the covered bridge across the Susquehanna ablaze as 1,400 militiamen retreated. Early's plan to attack Harrisburg from the southeast while Ewell brought the rest of the corps up from Carlisle was thwarted. Early pulled back to York, awaiting orders. Ewell sent a brigade of cavalry up the road from Carlisle toward Harrisburg, and on the night of the 28th, these horsemen bivouacked four miles from Pennsylvania's capital, the deepest penetration of Confederate arms into Northern territory during the Civil War.

However, by the 28th Lee still had heard nothing from Stuart. That evening, however, he received alarming news from a spy named Harrison, dispatched by Longstreet to Washington, DC, prior to the march northward. Harrison claimed that the Army of the Potomac was in fact on the march in Maryland and dangerously close to elements of Lee's scattered army. Lee issued orders to his corps commanders to concentrate in the vicinity of Cashtown and Gettysburg and prepare for battle against an enemy he believed was somewhere very close by.

Onwards to Gettysburg

While the Confederates prowled through Pennsylvania, Hooker submitted his resignation from command of the Army of the Potomac, protesting the decision denying his request that positions at Maryland Heights and Harpers Ferry should be abandoned and the 10,000 troops there reassigned to his command. General George Meade, who thought at first that he was being arrested, was notified of his elevation from corps to army command on 28 June. Meade strengthened the mutually supportive positions of his I, III, and XI Corps, those nearest the Confederate army, marching 25 miles to the Pennsylvania border the next day. General John Buford's cavalry division rode ahead, trotting into Gettysburg around 11am on 30 June.

The townspeople were excited; a Confederate force had just departed. This was General James Pettigrew's brigade, of General Henry Heth's division, Hill's Corps, looking for those precious shoes. Lee had issued orders not to bring on a general engagement while the Army of Northern Virginia was concentrating, and when Pettigrew saw the winding column of Buford's cavalry he chose to retire. He reported the sighting to Heth that afternoon. Hill joined the discussion, asserting that the Army of the Potomac was still miles away. With that, Heth gained permission to return to Gettysburg the next morning and finally "get those shoes".

As Buford's cavalry camped that night, he expected a Confederate attack at sunrise on 1 July and believed he would have to hold out until support arrived. Despite Lee's orders, Heth and Buford collided where neither army's commander had intended to fight, the little-known Pennsylvania town of Gettysburg. ★

General John Buford's Union cavalry opposed the infantry of Confederate General Henry Heth when opening shots were fired at Gettysburg

GETTYSBURG

The bloodiest battle of the American Civil War, Gettysburg claimed over 6,000 lives and is seen by many as the turning point in the bitter conflict

Images: Wiki/Adam Cuerden

At noon on 2 July 1863, the summer heat had already sapped the energy from every man, Union or Confederate, unable to find a piece of shade. Nearby, the deserted town of Gettysburg lay eerily quiet after the desperate fighting of the previous day, as the Union men had beat a hasty retreat through its streets and into the hills. General George Meade had steadied his men, forming up a tight defense that he now hoped would be enough to block his enemy's path to Washington, DC, the political heart of the United States. As shots were heard breaking out towards the Union's left flank, he realized that the attack had begun, but couldn't have any idea just how bloody the day would prove to be.

During the previous month, Robert E Lee, the Confederate's finest commander and arguably the greatest general of the American Civil War, had taken his Army of Northern Virginia, more than 72,000 men, to the north. Penetrating deep into Union territory, he predicted, would boost support for those calling for a peace deal to be brokered between the North and the South. A victory in this invasion so deep into the North would also put great pressure on President Lincoln, and could even allow Lee to march on Washington, DC, itself.

The relatively small town of Gettysburg, Pennsylvania, was only significant in that it saw the convergence of several key roads leading to the south, the north and elsewhere, from where Lee saw an opportunity to spread his army. Major General Joseph Hooker, commanding the Army of the Potomac, had shadowed Lee in his march north, following the rebel army to engage and destroy it. Three days before the battle, however, he was relieved of his command and General Meade was put in his place. The new general's sudden rise through the ranks earned him widespread mistrust among his officers, who questioned his ability to lead effectively.

The two armies met at Gettysburg on 1 July, with troops engaging at first in light skirmishes that soon escalated into a pitched battle, as limited Union regiments defended their line against advancing Confederates. With General Meade not yet on the field, Union officers took the initiative to control the defense of Gettysburg, but disaster struck when the senior officer, Major General John F Reynolds, was struck down by a sharpshooter's bullet.

Though they defended bravely, and delayed Lee's troops as much as they could, the Union soldiers were forced to run for their lives through Gettysburg's streets and up into the hills to the south, where a defensive line of artillery had been established. As more reinforcements arrived, the position on the high ground was fortified further and the Union generals could only wait to see what General Lee would do the next day.

With Gettysburg surrounded and taken on the first day, albeit with the lives of more men than he would have cared to give, General Lee was now as confident as he usually was of victory. He planned to outflank the Union position, killing its superior position on the high ground and forcing Meade to retreat from the field. The next two days would decide the fate of the United States, and would cost the lives of thousands of Americans. ★

09 PICKETT'S CHARGE

In the last major Confederate attack of the battle, General George Pickett is ordered to assault the Union center with his relatively fresh division with others under the command of General Longstreet. After a lengthy artillery bombardment from both sides, 12,000 Confederate soldiers attack, but are eventually broken.

02 SICKLES MOVES TO ATTACK

Major General Daniel Sickles moves his Third Corps, which holds the Union's left flank, to higher ground towards the west to an area known as Devil's Den, giving his artillery a better position. General Meade sends in his Fifth Corps to support Sickles.

05 BITTER FIGHTING IN THE DEN

The Devil's Den changes hands several times, with neither side able to hold it for long before being forced to retreat. About 1,800 casualties result from the fighting here. Further to the right of the Confederate attack, Alabama and Texas regiments begin assaulting Little Round Top, but encounter elements of the Fifth Corps General Meade has sent to support Sickles.

10 GENERAL LEE RETREATS

Confederate cavalry finally arrive on the battlefield but are too late to have any significant impact on proceedings. General Lee remains on the field to organize a rearguard for his army's retreat, anticipating a Union general advance on the rebels. However, General Meade keeps his army on Cemetery Ridge and Cemetery Hill.

03 LEE ORDERS THE FIRST ATTACK

With the bulk of his forces along Seminary Ridge, parallel to the Union's fish hook, General Lee orders Lieutenant General Longstreet to attack the enemy's left flank, General Ambrose Hill is to attack the center, while General Richard Ewell threatens the enemy's right. Lee plans for his forces to roll up on the Union left, flanking them entirely.

GETTYSBURG
1-3 JULY 1863
08 THE ARMIES REGROUP
As night falls on 2 July, there are more than 14,000 casualties of the battlefield. The Union now holds a defensive line along Cemetery Ridge, Cemetery Hill, and south to Little Round Top. In the evening, Confederate attacks on the right Union flank are barely repulsed, as the defenses are under-strength from supporting Sickles' position in the day. The next day, more attacks on Culp's Hill and around Spangler's Spring on the Union right flank are repulsed.
01 FORMING THE DEFENSIVE LINE
After the retreat from Gettysburg on 1 July, General Meade forms his troops into the shape of an inverted fish hook – with the curve facing north in the direction of the town and a long straight line facing the Confederates to the west. With the high ground and with each unit close enough to support one another, Meade is confident his Federal troops can hold off any attacks.
06 BATTLE FOR LITTLE ROUND TOP
With ammunition running low and having taken heavy casualties, Colonel Joshua Chamberlain orders his men to fix bayonets and charge the Confederate troops. The attack routs the attacking rebels.
07 THE END OF THE SECOND DAY
Sickles' Third Corps is pressed hard by the Confederate attacks, with the Wheatfield and Devil's Den finally falling into enemy hands. Sickles is wounded by a cannonball to the leg as his men retreat to Cemetery Ridge, where they hold. A huge gap in the Union center emerges after the Third Corps retreats, so the line is hastily reorganized to prevent the army being split in two.
04 LONGSTREET ADVANCES
Moving towards the Union's left flank, Longstreet's men encounter the Union Third Corps at the Devil's Den, a deadly position perfect for sharpshooting. Texas and Alabama regiments move towards Little Round Top to flank the Den.
Map: Rocio Espin

WEAPONS OF WAR

Men could die in any number of ways during the war, with a vast range of armaments at their disposal

WORDS **DAVID SMITH**

SPRINGFIELD MODEL 1861 RIFLED MUSKET

WEAPON OF CHOICE

With a 40-inch rifled barrel, the Model 1861 musket was a far deadlier weapon than its smoothbore predecessors. While smoothbore muskets had been notoriously inaccurate (hence the preference to fire them in massed volleys in the hope of hitting something), the rifled Model 1861 was far more lethal. It fired a Minié ball, the design of which allowed it to slip easily into a rifled barrel, as it expanded after firing to tightly fit the grooves.

Rate of fire was still low, at around three rounds per minute, but the shots were effective to a much greater range, typically 300 yards. This made the rifled musket the dominant weapon on the battlefields of the American Civil War and manufacture was licenced out to various contractors in order to keep up with demand. More than a million were produced during the war, with the weapon being used by both the Union and Confederate armies.

The rifled musket represented a great leap forward in weapons design

Image: Wiki Public Domain

MORTAR SIEGE SPECIALIST

The 12-pounder Napoleon may have been the main artillery piece on the battlefield, but for siege work, the mortar came into its own. These squat, ugly guns fired shells at a steep trajectory, allowing them to be lobbed over defensive walls. This enabled a besieging force to kill the garrison of a fort, or at least prevent them from easily manning their own defensive guns. Designated by their muzzle diameter, sizes ranged between 5.82 inches and 13 inches.

Gun crews operating a variety of mortars, including (front) an eight-inch design, which would fire a 44-pound shell

Image: Getty

BAYONET

OBJECT OF DREAD

The bayonet was a fearsome weapon, but few soldiers were actually wounded or killed by it. This does not mean it was ineffective, however, as a massed bayonet charge could be enough to scatter an opponent, assuming they were not able to stop it with accurate rifle or artillery fire. The bayonet was therefore more of a psychological weapon – the dread of being bayonetted meant that very few were brave enough to stand their ground if an enemy charge drew near.

***Left:** Rifles with bayonets attached*

Image: Getty

The saber is prominent in this depiction of a cavalry charge at the Battle of Yellow Tavern in 1864

CAVALRY SABER

WEAPON FROM A BYGONE AGE

Few weapons better symbolize the transition into modern warfare generally attributed to the Civil War than the cavalry saber. Although it had played a prominent role in battles for many centuries, the traditional sword still held its place in the armory of the Civil War. However, as cavalry charges became less common (as they often resulted in appalling losses), the new skirmishing role tended to dictate the use of pistols or carbines instead. Swords were often still carried, but not utilized as much.

With a blade of 32 inches, around 300,000 Model 1860 Cavalry Sabers were produced in the war

Image: Wiki

SHARPS CARBINE

STAPLE WEAPON OF THE CAVALRY

A full-length rifled musket was an impractical weapon for the cavalry forces of the war, and carbines had been in use for decades. The Sharps carbine was a shorter version of the company's rifle, and it proved much more popular, especially in the Union Army. Less cumbersome than the full-length rifle, the Sharps carbine could fire at a rate of ten shots per minute and still remained in use for years after the end of the war.

With a barrel length of just 22 inches, the Sharps carbine had a rather snub-nosed appearance

Image: Alamy

Sharps in use, from 1st Maine Cavalry Skirmishing by Alfred R Waud (Library of Congress)

Image: Wiki

A Gatling gun on display in Washington, DC, following the war

Image: Getty

Gatling Gun

THE SHAPE OF THINGS TO COME

Although the Gatling gun was actually used very sparingly during the American Civil War, it remains one of the iconic weapons of the conflict. A forerunner of the machine gun, it was fired by the operation of a crank and could release around 200 rounds per minute. The rotary design allowed rapid fire without overheating the barrel, because six barrels were in operation instead of one. Not officially adopted by the US government until after the war, a limited number were purchased privately and utilized by Union commanders.

Spencer repeating rifle

INFANTRY FIREPOWER REVOLUTIONIZED

The idea of a rifle firing more rapidly than the standard musket was tempting, but there was suspicion that it would promote wastefulness. Despite such concerns, the Spencer repeating rifle was manufactured in large quantities and was used conspicuously at the Battle of Chickamauga and at Gettysburg. Seven rounds could be fed in at once, with the cocking of a lever both ejecting a spent cartridge case and feeding in a fresh one.

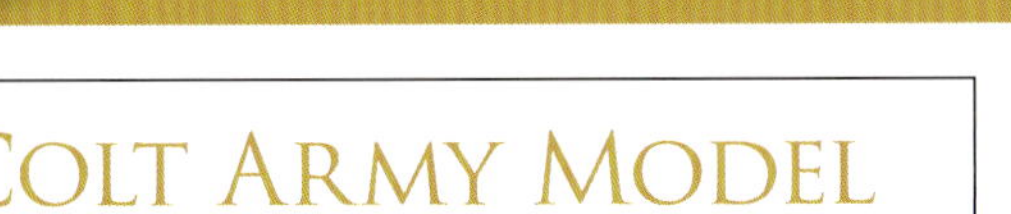

Image: Alamy

Around 200,000 Spencer repeating rifles were produced, giving the Union Army an advantage when they were available on the battlefield

Colt Army Model 1860 pistol

VERSATILE SIDEARM

Seeing service with infantry, artillery, cavalry, and navy, Colt pistols were among the most versatile weapons of the war. The 'Army' model, a .44 caliber design, was the most prolific. Loading was not as simple as with the familiar Colt .45 Peacemaker made famous by Hollywood. Paper cartridges were used and needed to be individually rammed home when loading. Once fully loaded, the Colt Army pistol could fire six shots with an effective range of up to 100 yards.

A modified Colt Army pistol with a 7.5-inch barrel

Image: Wiki

A British-made Bowie knife exported to the United States by George Wostenholm & Son Ltd

Image: Alamy

Bowie knife

REBEL FAVORITE

Although the name is very familiar, the 'Bowie knife' is actually ill-defined and generally refers to any large-bladed knife carried in a sheath. Originally almost identical to a butcher's knife, the Bowie remained a utility implement and was often favored over bayonets by Confederate soldiers. It pulled extra duty as a cooking implement and all-purpose tool, but was at its heart a fighting weapon. It was named after Jim Bowie, who allegedly used a knife of this type in a famous brawl known as the 'Sandbar Fight'.

Model 1857 'Napoleon' field gun

WORKHORSE OF THE BATTLEFIELD

This smoothbore 12-pounder was nearing the end of its working life by the time it became the most common piece of field ordnance during the American Civil War. Although rifled guns were available, it was the simplicity and reliability of the Napoleon (named after Napoleon III) that saw it wheeled into action by both sides.

Firing solid shot, shells or (at close range) canister, it was versatile but also endangered thanks to the increased range and effectiveness of infantry firepower. Made of bronze (some iron guns were still in use), it was not easy to maneuver on the battlefield and several smaller calibers were employed that were more portable. Despite no longer being the terror of the battlefield, however, a battery of Napoleons still packed a considerable punch, with an effective range of up to a mile.

Image: Alamy

Gun crews came to revere their 12-pound Napoleon guns for their reliability and effectiveness

Image: Alamy

A massed infantry charge still offered a tempting target for field guns, which would switch to canister at close range

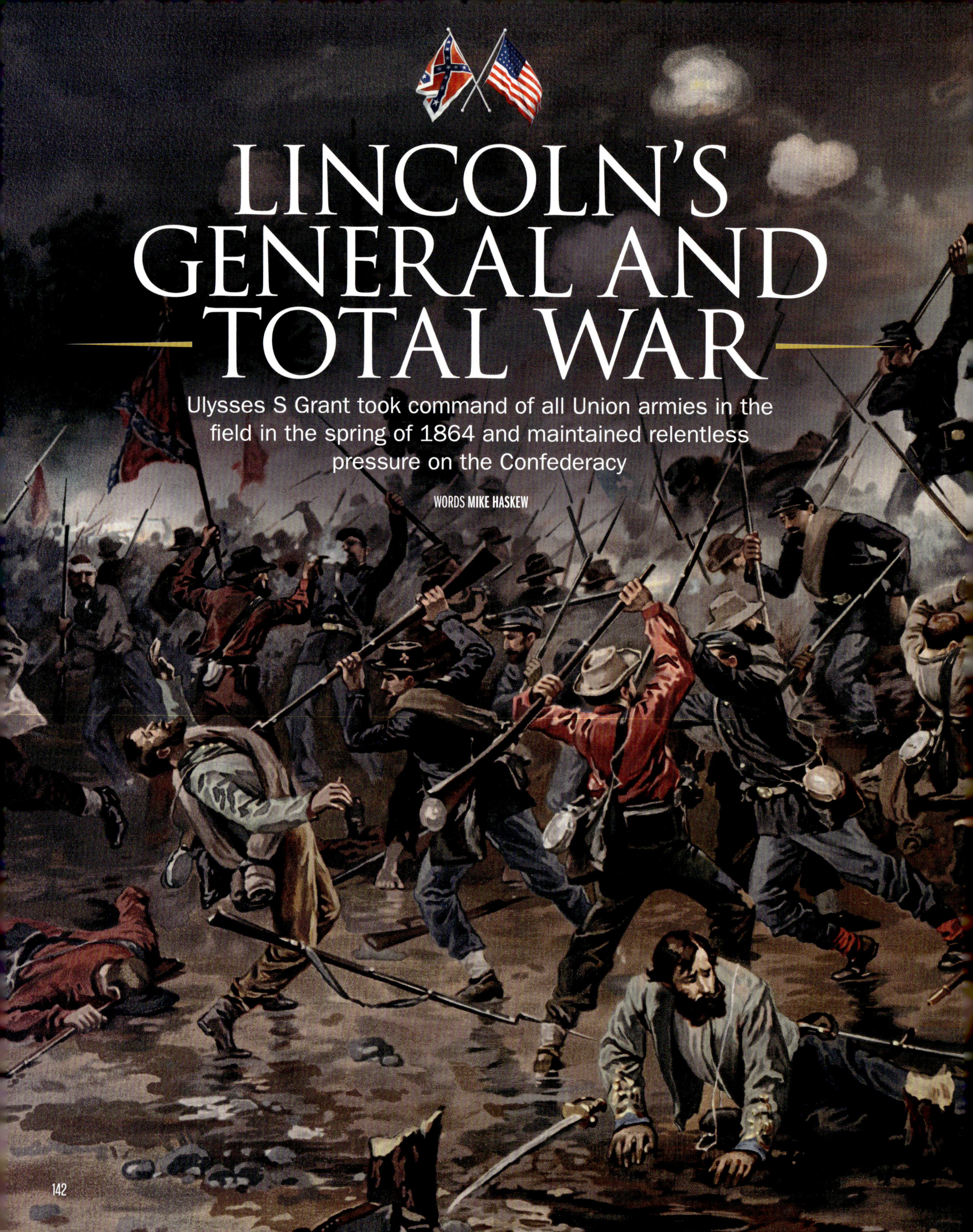

LINCOLN'S GENERAL AND TOTAL WAR

Ulysses S Grant took command of all Union armies in the field in the spring of 1864 and maintained relentless pressure on the Confederacy

WORDS **MIKE HASKEW**

The Union and Confederate armies lost a combined 30,000 killed, wounded, and captured during the Battle of Spotsylvania

Above *William Tecumseh Sherman had a reputation for restlessness and nervous energy that exhausted those around him*

The lobby of the Willard Hotel in Washington, DC, was a beehive of activity on the afternoon of 8 March 1864, so much so that no one noticed the nondescript Union Army officer in a disheveled uniform. With his 14-year-old son at his side, the officer listened as the clerk told him that only a room on the upper floor was available and luggage would have to be carried up several flights of stairs.

The officer agreed and dutifully signed the register, 'US Grant and son, Galena, Ill'.

When the clerk turned and read the signature, he was jolted to action. Immediately, there was a suite available on the second floor, and he personally took the officer's bags under his arms and started up the stairs. Ulysses S Grant was no ordinary officer. He had come from the Western Theater, a hero of this agonizing war, to take command of all Union armies in the field at the request of President Abraham Lincoln. Soon, Grant would command more than half a million men. Chief among his tasks was the defeat of the vaunted Confederate General Robert E Lee and his Army of Northern Virginia.

Ironically, Grant, who had managed to graduate from the US Military Academy at West Point in 1843, was a dismal failure at just about every undertaking in life until the coming of the Civil War. He served during the Mexican War but left the army in 1854, settling on a Missouri homestead owned by his father-in-law and struggling to earn a living at the place he called Hardscrabble Farm. Things got so tough that he sold firewood on the street in St Louis. A real estate partnership failed, and he took a job in his father-in-law's leather goods store.

Grant's fortunes changed in 1861. Since he had military experience, he was given a commission as a colonel in the Illinois Volunteers. Within months, he was a brigadier general. His troops won a small victory in Missouri and in February 1862, his name made

"LINCOLN WAS DISAPPOINTED THAT MEADE HAD FAILED TO PURSUE LEE AND DESTROY THE ARMY OF NORTHERN VIRGINIA. HE LOOKED TO GRANT TO DO THE JOB"

national headlines with the seizure of Forts Henry and Donelson in Tennessee. When the Confederate commander of Fort Donelson asked for surrender terms, he was told that only 'Unconditional Surrender' was acceptable. With that, the victor was dubbed 'Unconditional Surrender Grant'.

Delivering victories

When his army was surprised at Shiloh in April 1862, Grant and General William T Sherman rallied the troops the following day and won a victory. Then, after a long campaign and siege, the city of Vicksburg fell to Grant's army on 4 July 1863, giving the Union control of the length of the Mississippi River. Grant was a national hero, and his reputation was burnished even further with the raising of the siege of Chattanooga, Tennessee, an important rail center, in November. Chattanooga became the base of supply for Sherman's Atlanta Campaign and eventual March to the Sea.

Meanwhile, in Washington, DC, Lincoln was frustrated with events in the Eastern Theater. Robert E Lee had outthought and outfought a succession of Union commanders of the Army of the Potomac and other forces. True enough, Lee had suffered a major defeat at Gettysburg, Pennsylvania, as General George Meade and the Army of the Potomac turned back a Confederate invasion of the North in July 1863. But Lincoln was disappointed that Meade had failed to pursue Lee and destroy the Army of Northern Virginia. He looked to Grant to do the job.

The Army of the Potomac wintered at Brandy Station, Virginia, and on 10 March 1864, Grant paid Meade a visit. Meade expected to be fired and offered his resignation. Grant turned him down but did inform Meade that the overall commander would accompany the Army of the Potomac during the spring campaign. And it was an ambitious undertaking.

Unlike his predecessors, Grant grasped the strategic advantages he possessed and

Union General Ulysses S Grant (left) unleashed a campaign of total war against General Robert E Lee and the Confederate armies

Grand Strategy Grinding

While Grant attacked Lee, Sherman advanced in the West, but Butler was bottled up at Bermuda Hundred

As Grant prosecuted the Overland Campaign, General William T Sherman, his close friend, drove south from Chattanooga and successfully concluded the Atlanta Campaign, a bloody affair punctuated by severe battles at New Hope Church, Kennesaw Mountain, Peachtree Creek, Ezra Church, Jonesborough, and elsewhere, on 2 September 1864. By fall, Sherman was poised to launch his March to the Sea, concluding with the capture of the port of Savannah in December. Sherman was required to detach a portion of his command to deal with General John Bell Hood's ill-advised Confederate thrust to the northwest from the Atlanta area, which culminated in devastating defeats at the Battle of Franklin, Tennessee, in November and the Battle of Nashville in December.

Meanwhile, the performance of the Army of the James, which Grant had hoped would assault Petersburg and capture the rail center before the Army of Northern Virginia could fortify it, had failed to accomplish anything, primarily due to the lackluster performance of its commander, General Benjamin Butler. A political appointee, Butler lacked the initiative to assume the offensive, and Confederate forces under General PGT Beauregard occupied Petersburg. When Lee's army arrived, the opportunity had passed, contributing to Grant's decision to lay siege to the city. Grant had never placed much reliance on Butler's command ability. His hands were tied due to Butler's political connections, and his frustration was palpable. Butler was eventually relieved of command, but during this critical period his army remained virtually inactive, bottled up at Bermuda Hundred northeast of Petersburg.

A political appointee, General Benjamin Butler failed to take the offensive against Richmond with the Union Army of the James

intended to use them to bludgeon Lee into submission. Total war, Grant reasoned, inflicting hardship on the civilian population in the South and destroying its infrastructure, would be difficult, but a campaign of attrition would inevitably lead to victory. The industrialized North could produce virtually limitless quantities of supplies and armaments, while sustainable production in the South was always problematic. Manpower in the North was inexhaustible, while Lee's ranks were ever thinning. Further, Northern rail lines provided swift transportation and resupply, while Lee was constantly fighting to protect these essential arteries from destruction. When Grant suspended the program of parole and exchange that helped empty prisons North and South, he realized that many Union men would languish in Confederate confinement, but Rebels would no longer be released to rejoin the ranks of Confederate armies. Though tinged with an element of cruelty and decried in the Northern press, the move hastened the end of the war and probably saved lives.

Grant envisioned a bold grand strategy. The Army of the Potomac would cross the Rapidan River early in May and move against the Confederate capital of Richmond from the north. Simultaneously, the Army of the James, under General Benjamin Butler, would converge from the south. If Lee chose to fight, he would be defeated, and if he chose to retire to defend Richmond, the Union forces would draw a noose around the city and slowly strangle the Confederate capital. At the same time, an army under General Franz Sigel would venture up the Shenandoah Valley, the breadbasket of the Confederacy, cutting rail lines and destroying food and supplies intended for Lee's army. To the west, General Sherman would drive into Georgia with the Union armies, defeat Confederate General Joseph Johnston's Army of Tennessee, take Atlanta, march to the port of Savannah and turn north, sowing a path of destruction through the Carolinas. If any portion of the strategy was slowed or met with a temporary reversal, Grant knew that time was on his side. A steady, relentless campaign would ultimately end in success.

Confederate General JEB Stuart was killed at Brandy Station, Virginia, during a major cavalry battle of the Overland Campaign

Battle of the Wilderness

In spring 1864, however, the Army of Northern Virginia was still full of fight. Numbering about 65,000 troops, roughly half that of its adversary, Lee's command included General James Longstreet's I Corps, Stonewall Jackson's old II Corps now under General Richard Ewell, and the III Corps, led by General Ambrose Powell Hill.

Just across the Rapidan lay a tangle of brambles, thickets, and second-growth timber known as the Wilderness. The area was familiar to both sides, which had fought nearby at Fredericksburg and Chancellorsville in 1862-63. Grant hoped to cross the difficult terrain and hit Lee's right flank on better ground. Lee, however, was aware of Grant's movement. He responded quicker than Grant anticipated, and by noon on 5 May, the two armies were locked in a death grip.

The two-day Battle of the Wilderness was a bar-room brawl with rifle and cannon. The dense forest obscured vision and restricted troop deployments, somewhat neutralizing the Union advantage in manpower, just as Lee intended. The fighting began when Confederates of Ewell's Corps crashed into Federals of General Gouverneur K Warren's V Corps along the Orange Turnpike. Rapidly, the battle devolved into small groups of soldiers ambushing one another from the cover of thickets, some firing blindly amid the smoke and haze of battle. The blasts of artillery set the dry underbrush on fire, and the screaming of the wounded unable to move to safety as they were consumed by the flames brought a new horror to the fight.

Neither side had gained the advantage when darkness halted the fighting; however, Lee's right flank was vulnerable. Reinforcements arrived throughout the night, and Grant intended to hit the Confederates again at 4am, but his subordinates convinced him to delay the assault for an hour due to the difficulties of maintaining control of troop dispositions in the forest. Then, at first light on 6 May, General Winfield Scott Hancock's II Corps attacked Hill's Confederates along the Plank Road and initially pushed

"TOTAL WAR, GRANT REASONED, INFLICTING HARDSHIP ON THE CIVILIAN POPULATION IN THE SOUTH AND DESTROYING ITS INFRASTRUCTURE, WOULD BE DIFFICULT, BUT A CAMPAIGN OF ATTRITION WOULD INEVITABLY LEAD TO VICTORY"

Union troops used pontoon bridges such as this one across the James River during the Overland Campaign

In a sketch by Alfred Waud, 7th New York Heavy Artillery prepare to charge the Confederate line during the Battle of Cold Harbor

Image: Alamy, Getty

The Battle of Cold Harbor was a stunning setback for General Grant and the Union forces during the Overland Campaign

The Haunting Of Cold Harbor

THE SLAUGHTER OF COLD HARBOR DURING THE OVERLAND CAMPAIGN DISTURBED ULYSSES S GRANT FOR THE REST OF HIS LIFE

On the eve of their tragic charge at Cold Harbor, Union soldiers were aware that the attack would lead to widespread casualties and that many of them would not survive the harrowing advance. Lieutenant Colonel Horace Porter, a member of General Grant's staff, moved among the men on that somber evening and recalled, "As I came near one of the regiments that was making preparations for the next morning's assault, I noticed many of the soldiers had taken off their coats, and seemed to be engaged in sewing up rents in them… On closer examination it was found that the men were calmly writing their names and home addresses on slips of paper, and pinning them on the backs of their coats, so that their dead bodies might be recognized upon the field, and their fate made known to their families at home."

In 1885, Grant was dying of throat cancer. The former two-term president struggled to complete his two-volume memoir, which he hoped would provide an income for his family after his death. While writing, Grant acknowledged the horror of Cold Harbor and concluded, "I have always regretted that the last assault at Cold Harbor was made… At Cold Harbor no advantage whatever was gained to compensate for the heavy loss we sustained." The commander's position had been unenviable, and he was vilified by some in the North as 'Butcher Grant'. War, however, is a dirty business. Grant carried the scars of so many lost lives to his own grave.

the Rebels back. Longstreet bolstered Hill's wavering line and led a thunderous counter-attack about noon, only to fall with a serious shoulder wound due to friendly fire, common amid the confusion.

Hancock patched together a defensive line along the Brock Road, but in the gathering darkness General John B Gordon assaulted the exposed Union right flank, breaking through and sending panicked Union solders reeling toward Grant's headquarters. The Federals rallied to stave off disaster. The Battle of the Wilderness ended in a tactical draw with the Union racking up nearly 18,000 casualties and the Confederates 10,000. In the past after such a bloodletting, Union commanders withdrew to lick their wounds. Grant was different. During the night he ordered the weary Union Army to march south, toward the town of Spotsylvania Court House, keeping the pressure on Lee. When the troops realized they were not retreating, a collective cheer rose from the ranks.

Spotsylvania Court House

When Lee got word that Grant had indeed changed the game, he realized that Spotsylvania Court House was the Union objective. If Grant succeeded in taking the crossroads town, the Army of the Potomac would be between the Army of Northern Virginia and Richmond. The race was on, and Lee managed to reach Spotsylvania Court House first.

For two weeks the armies fought at Spotsylvania. The Confederates had erected breastworks of timber and stood firm against early assaults by Hancock's Corps on 9-10 May. On the 10th, Colonel Emory Upton led 12 Union regiments across open ground, braving furious artillery fire and grappling hand-to-hand with the defenders of an earthwork known as the 'Mule Shoe'. The attackers were thrown back. A major cavalry clash occurred at Yellow Tavern on the 11th, ending inconclusively but resulting in the death of Lee's trusted cavalry commander, General JEB Stuart.

That same day, Grant sent a telegram to a worried Lincoln, stating, "We have now ended the sixth day of very heavy fighting… the result up to this time is much in our favor. I intend to fight it out on this line if it takes all summer."

On 12 May, Hancock launched a human avalanche of 20,000 soldiers at the Confederate breastworks, fighting for 22 hours. The engagement was particularly brutal in an area that became known as the 'Bloody Angle'. Lee rode forward during the day, exposing himself to enemy fire, intending to personally lead a Confederate counter-attack. However, the soldiers refused to advance until the old commander was led to safety. Then, with

General John Bell Hood in the vanguard, the Rebel attack threw the Union troops back while the Confederate flanks stood firm. After an exhausting day, Lee ordered a general withdrawal to a new line to the rear.

Grant probed the Confederate defenses, and in a series of attacks and counter-attacks over several days, Lee's line stood firm. When Grant realized the futility of continued assaults, he again ordered his army southward. Two weeks at Spotsylvania Court House had cost the armies a combined 30,000 killed, wounded, and captured, 18,000 of them Union losses. As the casualty rolls lengthened, Grant continued to remain resolute.

On 21 May, the Union forces crossed the North Anna River, and Lee was again obliged to place his army between the enemy and the Confederate capital. Grant assessed that the Confederate defensive position at Ox Ford was impregnable and declined to attack. The Union Army splashed across the Pamunkey River on 26 May, still pressing toward Richmond. Lee stayed in step, entrenching along Totopotomoy Creek. The two armies brushed against one another inconclusively at nearby Bethesda Church on 30 May, and both armies stretched toward Cold Harbor, a scant ten miles northeast of Richmond.

Situated near the old 1862 battlefield of Gaines' Mill, Cold Harbor was yet another nondescript crossroads town. However, it gained a terrible place in the history of the Civil War when the armies concentrated there in the spring of 1864. Hancock's Corps failed to reach the field on 2 June as Grant had intended, forcing a tragic postponement of his planned attack. The day-long delay enabled Lee's beleaguered men to dig in at Cold Harbor, and on 3 June, Grant, possibly in sheer frustration at a lost opportunity, hurled elements of three Union corps, 50,000 men, toward the Confederate defenses. The result was disastrous.

Onwards to victory

Brave Union men fell in heaps at Cold Harbor. One Confederate recalled that they died "like rows of blocks or bricks pushed over by striking against one another." Rebel General Evander Law was succinct: "It was not war; it was murder." A single Union brigade lost 1,000 men in only 20 minutes. Estimates of the day's loss to the Army of the Potomac range as high as 7,000. For nine more days, the two armies faced one another at Cold Harbor, with Union casualties near 13,000. Grant still persevered.

On the night of 12 June, Grant pulled the Army of the Potomac out of its lines and moved by the right flank toward the James River, crossing aboard pontoon boats and long foot bridges. He did not turn directly toward Richmond, instead heading for the rail center of Petersburg, 23 miles to the south, to cut supply lines into the capital city. The move made Lee's greatest fear a reality. The loss of Petersburg would doom the Confederate capital and probably the entire war effort in the east. Through mid-June, Lee avoided a decisive battle, and he prevented Grant from seizing Petersburg outright. Still, he was obliged to defend both Petersburg and Richmond.

The Overland Campaign had cost the Army of the Potomac 60,000 casualties and the Army of Northern Virginia an irreplaceable 35,000, but the Rebels had been brought to ground. The war of maneuver was over, and Grant redefined his offensive, laying siege to Petersburg, pinning Lee down for nine months in a grinding defense that ultimately led to the fall of Richmond and victory. ★

Ulysses S Grant built this cabin for his family on the Missouri homesite he dubbed Hardscrabble Farm

Despite the Union Army's numerical advantage, the Battle of the Wilderness ended in a tactical draw

Image: Alamy, Getty

In this photo of Andersonville prison camp taken on 17 August 1864, Union captives live in squalor

LIVING AND DYING IN CAPTIVITY

Prisoners of war endured wretched conditions and harsh privations during the Civil War – many died in the camps, both North and South

WORDS **MIKE HASKEW**

Images: Alamy

Captain Francis Marion Headley of the 8th Kentucky Mounted Infantry wanted to go home to care for his children after his wife died. But his resignation from the Confederate Army was denied. Instead, he was sent back to the Bluegrass State to recruit more men.

The effort was virtually fruitless, but worse was to come for Captain Headley, a veteran of fighting in Tennessee and Mississippi. Headley found himself on the run, then surrounded by Union sympathizers, former friends who saw the situation in Kentucky differently. His captors wanted to shoot him, but a Union officer came to his aid and Headley was packed off to captivity.

It was his second journey into the unknown as a prisoner of war. Captured earlier at Champion Hill, Mississippi, Headley was exchanged. This time, though, his confinement was for the rest of the war, at the federal prison on Johnson's Island, near Lake Erie, a few miles from Sandusky, Ohio. Johnson's Island had opened in April 1862, on a 1.65-acre tract with 12 two-storey barracks, a hospital, and a stockade fence 15 feet high. Intended to house 2,500 prisoners, Johnson's Island eventually hosted 15,000 Confederates, who endured sub-freezing temperatures in the winters.

Remarkably, only 300 prisoners are known to have perished there. Headley returned home after the war, but the experience drastically affected his health for the rest of his life. Still, he might be considered among the fortunate.

For most, the prisoner experience was brutal and too often terminal. Prisoners suffered the common privations of too little to eat, inadequate shelter, and threadbare clothing. While the horrors of Southern prison camps, particularly the hell of the notorious Andersonville, are better known, the plain truth is that both Union and Confederate prisoners suffered mightily in wretched captivity.

Fate worse than death

Between 1861 and 1865, more than 150 prisons were established by order of the Union and Confederate governments. While estimates of the number of prisoners held

The African-American Prisoner Perspective

THE VIEWPOINTS OF SOLDIERS AND STATESMEN NORTH AND SOUTH VARIED ON THE TREATMENT OF AFRICAN-AMERICAN PRISONERS

Early in the Civil War, the Confederate Congress declared that the food rations "furnished prisoners of war shall be the same in quantity and quality as those furnished to enlisted men in the army of the Confederacy". These words rang hollow as shortages affected the civilian and military populations of the Confederacy and then, inevitably, the fortunes of Union prisoners.

They meant absolutely nothing to the African-Americans that donned the blue uniform and struck a blow for freedom as soldiers of the US Army. On 1 May 1863, a joint Confederate Congressional resolution read, "That every white person being a commissioned officer… who shall command Negroes or mulattoes in arms against the Confederate states… shall be deemed as inciting servile insurrection, and shall if captured be put to death or otherwise punished at the discretion of the Court." Further, the Congress condoned the execution of African-American prisoners, stating all "negroes or mulattoes" taken prisoner were subject to the death penalty.

President Abraham Lincoln responded that there was no distinction of color among prisoners of war and that the US would put a prisoner to hard labor for every African-American returned to slavery in the Confederacy.

In practice, the Confederacy did not acknowledge African-American captives as prisoners of war, instead encouraging former slave owners to reclaim their 'property'. Troops, however, are documented as executing some African-American prisoners. Others were held in at least nine Southern camps. The records at Andersonville mention about 100 segregated along with their white officers.

Libby Prison in Richmond, Virginia, was well-known as a place of internment for Union officers during the Civil War

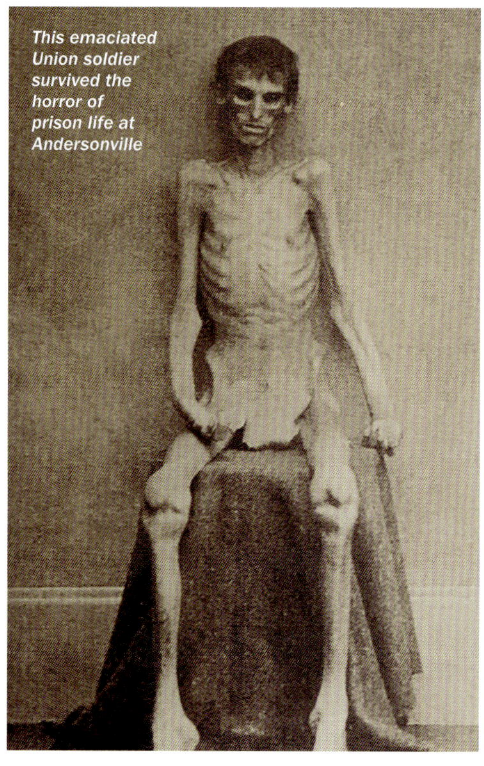

This emaciated Union soldier survived the horror of prison life at Andersonville

at any time vary, the war's Official Records acknowledge a total of 347,000 men – 127,000 Union and 220,000 Confederate – taken prisoner. More than 49,000 died in captivity, and the numbers are strikingly parallel, 22,580 Union and about 26,440 Confederates. The overall mortality rate was roughly 14 percent.

Neither side was prepared for the flood of prisoners produced during four years of conflict, a devastating war most observers had believed would last only weeks or months. Resources were stretched everywhere. The grim reality left those captured to contemplate the possibly preferred outcome of a swift death on the battlefield. Those captured languished with the slow passage of time, hoping deliverance would come as they cared for the sick, shivered and starved, and buried their dead.

An on-again, off-again system of prisoner exchange had been implemented in 1862, and both the Union and Confederate governments pledged to treat prisoners humanely. The system, however, became unsustainable, and the ability to provide for prisoners adequately was impossible, particularly in the South, which suffered from continual shortages of supplies.

Hell on Earth

By 1864, General Ulysses S Grant, Union commander, suspended the prisoner

This expansive view of the prison at Andersonville was published 25 years after the war

exchanges to prevent released Confederates rejoining the enemy ranks. The pragmatic Grant understood that attrition was a necessary aspect of total war, which would hasten the Union victory. He stated, "It is hard on our men held in Southern prisons not to exchange them, but it is humanity to those left in the ranks to fight our battles. Every man released on parole or otherwise becomes an active soldier against us at once, either directly or indirectly. If we commence a system of exchange which liberates all prisoners taken, we will have to fight on until the whole South is exterminated."

As politicians and military leaders debated, lives were at stake, and the suffering continued. Though others were established before it, the most infamous prison on either side in the Civil War was Andersonville, 60 miles southwest of Macon, Georgia, in the wilderness of Sumter County. Andersonville took in 600 Union prisoners on 24 February 1864, and shortly after Grant's suspension of exchanges in April, the number swelled to more than 20,000. The original stockade occupied 16.5 acres, and Sweetwater Creek ran through its footprint. By July, Major Henry Wirz, the commandant, ordered a ten-acre expansion. In August, just five months after receiving its first prisoners, Andersonville was the scene of 2,994 deaths. Disease was rampant, the creek became fetid, and drinking the water left men with dysentery. Vermin spread typhoid and other afflictions that ravaged the population.

Private Prescott Tracy of the 82nd New York Infantry Regiment recalled, "The newcomers, on reaching this, would exclaim: 'Is this hell?' yet they soon would become callous, and enter unmoved the horrible rottenness..." By the end of the war, nearly 13,000 prisoners had died at Andersonville, roughly 28 percent of the prison population, and a toll representing 57 percent of all Union prisoner deaths in the entire conflict. The corpses were buried in mass graves. In the wake of the horror, Wirz was tried and convicted of war crimes and hanged in the yard of the Old Capitol Prison in Washington, DC, the only individual on either side to pay such a price for atrocities committed against prisoners. Swiss-born and speaking with a foreign accent, Wirz was a likely target for retribution, and questions persist as to his culpability amid circumstances in which the guards could barely feed themselves at times.

"COLONEL DELAND ORDERED THREE MEN TO BE HUNG BY THEIR THUMBS FOR AN HOUR"

Death and disease

Among other prominent Southern prisons, Libby Prison, in Richmond, Virginia, the Confederate capital, stands out. A former tobacco warehouse complex of three buildings, each four storeys high, Libby became operational after the First Battle of Bull Run in 1861, and more than 50,000 captive Union officers passed through, no fewer than 1,200 at any time. A *New York Times* story that appeared in November 1863 described the conditions at Libby Prison. "The prevailing diseases are diarrhea, dysentery, and typhoid pneumonia. Of late the percentage of deaths has greatly increased, the result of causes that have long been at work – such as insufficient food, clothing and shelter, combined with that depression of spirits brought on so often by long confinement."

Libby Prison was also the site of the largest prisoner escape of the Civil War. More than 100 Union officers broke out on 9 February 1864, and 59 of them eluded recapture.

Of course, Andersonville and Libby were not alone among Southern prisons. One captive called the Confederate camp at Salisbury, North Carolina, a "dark hole". Also in the Richmond area, Castle Thunder held political prisoners, spies, and individuals accused of treason, while Belle Isle in the James River housed Union-enlisted prisoners.

Human suffering chooses no side in wartime, and across the Northern states Confederate prisoners suffered in large

Images: Wiki Public Domain

Henry Wirz, the commandant of the infamous Andersonville Prison, is hanged for war crimes in Washington, DC, following the end of the war

Confederate prisoners at the notorious Camp Douglas in Chicago

Confederate prisoners at a railroad depot in Chattanooga, Tennessee, in 1864

numbers. While Johnson's Island was well known, the population of Camp Chase, on the outskirts of Columbus, Ohio, peaked near 10,000, and 2,260 died in the six-acre enclosure. A federal inspector once noted that open latrines and cisterns contributed to an outbreak of smallpox. At Rock Island, Illinois, 2,000 of 12,000 Confederate prisoners died, while Point Lookout, Maryland, took in 50,000 captives, 4,000 of whom died. After the Battle of Gettysburg in July 1863, the roll at Fort Delaware on Pea Patch Island in Newcastle County, Delaware, increased to 30,000, and 2,500 died. One Confederate prisoner was emaciated, dropping from 140 pounds to 80. Another prisoner wrote, "The bacon was rusty and slimy, the soup was slop... filled with white worms a half-inch long."

Torment and tragedy

The prison at Elmira in Upstate New York is worthy of special mention. Known to the Confederates as 'Hellmira', its 25 percent death rate – about 3,000 of 12,000 prisoners – rivaled that of Andersonville.

In the North, though, no prison experience surpassed the horror of Camp Douglas, opened in 1861 in Chicago, Illinois. More than 26,000 Confederate prisoners were held there during the war, and the death toll is estimated at 4,500 to 6,000, a mortality rate between 17 and 23 percent. Amid the harsh winter of 1862, about 200 prisoners were crowded into a single barracks measuring no more than 20 by 70 feet. Prisoners were made to stand in ranks in deep snow, and the death toll that winter alone reached 1,700.

While several commanders were in charge at Camp Douglas, most infamous was Colonel Charles V DeLand. On another occasion, he ordered three men to be hung by their thumbs for an hour with their toes barely touching the ground. While blankets and supplies were sometimes available, such items were regularly withheld from prisoners as retribution for the treatment of Union prisoners in the South.

Thousands languished in camps from 1861 to 1865, both through purposeful intent and the universal privations accompanying prolonged conflict. Their suffering adds another gut-wrenching chapter to the tragedy of the Civil War. ★

Elmira Prison in Upstate New York was given the nickname 'Hellmira' by Confederates

THE MARCH TO THE SEA

On 15 November 1864 a Union army set forth from Atlanta on what became one of the most controversial military campaigns ever staged

WORDS **DAVID SMITH**

The struggle for Atlanta had been a cagey, cat-and-mouse affair, dragging on through the summer of 1864. Confederate forces under General Joseph E Johnston had repeatedly withdrawn in the face of William Tecumseh Sherman's Union army, and frustration was growing on both sides.

War-weariness was a genuine concern in the North. The procession of costly battles – names like Shiloh, Antietam, Fredericksburg, Chancellorsville, Gettysburg, and Chickamauga still resonate today – showed no signs of coming to an end. Half a million men had died in the fighting so far.

As well as the drawn-out campaign against Atlanta, Ulysses S Grant was bogged down in trench warfare at Petersburg, Virginia. The war seemed to be dragging on with no end in sight. Adding pressure was a presidential campaign, with Abraham Lincoln seeking re-election. Democratic candidate George Brinton McClellan, a former commander-in-chief of Union forces, was running against Lincoln on a so-called 'peace-platform' and there was real fear that Lincoln might be defeated and a negotiated settlement reached.

The Confederate armies had their own worries to contend with. Johnston seemed unwilling to stand and fight and it looked as if he might eventually give up Atlanta without a battle. Despite his success in dragging out the campaign at this critical juncture, the Confederate leadership could not stomach a seemingly endless defensive. Johnston was replaced as commander of the Army of Tennessee by the firebrand John Bell Hood, who immediately embarked on a series of costly and unsuccessful offensives. The battered Confederate army was forced to evacuate Atlanta, providing a shot in the arm for Lincoln's campaign. "Atlanta is ours" Sherman telegraphed the president, "and fairly won".

With tension eased by the capture of Atlanta, Sherman pondered his next move. The following campaign would win him fame or infamy, depending on your viewpoint.

The hard hand of war

Sherman's idea was to march his army through Georgia. It was to be a deliberate and calculated

Sherman was a formidable commander, but his most audacious decision would be to focus his attentions on the civilian population of the South

act to cow the state and destroy its war-making capabilities. In a telegram to Grant, he wrote of his plan for the "utter destruction of its roads, houses, and people," and how this would "cripple their military resources".

Much has been written of Sherman's decision to confront civilians with the realities of war, but he was willing to consider less oppressive methods to achieve his goal. Writing to Governor Joseph Brown, he offered to march peacefully through the state if Georgia would withdraw from the rebellion. If it did not, then Sherman would "be compelled to go ahead, devastating the State in its whole length and breadth".

Sherman was still waiting for permission from Grant to begin his march, and Hood had 40,000 soldiers in the vicinity to contest his progress. On 21 September Hood took the imaginative decision to attack Sherman's supply lines, forcing plans for the march to be shelved, as Union troops backtracked through the state to counter Hood's move. Sherman, seething with frustration, persuaded Grant that chasing Hood was pointless.

On 2 November he was granted permission to abandon the pursuit of Hood and march to the coast. It resulted in a peculiar spectacle, as Sherman himself fully appreciated: "Two hostile armies marching in opposite directions, each in the full belief that it was achieving a final and conclusive result in a great war."

Forces in Georgia

The prospect of marching hundreds of miles through hostile territory, with no communications, no supply line, and no chance of rescue appeared daunting. Some envisioned an apocalyptic scenario in which the Union army would be whittled down by guerrilla actions, starved and harried and destroyed entirely by swarming militia. It was not a prospect for the faint-hearted. Nor was it one for the infirm or injured – a thorough medical examination weeded out almost 800 weak and sickly men before the march even started.

The army was organized into two wings, each of two corps – XIV and XX Corps for the left wing, XV and XVII Corps for the right. Sherman knew that Confederate resistance would be limited and he intended to make it even less effective through deception. Each wing would threaten a town or city, but if Confederate forces massed to resist, the wings would shift course to a different destination. With limited manpower, the Confederates could not hope to protect every potential target along the Union march.

"THE CONFEDERATES COULD NOT HOPE TO PROTECT EVERY POTENTIAL TARGET ALONG THE UNION MARCH"

SHERMAN'S MARCH

THE TWO WINGS OF SHERMAN'S ARMY MADE EASY PROGRESS THROUGH GEORGIA, GOING WHERE THEY WANTED, WHEN THEY WANTED

Although some talked gloomily of a scorched-earth policy being employed, Sherman had no doubt that his men would prevail. The march was easier during its first stage. With Atlanta situated in the Piedmont plateau, characterized by low rolling hills, the ground was firm, and there was also a certain novelty to the campaign, which kept the spirits of the marching columns high. Some of the men on the march talked of it in terms of a pleasure excursion.

The second phase of the march saw the landscape become bleaker as the plateau gave way to the coastal plain. Sandy and then marshy ground made progress difficult, and many soldiers noted that the march had become tiresome.

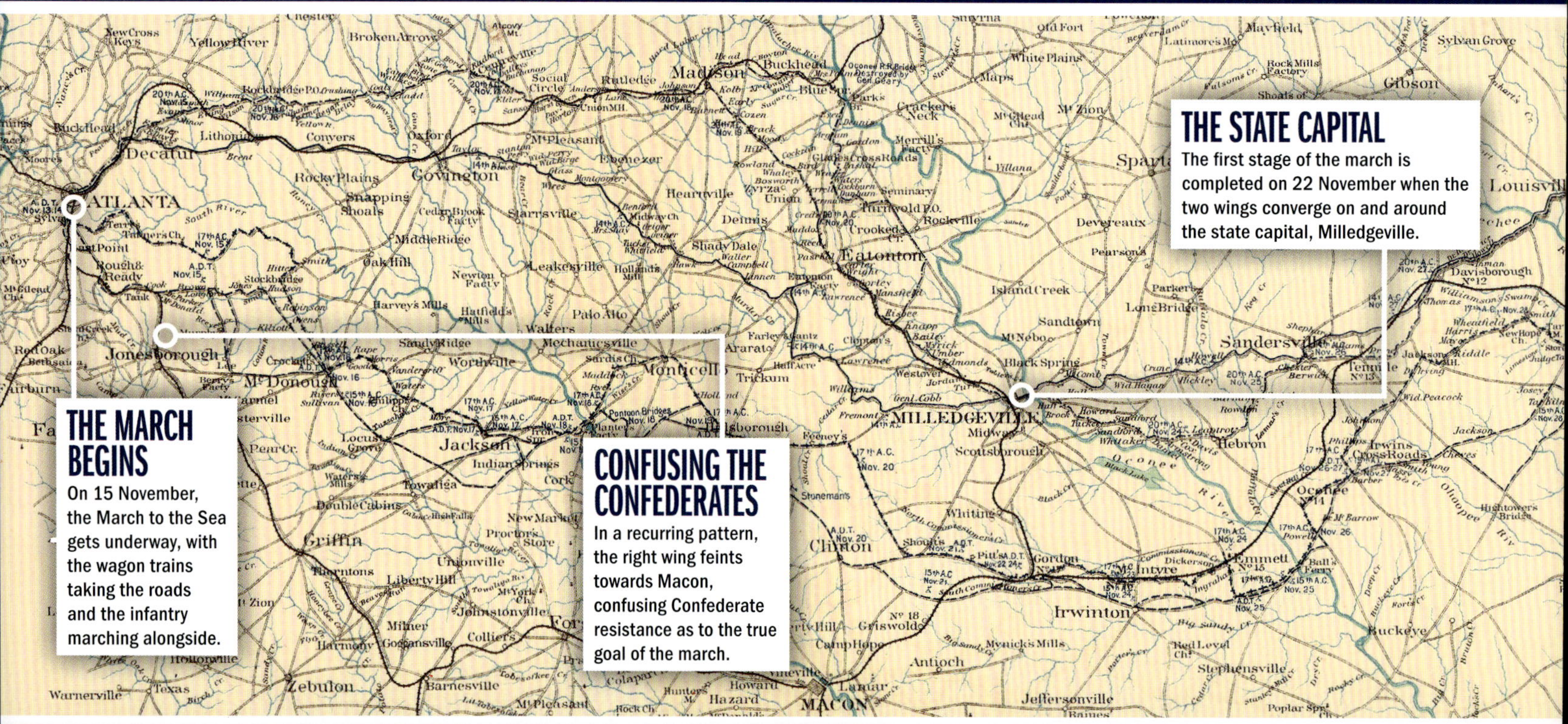

THE MARCH BEGINS
On 15 November, the March to the Sea gets underway, with the wagon trains taking the roads and the infantry marching alongside.

CONFUSING THE CONFEDERATES
In a recurring pattern, the right wing feints towards Macon, confusing Confederate resistance as to the true goal of the march.

THE STATE CAPITAL
The first stage of the march is completed on 22 November when the two wings converge on and around the state capital, Milledgeville.

The destruction of railroads (twisting the rails into 'Sherman's neckties') was one of the main activities on the march

Image: Getty, Source: Wikipedia Commons / Public Domain

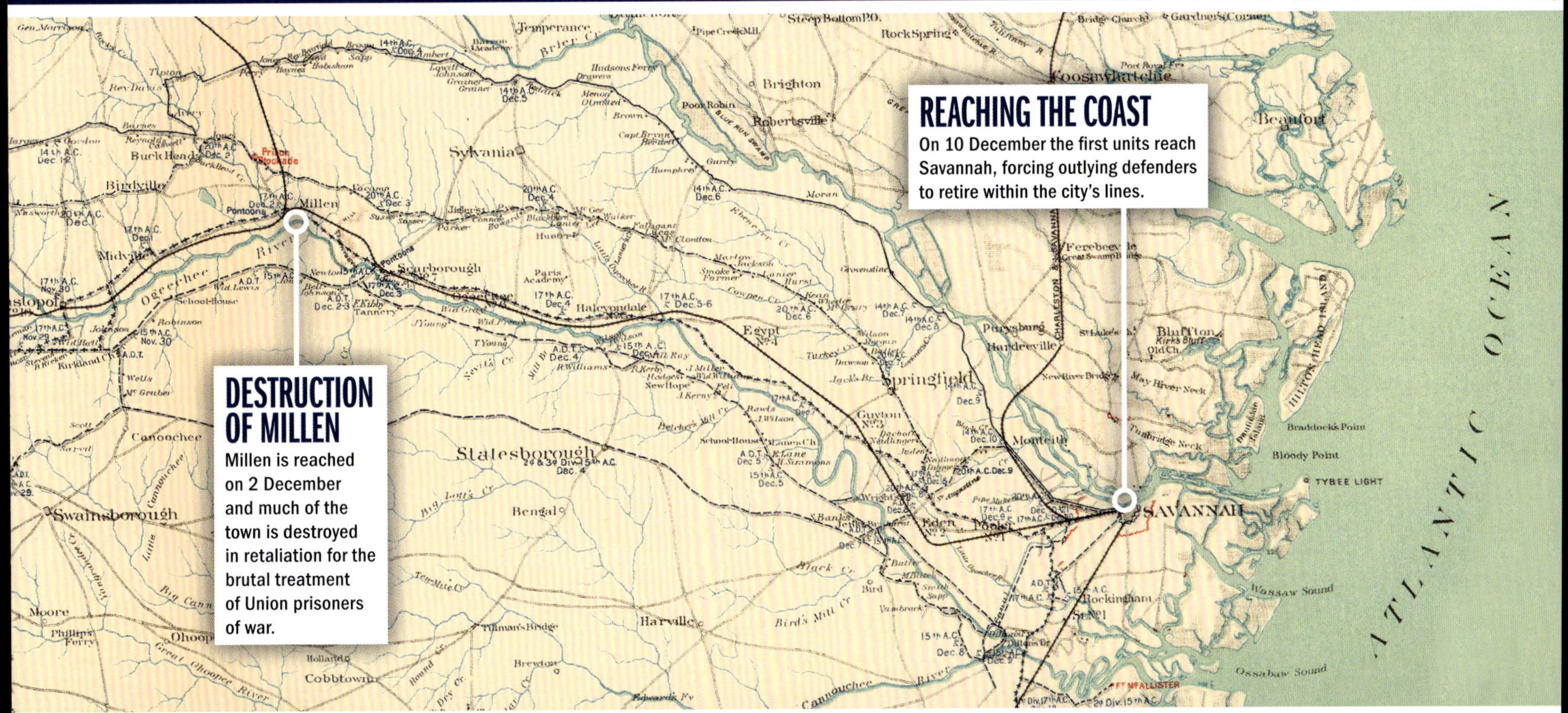

DESTRUCTION OF MILLEN

Millen is reached on 2 December and much of the town is destroyed in retaliation for the brutal treatment of Union prisoners of war.

REACHING THE COAST

On 10 December the first units reach Savannah, forcing outlying defenders to retire within the city's lines.

Despite his formidable reputation, Sherman routinely offered defeated Confederates generous terms

Each wing of the army numbered more than 27,000 men, and there was also a 5,000-strong cavalry division, commanded by the hot-headed Hugh Judson Kilpatrick, known as 'kill-cavalry' thanks to his excessively aggressive nature.

With Hood taking out of the picture the only major Confederate army available to protect Georgia, defense was left to whatever units could be scraped together. A cavalry force of 3,500 under 'Fighting Joe' Wheeler was potentially the biggest problem, if it could avoid the superior numbers of Union cavalry protecting Sherman's army. There was also state militia, some line regiments, a little artillery and a selection of largely untrained cadets. Scattered around the state, they were unable to do much other than fall back in the face of an overwhelming enemy.

The march begins

Sherman's men traveled light. Only 20 days' worth of rations were carried in the long wagon trains that followed the roads out of Atlanta in the middle of November, heading southeast. Only five days' worth of forage was carried for the thousands of animals used to haul those wagons – six mules for each one of the 2,500 wagons, and two horses for each of the 600 ambulances. One gun was taken for every 1,000 men, but Sherman was not envisioning any major pitched battles.

Before leaving, Atlanta was destroyed, with a fire adding to the devastation on the night of 14 November. Sherman's men then began to cut a swathe of destruction through Georgia. The railroad was a prime target. Sleepers were ripped up, piled into a bonfire and set on fire. The rails themselves were then heated on the fires until they softened, at which point they were twisted or bent beyond hope of repair. At the same time crops, livestock and other supplies were commandeered or destroyed and slaves were freed.

The Confederate response was mainly a futile call for the civilian population to rise up, and a hope that somehow faith would save them. The first serious fighting of the march

Sherman's March to the Sea was characterized by devastated infrastructure and property. The railroads were sabotaged and stores burned, while slaves were set free by the Union forces

took place on 22 November, when a mixed bag of around 3,000 Confederates, including state militia, stumbled upon a Union force half its size. Perhaps encouraged by this disparity in numbers, the Confederates chose to attack in what is known as the Battle of Griswoldville, but which was in fact little more than a slaughter. The untested Southern troops, many of them boys or old men, had no business launching a frontal assault against trained and entrenched troops, and the Union soldiers were also armed with Spencer repeating rifles. The battle was one-sided, resulting in around 600 Confederate casualties, against less than 100 for the Union troops. It had been a show of resistance at least, but it achieved nothing.

The 'bummers'

Sherman's orders to his men were to "forage liberally on the country", but he could not risk letting loose his entire army of 60,000 men. Foraging parties were instead organized by each brigade. These usually numbered between 30 and 50 men, with a single officer to retain some

The interior of Fort McAllister, whose heavy earth walls were meant to absorb naval gunfire rather than withstand an infantry assault

sort of order. Private property was not supposed to be entered, and civilians were to be left with enough food to get them through the winter, but the men were also to destroy most of what they could not carry back to the marching columns.

Known as 'bummers', Sherman's foragers earned a dark reputation among the Southern population. The general would later claim to have heard of only two rapes during the entire march, but the true toll was vastly higher. Private properties were also routinely ransacked and possessions stolen or destroyed.

Whether Sherman turned a deaf ear to reports of such activity, or whether he thought it was nothing more than the South deserved for starting the war, he tended to speak with approval of the foraging parties. They would set out in the morning on foot and invariably return in the evening riding requisitioned animals.

The idea of the march becoming another retreat from Moscow soon began to seem ludicrous. In fact there was just too much for the army to take, and massive amounts of provisions were left behind or simply destroyed. Sherman would later estimate that his army had done $100 million worth of damage to the state, with only 20 percent of that actually used by the Union troops. "The remainder", he admitted, "is simple waste and destruction".

The Battle of Nashville

As Sherman's men made progress, calls for Hood to return with the Army of Tennessee grew desperate, but he had other ideas. With just over 40,000 men, he intended to take on Union forces in Tennessee, capturing Nashville and moving northwards. He hoped this would force Sherman to reverse course.

The chance of success was slim, and they were not helped by Hood's reckless handling of his army. At Franklin on 30 November, he launched a suicidal frontal assault against prepared defenses, taking over 6,000 casualties, including a number of generals. Greatly weakened, his army was then overwhelmed and shattered during two days of fierce fighting at Nashville on 15-16 December.

Whether or not Hood's men would have been strong enough to oppose Sherman's march is debatable, but they would certainly have been able to offer more resistance. As it was, most of the Union troops marching through Georgia had little more to worry about than covering their 15 miles a day.

The second stage

It had taken just ten days to cover half the distance to Savannah, and one Union captain commented that it was "the most gigantic pleasure excursion ever planned". Even the

Sherman's army covered as many as 15 miles per day during the march through Georgia

men in the foraging parties, the most obvious targets for Confederate resistance, were largely unscathed. Only 64 of them were killed during the march.

Still, there was trepidation in the North. With Sherman out of contact there was no way of knowing if he was making smooth progress or getting bogged down in guerrilla actions. There would be no firm news until Sherman reached the coast and re-established communication.

The second stage of the march began with a feint towards Augusta. Once more, this was just a ruse to draw Confederate defenders, and Union cavalry under Kilpatrick moved towards the town to strengthen the deception. In clashes with defending Confederate cavalry, Kilpatrick's men were forced into a series of retreats. It was the most effective resistance of the entire march, but it changed nothing. A corridor was being swept through the state, with infrastructure being destroyed. Tellingly, the Union troops also targeted any building that could be "easily converted" to military use.

By late November the excursion atmosphere was starting to fade. The land was turning marshy, with pine forests proliferating. Sherman later wrote about the invigorating scent of pine wood on the campfires at night, but his men were not impressed: "I never saw such a lonesome place," an Illinois captain remarked, "Not a bird, not a sign of animal life, but the shrill notes of the tree frog... no vegetable life but just grass and pitch pine."

Kilpatrick's cavalry clashed once more with their Confederate counterparts at the Battle of Waynesborough, driving them away. Kilpatrick then hoped to rescue captive Union soldiers at the notorious prison at Millen, but the inmates had already been moved by the time he arrived. The Union troops noted the appalling conditions of the camp and a mass-burial pit holding 650 bodies, and the mood of the march soured.

The fall of Savannah

Military actions remained rare. On 1 December a captain noted that he had not heard enemy gunfire for the previous nine days. Thoughts were turning to Savannah, where a garrison of around 10,000 was expected to offer at least some resistance. Before getting there, communications needed to be reopened, and that required the capture of Fort McAllister. Originally developed to defend the coast from Union shipping, Fort McAllister had not been designed to withstand an assault from the land and was manned by just 150 Confederates, but it still represented an obstacle. On 13 December nine Union regiments stormed the fort and took it in 15 minutes. Sherman was then able to converse with the captain of the Union steamer Dandelion, re-establishing communications with the North.

"SHERMAN OFFERED SAVANNAH TO THE PRESIDENT AS A CHRISTMAS GIFT"

Savannah now waited, and its fall was inevitable. Despite an extensive series of defensive works, including 81 pieces of artillery, there was no hope of holding out for long. Only the need to bring up heavy guns (his army had marched with only field pieces) delayed Sherman's assault, and Confederate forces took the opportunity to quietly evacuate the city on the night of 20 December. In a light-hearted, almost giddy telegram, Sherman offered Savannah to the president as a Christmas gift. Lincoln replied with heartfelt thanks.

The 'March to the Sea' had been completed, at a cost of just 1,888 men killed, wounded in action, captured, or missing. Only 32 deaths had been suffered due to disease, testimony to the wisdom of undertaking a health check

Although Sherman was unenthusiastic about freed slaves following his army, an estimated 25,000 flocked to his columns during the course of the march

Sherman marched on into South Carolina in 1865, wreaking even more destruction, including the burning of McPhersonville

of the men before starting the march, and also to the benefits of outdoor life and regular exercise. Sherman, however, was far from done, and controversy over his epic march was just beginning.

Sherman marches on

Progress through Georgia had been so easy, the Union general determined to repeat the process in South Carolina. Regarded as the seat of secessionism, antipathy towards South Carolina was far greater than it had been towards Georgia. This second march began on 1 February 1865, and the message to the Confederate states was clear. In case it needed underlining, Lincoln made a speech to Congress in which he stated, "We are gaining strength, and may, if need be, maintain the contest indefinitely."

The South, on the other hand, was losing men, supplies, and war-making infrastructure. In South Carolina, the destruction wrought by Sherman's men was even worse. An unusually harsh winter barely slowed them as they bridged rivers and trudged through mud at a remorseless ten miles a day. The march then continued into North Carolina, but much of its fury had abated as the war stumbled to its close. The ultimate aim, that of linking up with Grant's men besieging Petersburg, was never realized, as Grant achieved victory before Sherman could arrive.

The American Civil War was effectively over, but resentment would linger for years, much of it stoked by the harsh treatment of Confederate states by Sherman's men. There was concern that an interminable guerrilla war might break out, with small pockets of still-committed Confederates engaging in resistance-style sabotage and ambushes. Such a dire prospect was embraced by the Confederate cavalry commander Nathan Bedford Forrest, who took part in Hood's disastrous Tennessee campaign. "Be not allured by the siren song of peace," he implored the South. "You can never again unite with those who have murdered your sons, outraged your helpless families, and with demonic malice wantonly destroyed your property, and now seek to make slaves of you."Forrest's exhortations were in vain, but anger over the March to the Sea would last for decades.

The verdict

History has not viewed Sherman kindly. His marches have been condemned by some as war crimes, although events in the 20th century have cast new light on his actions. The march through Georgia now seems positively tame when compared to the deliberate targeting of civilian populations in World War II, and unleashing foragers on the countryside seems mild compared to the dropping of atomic bombs.

Sherman had no doubt that he was actually waging a more humane form of warfare. Destroying the ability of a region to support an army was better, in his mind, than fighting that army and inflicting 15,000 casualties. While marching through South Carolina, he made this clear, commenting to one lady that he was destroying her plantation so that he wouldn't have to kill her husband on the battlefield.

He was also acting within the law, under the terms of the Lieber Code, framed by the legal scholar Franz Lieber and established in 1863. The code stipulated that "to save the country is paramount to all other considerations" and this allowed for acts such as the destruction of civilian property. Sherman, in any case, believed the war itself was an illegal act and needed to be terminated as quickly and as ruthlessly as possible.

Many will never be convinced, and there is no doubt that Sherman intended to inflict suffering on the civilian population of the South. He had left no doubt on that score when he lobbied Grant for permission to start his march, back in October 1864. "I can make the march," he had written to Grant in a telegram, "and make Georgia howl". ★

Image: Alamy, Getty

NASHVILLE

A veteran Confederate army desperately tries to change the course of the war in its final months

WORDS **WILLIAM E WELSH**

Union troops break through the Confederate line on the second day of the battle, sparking a Confederate retreat south

On the fog-shrouded morning of 15 December 1864, the soldiers of the 14th US Colored Troops broke through the thin screen of Confederate skirmishers posted in the rifle pits, in front of the Chattanooga & Nashville Railroad. After regrouping, they surged across the railway tracks in a bid to outflank the right of the Confederate lines on the outskirts of Nashville.

Suddenly, Confederate 12-pounder smoothbore guns in a lunette adjacent to the tracks erupted with canister – tin cans filled with deadly iron balls – which shredded the regiment's ranks. Confederate infantry, which had been hiding in a stand of timber, fired a thunderous volley into the Union regiment's ranks. The survivors fled in the direction from which they had come – within ten minutes they had lost 117 men.

It was the kind of tactical success that Confederate General John Bell Hood so desperately sought when he lured Union Major General George Thomas to attack his earthworks on the south side of Nashville after a nearly two-week standoff between the armies.

In the war-ravaged South in the final months of the conflict, Hood lacked the troops that would be needed to capture Nashville. Because of this, the best he could hope for was to inflict heavy casualties on Thomas's army, which had been cobbled together from various Union commands in the Western Theater to take on the crack troops of Hood's Army of Tennessee. If the Confederates could continue throughout the day to repulse other piecemeal Union attacks with similar success, Hood just might win a tactical victory against a much larger Union army.

Long odds for success

The battered armies of the Confederate States of America faced near-certain defeat by fall 1864. After years of campaigning, General Robert E Lee, commanding the Army of Northern Virginia, was besieged in the Richmond-Petersburg sector by the Army of the Potomac under the watchful eye of General Ulysses S Grant, who president Abraham Lincoln had made the commander of all Union armies in March 1864.

The Army of Tennessee under the command of General Joseph Johnston had been steadily retreating through northern Georgia since Major General William T Sherman began his offensive to capture Atlanta in March 1864. Sherman had a grand army composed of three formerly regional armies named after the Ohio, the Cumberland, and the Tennessee rivers that totaled 112,000 troops.

Sherman had reached the Chattahoochee River just north of the city in early July. Confederate President Jefferson Davis, who was disappointed with 57-year-old Johnston's performance, sacked him on 17 July and replaced him with the much-younger Hood.

Hood, a 33-year old Kentuckian who had graduated in West Point's Class of 1853, had a reputation as a fighter from his days commanding a brigade and later a division in the Army of Northern Virginia. While Hood's fighting spirit was undiminished, his body had been ravaged by injuries suffered in battle. He had lost the use of his left arm when it was hit by shrapnel at Gettysburg, Pennsylvania, in July 1863, and his right leg had been amputated at Chickamauga, Georgia, two months later.

Initially Hood had 60,000 troops with which to fight off Sherman's legions. He attacked various parts of the Union juggernaut at different points around Atlanta between 20 July and 31 August. After these four bloody clashes, the fiery Confederate commander had nothing to show for his efforts. The grinding battles resulted in 16,000 Confederate casualties.

As August drew to a close, Hood abandoned Atlanta and Sherman took possession of it on 2 September. In late October Hood devised a plan to invade Tennessee in the hope of forcing Sherman to follow him. If Hood could capture Nashville it would boost Confederate morale and perhaps enable Hood to continue north into Union territory. With Confederate president Davis's approval, Hood prepared to invade Union-controlled Middle Tennessee.

Thomas must defeat Hood

While Sherman prepared to march the best 60,000 troops in his army from Atlanta through the heart of Georgia to Savannah, he tasked

Image: Alamy

***Above** Union infantry storms Shy's Hill on the second day of the Battle of Nashville*

01 UNION DIVERSIONARY ATTACK FAILS

A diversionary attack by Union forces against the Confederate right on the morning of 15 December encounters fierce resistance from entrenched veteran troops.

02 CONFEDERATE LEFT FLANK THREATENED

Union cavalry armed with repeating carbines working in tandem with infantry capture Redoubts No. 4 and No. 5 in the early afternoon of the first day. This enables the cavalry to begin to turn the Confederate left flank.

03 HOOD REINFORCES HIS LEFT

General Hood pulls Major General Edward Johnson's division from the Confederate center and sends it to the left where two brigades of soldiers, the first to arrive, deploy behind a stone wall along the Hillsboro Pike in an effort to shore up the endangered flank.

04 BLOODY FIGHT FOR MONTGOMERY HILL

Charging masses of Union infantry carry the first line of Confederate trenches on the crest of Montgomery Hill, only to run headlong into a wall of resistance on the reverse slope. Confederates fire heavy volleys that check the Union advance.

05 FEDERALS STORM CONFEDERATE SALIENT
Soldiers from two Federal divisions charge the salient where Redoubt No. 1 is situated in the late afternoon of the first day. As they sweep over the entrenchments, they find that the Confederates are disengaging.

06 FIRST DAY ENDS WITH CONFEDERATE RETREAT
Johnson's troops panic as they are outflanked by Federal cavalry and under heavy attack from the Union XVI Corps. This precipitates a retreat of the entire Confederate left wing one mile to the Granny White Pike, where Hood rallies the troops.

07 UNION ATTACK RESUMES AGAINST OVERTON HILL
A Union attack at mid-afternoon on the second day of the battle against well-entrenched Confederates on Overton Hill fails to make any headway.

08 COORDINATED UNION ATTACK SHATTERS CONFEDERATE ARMY
The Union army assails all points of the Confederate line in the late afternoon of the second day. When the Confederate position on Shy's Hill crumbles, the Confederate army begins a rapid retreat south along the Franklin Pike.

General John Bell Hood commanded the Confederate Army

Thomas with preventing Hood from retaking occupied territory in Middle Tennessee. Of his remaining troop, Sherman left some to garrison Atlanta and sent the rest to Thomas.

Thomas, who had graduated from West Point in 1840, had a knack for defensive tactics, as shown by his brilliant rearguard action as a corps commander at Chickamauga in September 1863. He had single-handedly saved Major General William Rosecrans' Union Army of the Cumberland from destruction. In recognition of his achievement, President Lincoln replaced Rosecrans with Thomas in October 1863.

Thomas arrived in Nashville in late October to oversee its defense and defeat Hood. The forces under his control were scattered throughout the region. They included 8,000 garrison troops in Nashville; a Provisional Detachment of 8,500 troops in Chattanooga led by Major General James Steedman; and 30,000 veteran troops in Major General David Stanley's IV Corps and Major General John Schofield's XXIII Corps in Pulaski, Tennessee. In addition, Major General Andrew J Smith's 9,000-man XVI Corps received orders to march from Mississippi to join Thomas in Nashville. Thomas also had 9,000 cavalrymen under the command of Brigadier General James Wilson, but they needed to be refitted with fresh horses and new carbines for the coming campaign.

Rash decision at Franklin

Hood's army set out for Nashville on 20 November. His army numbered 32,000 infantry organized into three corps and 6,000 cavalry. Hood hoped that his march into Middle Tennessee would compel Sherman to pursue him, but Sherman had already given Thomas the forces necessary to contain Hood. Thomas instructed Schofield to offer battle to Hood if necessary to slow his advance northward to allow time for more Union reinforcements to arrive in Nashville. Schofield had great respect for Hood's capabilities as a commander. "He'll hit you like hell, before you know it," he had told Sherman during the Atlanta campaign.

Hood's army easily bypassed Pulaski to the west, reaching Spring Hill, Tennessee, on 29 November in the rear of Schofield's position. Expecting Schofield to force his way through the Confederate army, Hood planned to ambush Schofield's army but his corps commanders failed to successfully carry out his orders. Hood shared the blame for the debacle in

General John Bell Hood hoped to lure the Union army out of its strong fortifications of Nashville

The vast Union encampment at Nashville attested to the strength of Major General George Thomas's reinforced Army of the Cumberland

that he had retired for the night and was not present at the front when Schofield marched right past the Confederate bivouac that night. "The best move in my career as a soldier… came to naught," Hood wrote afterwards.

Schofield reached Franklin, which was 20 miles south of Nashville, the following morning. Hood, who was furious that his generals missed an opportunity to destroy or heavily damage Schofield's army, ordered what turned out to be a very costly frontal attack against Schofield's troops in pre-existing earthworks at Franklin. Among more than 6,000 Confederate dead and wounded were a number of Confederate generals. Hood's decision to risk a costly attack against entrenched troops showed not only that he was rash, but also that he lacked the skills and experience necessary for high command.

Hood entrenches at Nashville

Federal forces had held the capital of Tennessee since February 1862. By December 1864 the city was protected by an inner and outer fortified belt, the flanks of which were anchored on the Cumberland River.

Schofield reached Nashville on 1 December, and Hood arrived the following day. The Confederate commander undertook a partial siege of the city, entrenching his army on a four-mile front along an arc of hills south of Nashville. Lieutenant General Alexander Stewart's corps held the Confederate left along Hillsboro Pike, Lieutenant General Stephen D Lee's corps held the center, and Major General Benjamin Cheatham's corps held the right along the Nashville & Chattanooga Railroad.

The Confederate left was the most vulnerable to attack because beyond the Hillsboro Pike there was ample room for Thomas to maneuver his troops for a large-scale attack. Hood instructed Stewart to refuse his flank and strengthen his earthworks by constructing five redoubts, each of which housed two or four cannon and 100 infantry.

Hood's siege lines were from between 0.6 to 1.9 miles south of the Union fortifications protecting Nashville. Hood hoped that in the coming days Thomas would wreck his army trying to dislodge the Confederates from their position.

Hood sent Forrest's cavalry to the southeast to tear up sections of the Nashville & Chattanooga Railroad. Thomas decided not to send Wilson's cavalry to engage Forrest because of its poor condition. He therefore sent the Union cavalry across the Cumberland River to Edgefield to rest and refit.

Grant browbeats Thomas

When Thomas informed Washington that it would be at least ten days before he launched offensive operations against the Confederate Army of the Tennessee encamped outside his fortifications, Grant demanded immediate action in order to prevent Forrest's troopers from destroying bridges and track along the Nashville & Chattanooga Railroad.

With each passing day that Thomas failed to attack Hood, Grant grew more incensed. "Attack Hood at once and wait no longer for a remount of your cavalry," Grant telegraphed Thomas on 6 December. Bowing to Grant's wishes, Thomas scheduled an attack for 7 December, but an ice storm struck the region, making it unrealistic to take offensive action until the weather improved.

During this time, Thomas put the final touches to his battle plan. Steedman's Provisional Detachment would launch a diversionary attack against the Confederate right wing to pin down Cheatham's corps. The main attack would consist of a "left grand wheel" to strike that portion of Stewart's line along the Hillsboro Pike. Brigadier General Thomas Wood's IV Corps and Major General Andrew J Smith's XVI Corps would lead the attack, and Schofield's XXIII Corps would follow in reserve. Wilson's cavalry would cover the army's southern flank against a possible attack by Forrest.

"Delay no longer for weather or reinforcements," Grant wired Thomas on 12

The Union army deployed cannon on the grounds of the state capitol during the Battle of Nashville

General Sherman at Kennesaw Mountain during the Battle of Allatoona Pass, the first major engagement of the Franklin-Nashville campaign

December. The weather began to improve the following day, but Thomas still did not launch his attack. At that point, Grant made plans to travel from Petersburg, Virginia, to Nashville to take command himself. But Thomas attacked Hood before Grant entrained for Tennessee.

Yankees storm rebel redoubts

Thomas took up a position in the center of the outer fortified belt to observe the progress of the Federal attack. A thick fog clung to the landscape on the morning of 15 December as the ground continued to thaw. Steedman's diversionary attack in the morning stalled in the face of determined Confederate resistance, and his effort failed to prevent Hood from shifting forces later in the day from the right wing to the left one.

As the three Union infantry corps began their left grand wheel, Stewart's 4,800 Confederates, who were outnumbered five to one, watched with apprehension as a 1.9-mile-long Union line of battle thick with regimental flags and guidons headed their way.

Wood's divisions attacked the northern half of Stewart's line, while Smith's divisions attacked the southern half of his line. Before Smith's men could attack the earthworks, though, they had to clear the Rebels from Redoubts 3, 4, and 5, which were situated outside of the main line of trenches.

While veteran Confederate soldiers in the north held their ground against the Federals, the southern end of Stewart's line came under attack from cavalry and infantry backed by rifled guns firing solid shot and fused shells. Wilson's troopers on the extreme right of the Union line had an advantage in that they were armed with newly issued Spencer carbine repeaters.

When Thomas observed a large gap open as the two forward infantry corps veered away from each other, he ordered Schofield's XXIII Corps to fill the space between them and add its weight to the attack.

Hood reinforces wavering flank

Hood ordered Major General Edward Johnson's Division of Lieutenant General SD Lee's corps in the center to reinforce the left flank when he saw that it was the target of the Union army's main attack. The first two brigades to arrive deployed on the south end of Stewart's line where they were desperately needed to prevent his flank from being turned.

Smith attacked Redoubts No. 4 and No. 5 with overwhelming force. Dismounted troopers of the 2nd Iowa Cavalry with their repeating carbines spearheaded the attack on Redoubt No. 5 and were assisted by Smith's infantrymen. After a brief melee

Major General George Thomas holds a council of war during the Battle of Atlanta that preceded the Nashville campaign

inside the redoubt, the surviving Confederates retreated to the main line along the Hillsboro Pike. The combined force of the 5th Cavalry Division and elements of the Union IV Corps captured Redoubt No. 4 shortly afterwards.

As Colonel Sylvester Hill of Smith's Corps prepared to lead his infantry brigade in a charge to capture Redoubt No. 3, his commanding officer, Brigadier General John McArthur, advised him to wait for additional troops to support him. Hill ignored the general's advice. "Our brigade will go right up there," Hill told Smith. "Nothing can stop them."

Although his men captured the redoubt, a Rebel marksman shot Hill in the head, killing him as he was preparing to lead his troops in a charge against Redoubt No. 2. Angered by Hill's death, Colonel William Marshal, the commander of the 7th Minnesota regiment, led his 200 men in a spirited charge that so intimidated the Confederates in Redoubt No. 2 that they fled without putting up any resistance.

The riflemen of Johnson's two advance brigades on the far end of Stewart's line found themselves under heavy artillery fire from the rifled Union guns. With the shells exploding among them, these troops fell back unexpectedly. "These Rebels appeared panic-stricken and fired badly," said a Union officer whose troops had exchanged fire with them.

The rout of Johnson's advance brigades triggered the collapse of Stewart's entire line at 4pm. Stewart ordered his division commanders to reform their troops nearly a mile east along the Granny White Pike. Complete disaster was diverted not only by the arrival on the Confederate left of Johnson's two remaining brigades, but also by the arrival of 1,500 more troops from Cheatham's corps that Hood had hurried to the point of crisis. Nightfall put an end to the fighting.

Union officers in the US Army's telegraph office in Washington on 15 December received a message late that night from Thomas stating that his troops had driven back the enemy from one to three miles over the course of the day's fighting. "The whole action of today was splendidly successful," wrote Thomas.

Confederates shorten the line

Hood's army, which already was at a great disadvantage, was extremely low on manpower by the end of the day on 15 December. Hood had suffered 2,200 killed, wounded and captured on the first day of the battle. Thomas and his corps commanders had every confidence that they would crush Hood's weakened army if he offered battle again on the following day.

True to his nature, Hood intended to stand his ground because at that point he had few strategic options remaining. He believed that he could still bleed the Union army if his troops could hold a contracted line that stretched for 1.9 miles from Shy's Hill on the west to Overton Hill on the east.

In preparation to receive a renewed Union assault on the following morning, Hood placed Stewart's badly battered corps in the center. The Confederates held strong positions on fortified hilltops on each flank. Cheatham's corps deployed on the left side of the Confederate battle line atop Shy's

The Battle of Franklin proved very costly to Confederate chances at Nashville

This photo shows the inner line of Union Army defenses at the Battle of Nashville

Hill, and SD Lee's corps took up positions on Overton Hill on the right side.

Union troops rout Confederates

Thomas opened his attack the following day by sending elements of Wood's IV Corps against Major General Carter Stevenson's Division of SD Lee's corps atop Overton Hill. The Union troops advanced at the enemy in three ranks. Well-entrenched Confederate troops backed up by massed Confederate artillery repulsed Wood's attack. Next, Thomas ordered Steedman's Colored Troops to assail the hill at midday, but this second attack also floundered in the face of determined Confederate resistance.

Union attacks, some ordered by Thomas and some spontaneous, occurred along the entire length of the Confederate position in the late afternoon. When Union troops from the XVI and XXIII corps attacked Cheatham's men on Shy's Hill at 4pm, his troops could not hold them off. At the same time, Wilson's cavalry rode around Cheatham's flank. At that point, the Southern troops on the left and center fled towards Franklin Pike. Realizing he was defeated, Hood ordered a general retreat south along the Franklin Pike.

Hood suffered 1,500 killed and wounded, as well as 8,500 captured in the two-day battle. Altogether, he had lost nearly one-third of his army in the bloody battles at Franklin and Nashville. Although Thomas suffered 3,000 casualties at Nashville, his much larger army could more easily afford the losses. On 18 December Grant telegraphed his congratulations to Thomas for what he called a "great victory".

Forrest ambushes Union pursuers

The Union pursuit of the retreating Confederate army began immediately. Hood sent orders to Forrest to cover his retreat. The 'Wizard of the Saddle', as Forrest was known, carried out a series of well-laid ambushes that bought Hood the time he needed to get the rump of his army to safety. Even so, Union troops leading the pursuit rounded up thousands of Confederates who were too weary to keep up with the main body.

By 26 December the Army of Tennessee had succeeded in crossing the Tennessee River. Of the 37,000 Confederate troops that had set out for Nashville in late November, only 20,000 remained when it reassembled in northeastern Mississippi. Davis sacked Hood in January 1865.

Through careful planning and skillful handling of his forces, Thomas had eviscerated the Army of Tennessee and it played no significant part in the remainder of the war. ★

STATE OF PLAY 1865

With the fourth year of the American Civil War, the Confederacy's days are numbered as Union forces march to victory

In the spring of 1865, Robert E Lee's Army of Northern Virginia is finally forced out of its defensive position around the rail center of Petersburg and the Confederate capital of Richmond, Virginia, a few miles to the north. The climactic campaign of the American Civil War ensues as three Union armies, under the overall command of General Ulysses S Grant, pursue the ragged Confederate forces westward towards the village of Appomattox Court House, where they raise the white flag. Lee's army suffers a substantial defeat at Five Forks, on 1 April. Then, at Sailor's Creek five days later, a quarter of the army, including six generals, surrenders. Lee's effort to reach the rail line at Lynchburg is thwarted, and he surrenders at Appomattox Court House on Palm Sunday, 9 April 1865.

A Confederate delegation, meanwhile, journeys to Washington, DC, to discuss peace terms with President Lincoln, but the talks break down and the fighting continues.

To the south, General William T Sherman leads his large Union army northward into the Carolinas, chasing the remnants of three Confederate armies under General Joseph E Johnston. Sherman accepts Johnston's surrender near Durham, North Carolina, on 18 April. Fighting continues, particularly in the west, but hostilities cease in the coming weeks, effectively ending the Civil War.

While the war winds down, President Lincoln discusses his vision for reconciliation and the restoration of the Union. However, he is shot by assassin John Wilkes Booth on 14 April, dying the following morning. The South is destined to endure a harsh period of Reconstruction. ★

The McLean House in Appomattox Court House, Virginia, is the site of Robert E Lee's surrender to Ulysses S Grant

Jefferson Davis, former president of the Confederacy, was confined to prison after his capture and eventually released

The locomotive of President Abraham Lincoln's funeral train bore a portrait of the slain leader during its journey

LINCOLN LAID TO REST

After lying in state in major Northern cities – with throngs of mourners paying their respects – and a state funeral in Washington, DC, President Abraham Lincoln is laid to rest in Oak Ridge Cemetery near Springfield, Illinois. The coffin of his young son, Willie, who died in 1862, is also placed aboard the funeral train to Springfield, and the two are interred together.

CONSTITUTIONAL AMENDMENT ABOLISHES SLAVERY

Although passed by the US Congress on 31 January 1865, the 13th Amendment to the Constitution, abolishing slavery and involuntary servitude in the United States, is finally ratified by the required number of states to become the law of the land on 6 December 1865. The votes of several Southern states, then in the throes of Reconstruction, tip the balance for ratification.

LAST CONFEDERATE FIELD ARMY SURRENDERS

On 2 June 1865, General Edmund Kirby Smith – the last Confederate general officer with a major field army under his command – surrenders his force to Union authorities at Galveston, Texas. After escaping to Mexico and then Cuba to avoid arrest, Smith eventually returns to the US after his wife concludes amnesty negotiations. He later becomes a university professor in Tennessee.

CONFEDERATE FLIGHT TO DANVILLE

After evacuating Richmond by rail, the Confederate government flees toward the town of Danville, Virginia, hoping to avoid capture by Union forces that have occupied the capital city. President Jefferson Davis reaches the Carolinas and later travels to Georgia with an escort of Confederate troops. His luck runs out near the town of Irwinville, Georgia, where he is captured by Union cavalry on 10 May 1865.

THE FINAL CAMPAIGN

Robert E Lee's Confederate Army of Northern Virginia retreats from Richmond and Petersburg, attempting to reach the railroad at Lynchburg for resupply and then to possibly link up with forces under General Joseph E Johnston in North Carolina. However, the dogged pursuit of General Ulysses S Grant's Union armies foils the effort. Lee surrenders at Appomattox Court House on 9 April 1865.

Image: Alamy, Getty, Wikipedia Commons / Public Domain

The city of Richmond burns as Confederate troops and civilians flee the capital in advance of approaching Union troops

LAST DAYS OF THE CONFEDERACY

In the spring of 1865, Confederate forces under Robert E Lee and Joseph Johnston finally yielded to the overwhelming might of the Union armies

WORDS **MIKE HASKEW**

The landscape around the city of Petersburg, Virginia, was desolate, resembling the scarred battlefield of the Western Front in World War I a generation later. For nine months General Robert E Lee and the beleaguered Confederate Army of Northern Virginia defended a line that eventually stretched an astounding 53 miles from the capital city Richmond south to Petersburg and beyond, protecting the crucial rail and road terminus, the lifeline of supply from the South.

General Ulysses S Grant, commander of all Union armies in the field, had been frustrated in early to mid-1864 as repeated attempts to capture Richmond had failed. Each thrust of the Overland Campaign, the Wilderness, Spotsylvania Court House, along the North Anna River, and Cold Harbor, had been parried by Lee during bloody weeks of maneuver punctuated with sharp inconclusive battles. Grant now changed his focus to Petersburg, south of the James River, where the Southside Railroad ran from Lynchburg westward, the Norfolk & Petersburg line ran up from the southeast, and the Weldon Railroad approached from North Carolina. With Petersburg in Union hands, the Confederates would have to abandon Richmond and then fight against overwhelming odds.

Again, though, efforts to capture Petersburg met with frustration due to Confederate resourcefulness and Union miscommunication. By the end of June, the lines had stagnated. The war of rapid movement had become a siege, Lee with barely 36,000 men at Petersburg and 20,000 in Richmond, while the Union host numbered more than 100,000. For months, fighting moved in fits and starts, at times troops on both sides using pick and shovel more than the rifle and cannon. Grant forced Lee to extend his defensive lines, moving south and west to cut the roads and rail lines into the city.

Meanwhile, to the south Union General William T Sherman had made good on his vow to "make Georgia howl," concluding his destructive march from Atlanta to the sea. Sherman captured the port of Savannah in December and cabled President Abraham Lincoln: "I beg to present you as a Christmas gift the city of Savannah with 150 heavy guns and plenty of ammunition and also about 25,000 bales of cotton."

In late January 1865, Sherman turned his armies of the Tennessee, the Ohio, and Georgia northward into the Carolinas. Opposing his offensive was the ragged Confederate Army of Tennessee under General Joseph E Johnston, at times numbering fewer than 20,000 soldiers and facing up to 90,000 Union troops at any given time. On 3 February, Sherman's vanguard brushed aside an effort to drive the Union right flank back at Rivers' Bridge on the Salkehatchie River. Two weeks later, Union troops captured Columbia, South Carolina, capital of the state labeled the 'Mother of Secession'. A fire of unknown origin swept through the city.

Beginning of the end

On 22 February, the port of Wilmington, North Carolina, fell to Union forces, and troops under General John M Schofield advanced inland against Confederates under General Braxton Bragg. On 16 March, a sharp clash at Averasborough delayed the Union advance for 48 hours. Three days later, Bragg joined Johnston at Bentonville, their combined strength totaling 21,000. Johnston attacked, driving Union forces back. Rapid reinforcement stopped the Confederates, and Johnston held his ground for more than a day before a flanking movement forced his retreat toward Raleigh, the North Carolina capital.

Johnston fell back to Greensboro and met with Confederate President Jefferson Davis on 12-13 April, frankly admitting: "Our people are tired of war, feel themselves whipped, and will not fight [...] My small force is melting away like snow before the sun." On the 18th, Johnston met with Sherman at Bennett Place, near Durham Station. The western forces of the Confederacy

"THE LAST CONFEDERATE CAVALRYMAN TO CROSS MAYO'S BRIDGE TIPPED HIS HAT AND ORDERED THE SPAN ABLAZE"

Image: Getty

Union troops brought forward a huge mortar nicknamed the 'Dictator' to bombard Confederate positions during the siege of Petersburg

were vanquished, but confusion reigned; Sherman's surrender terms were generous, replete with political overtones he had no authority to negotiate. The commanders met again on 26 April, clarified the military terms of surrender, and it was accomplished.

The drama of the endgame in Virginia had played out by that time. Robert E Lee and the Army of Northern Virginia were steadily being strangled as Grant's forces slugged their way around the Confederate right flank. Starvation and disease wracked the army, and from mid-February to mid-March 2,934 men, eight percent of Lee's fighting strength, deserted. By early March, only the South Side Railroad remained open. General John B Gordon, commander of the II Corps, Army of Northern Virginia, asked Lee: "'What, then, is to be done, general?' He replied that there seemed to be but one thing we could do – fight. To stand still was death. It could only be death if we fought and failed.'" Grant knew this as well. Lee would eventually have to abandon his trenches at Petersburg and fight for his life.

Following Lee's directive, Gordon chose Fort Stedman, 150 yards from the Confederate lines, as the focus of an attack. In the predawn darkness of 25 March 1865, the assault initially made good progress. By daybreak, however, the Confederates were in danger of being cut off. Lee ordered a withdrawal.

Grant realized the best hope for Lee to survive was a junction with Johnston's forces in North Carolina. He took steps to prevent such a movement. General Phil Sheridan rejoined his command after a foray into the Shenandoah Valley and would soon play a key role in the final victory. Grant ordered

"LEE WOULD HAVE TO ABANDON HIS TRENCHES AT PETERSBURG AND FIGHT FOR HIS LIFE"

continuing movement to the west, around Lee's flank, and sent Sheridan towards the vital road junction at Five Forks, Lee's best route towards North Carolina. Soon enough, Lee realized his right and rear were in peril. He dispatched a division under General George Pickett to slow the Union advance and "hold Five Forks at all hazards." On 1 April, the Battle of Five Forks ended in disaster for the Confederates. Sheridan's cavalry had been joined by a large Union infantry, and the spirited attack flanked Pickett's position. The fight was quickly won. Union troops controlled the precious crossroads, and 5,000 prisoners were taken along with 11 Confederate battle flags.

Road to surrender

Lieutenant Colonel Horace Porter, a Union staff officer, wrote later that the victory was "the beginning of the end, the reaching of the 'last ditch.' It pointed to peace and home." Grant ordered a general assault. With the loss of Five Forks, Lee's positions at Petersburg and Richmond were unhinged. On Sunday morning, 2 April, the old general notified President Jefferson Davis that the army was abandoning its defense and the government should flee Richmond.

That same morning, the Union VI Corps broke through General AP Hill's Confederate line, and the 39-year-old Hill was killed. Lee ordered General James Longstreet to patch together a new line at Fort Gregg and Battery Whitworth to protect bridges across the Appomattox River. He had to hold Petersburg through the night to allow the remnants of the Army of Northern Virginia to escape. Gordon attacked the Union defenders of Fort Mahone, but as Longstreet's men sacrificed themselves he received word that Hill's line had collapsed. Lee managed miraculously to move his army west toward Amelia Court House. President Davis and the Confederate government pulled out of Richmond aboard rail cars late on 2 April. Mayhem gripped the city, and fires erupted. The last Confederate cavalryman to cross Mayo's Bridge tipped his hat and ordered the span ablaze shouting, "All over, goodbye; blow her to hell!" Skirmishes occurred the next day, Lee only hours ahead of his pursuers. He intended to remain at Amelia Court House long enough to provision his starving soldiers. Forage wagons returned mostly empty. Marching into the resort town of Amelia Springs, the Confederates skirted Union troops at Jetersville, and Lee received word that provisions were waiting at Farmville. His ragged command stumbled ahead through darkness and pelting rain.

Longstreet's rear guard held the High Bridge across the Appomattox River for a time, but a debacle ensued at Sailor's Creek on 6 April. Lee watched in disbelief as nine Confederate generals were captured and 9,000 soldiers, a quarter of his army, taken prisoner. "My God!" Lee gasped. "Has the army been dissolved?"

Still, the road to Farmville was temporarily open. The Confederates failed to destroy

This Confederate soldier was killed in the fighting at Fort Mahone as the Siege of Petersburg ended

During General William T Sherman's Carolinas campaign, the city of Columbia, South Carolina, burns furiously

the High Bridge or a nearby wagon bridge, and the Union pursuit continued. Sheridan's cavalry rode ahead, attempting to block Lee's columns. At Farmville, Lee's soldiers reached into boxcars for provisions, only to come under attack by Union cavalry before many could gather anything. Lee had altered his plan, marching for Lynchburg, where he might turn south into North Carolina. The road led through the village of Appomattox Court House.

Union troops crossed the High Bridge on the morning of 7 April, and fighting erupted around Cumberland Church, ending at dusk. That night, Lee's army continued towards Appomattox Court House, 26 miles distant. By 8 April, communications between Grant and Lee regarding a possible surrender had begun. Throughout the day, the Army of Northern Virginia marched towards Appomattox Court House, but Union cavalry under General George A Custer captured rail cars full of provisions and cut the Richmond-Lynchburg Stage Road, slamming the door on Lee. Camped at Rocky Run to the north, Lee held a war council. A daylight attack would dislodge the enemy if they faced cavalry alone. The presence of Union infantry meant the end.

General John B Gordon advanced his II Corps the next morning, and the Battle of Appomattox Court House led directly to the surrender of the Army of Northern Virginia on the afternoon of 9 April 1865. This surrender marked the effective end of the Confederate States of America, and the end of a four-year-long civil war. ★

A Visit To Richmond

PRESIDENT ABRAHAM LINCOLN VISITED RICHMOND JUST HOURS AFTER THE CONFEDERATE CAPITAL FELL TO UNION FORCES

President Abraham Lincoln anxiously awaited word of the Union armies' progress in April 1865, spending much of the month away from Washington, DC, at the vast supply base of City Point, Virginia.

On 3 April, Lincoln and his 12-year-old son Tad left City Point to meet General Grant in Petersburg. Along the way they stopped at Fort Mahone, which had been the scene of intense fighting just hours earlier.

The dead had yet to be buried, and bodies were strewn across the ground. By afternoon, the president was back at City Point after conferring with Grant. He cabled Secretary of War Edwin M Stanton: "[...] It is certain now that Richmond is in our hands, and I think I will go there to-morrow. I will take care of myself." On the morning of 4 April, Lincoln and his small entourage, including Tad, boarded a steamer for the short trip up the James River to the smouldering former capital of the Confederacy.

When he came ashore there was little in the way of armed guard for protection, and an astounded crowd of former slaves assembled. "My poor friends, you are free – free as air," he told them. A few Union cavalrymen appeared, escorting Lincoln, who walked about two miles to the nearest army headquarters, the former Confederate White House.

The president entered, sat in a chair with his legs crossed, gazed dreamily, remarked that it must have belonged to Jefferson Davis, and asked for a glass of water. He toured the rest of the house and was never exultant.

Former slaves shout with joy as President Abraham Lincoln strides through the city of Richmond on 4 April 1865

THE END COMES AT APPOMATTOX

Doggedly pursued by three Union armies, the Confederate Army of Northern Virginia fought its last battle and furled its flags at Appomattox Court House

WORDS **MIKE HASKEW**

Generals Robert E Lee and Ulysses S Grant discuss surrender terms at the McLean House on 9 April 1865

"THERE REMAINED ONE FORLORN HOPE FOR GENERAL LEE – TO PUSH THROUGH TO LYNCHBURG. THE PRESENCE OF UNION INFANTRY, HOWEVER, WOULD MEAN THE END"

The tone was desperate and the implications were clear. "Tell General Lee that my command has been fought to a frazzle and unless Longstreet can unite in the movement, or prevent these forces from coming upon my rear, I cannot long go forward."

The message to his commander-in-chief, sent by General John B Gordon, whose beleaguered and understrength II Corps of the Confederate Army of Northern Virginia had engaged Union troops barring the route of march towards the rail line and rations at Lynchburg, sounded the death knell of the proud rebel army that had waged war for four agonizing years.

A week earlier, General Robert E Lee had been compelled to abandon the defenses of Petersburg, an important rail center, and Richmond, the Confederate capital city, in the face of overwhelming attacks by Union troops. General Ulysses S Grant, commanding all Union armies arrayed against the Confederacy, then pursued Lee across central Virginia, maintaining a parallel track, checking his adversary's every move, and sending the hard-riding cavalry of General Philip Sheridan ahead to finally cut the Confederates off.

On the afternoon of 8 April 1865, General George Armstrong Custer's cavalry division had thundered into Appomattox Station on the South Side Railroad, about two miles from the village of Appomattox Court House, and seized four trains trailing boxcars of foodstuffs and other supplies meant for Lee's army. The object of the Confederate general's march towards Appomattox was gone. He had hoped to provision his famished troops and then turn again to the south to link up with Confederate forces in North Carolina under General Joseph E Johnston. But it was not to be.

That evening, Lee called his subordinate commanders together. There were no chairs or tents available – all had been seized by the marauding Union cavalry. In fact, three Union armies – Lee's old nemesis, the Army of the Potomac, and two smaller forces, the Army of the James and the Army of the Shenandoah – were in pursuit and close at hand. There remained one forlorn hope. If only Union cavalry blocked the road to Lynchburg, Gordon's corps and the cavalry under General Fitzhugh Lee, the old general's nephew, might push the enemy aside and open the route for the rest of the army. The presence of Union infantry, however, would mean the end.

As the Confederate generals assessed the dismal situation, a dialogue surrounding surrender terms had already begun, with Generals Lee and Grant exchanging messages by courier. Lee had looked to buy time, while Grant, suffering from a debilitating headache, dashed off a reply to the Confederate commander's latest communication on the morning of 9 April. He then mounted Cincinnati, one of three horses he rode during the spring of 1865, along with Egypt and Jeff Davis, and galloped off toward Sheridan.

Before sunrise, Grant's trusted cavalry commander had ordered the dismounted brigade of General Charles H Smith to occupy a low ridge about a mile west of Appomattox Court House. From that vantage point, the veteran cavalrymen of New York, Ohio, and Maine covered the Richmond-Lynchburg Stage Road and the Bent Creek Road running north. The troopers dug shallow trenches and waited. Lieutenant James Lord brought a pair of cannon to the ridge, and soon these guns were firing at the distant Confederate positions, just visible through a thick shroud of fog. More Union cavalry, four full divisions, arrived, and Sheridan was confident of victory.

A futile fight

Gordon patched together an infantry battle line with what was left of three divisions, under Generals Clement Evans, James Walker, and Bryan Grimes. The understrength division of General William H Wallace remained slightly to the rear as an immediate reserve, and Fitzhugh Lee's cavalry, led capably by the battle-hardened Thomas Munford, Thomas Rosser, and WHF 'Rooney' Lee, the old general's second son, moved to the right flank. Artillery under Colonel Thomas Carter rolled into position.

As first light streaked the eastern sky, Gordon and Fitzhugh Lee could see the blue-clad enemy along the ridge, but the distance made it unclear whether the soldiers were cavalry or infantry. If they were cavalry, Lee would lead the advance; if infantry, the chore would fall to Gordon. While the two men engaged in a heated exchange, Grimes rode forward and boldly stated that the job belonged to someone. "I will undertake it," he declared.

Gordon offered, "Well, drive them off!" When Grimes responded that his division alone was not sufficient, Gordon retorted, "You can take the other two divisions of the corps!"

At 5am, the Confederates began forming for battle. Three hours later, the rebels raised their familiar "Yip! Yip!" yell and stepped forwards. North Carolina cavalrymen seized Lord's two Union guns, while the infantry pivoted to the left like a gate on a hinge, flanking Smith's forward positions. Crossing the Richmond-Lynchburg Stage Road, the rebels surged south and west towards a much stronger second Union line commanded by General

Image: Getty

George Crook. Heavy fighting, some hand-to-hand, erupted, and opposing cavalry forces clashed with sabers and wielded pistols. Munford and Rosser spurred their horsemen further west to widen the escape corridor.

Sheridan heard the gunfire and rode forwards. He realized that infantry of the XXIV Corps of the Army of the James, commanded by General Edward OC Ord, was nearby along with the V Corps of the Army of the Potomac, under General Charles Griffin, and two brigades of United States Colored Troops of the XXV Corps. He issued a flurry of orders for the cavalry to make way. As the Union horsemen executed their fighting withdrawal, the Confederates rushed into the gap on the precious road, some of them cheering. The moment of exultation was short-lived. As they reached the crest of another low ridge, they saw the spectacle of Union infantry deploying into line of battle.

Gordon quickly realized that his flank and rear were vulnerable as Griffin slanted northward toward the Court House building. Moments later, Colonel Charles Venable – an aide sent forward by General Lee to find out what was happening – received Gordon's disturbing report. The Confederate cavalry could not stand up to massed infantry and began to disengage. The balance of the Confederate army, under General James Longstreet, could not assist Gordon as a new threat from the Union II and VI Corps, under Generals Andrew Humphreys and Horatio Wright respectively, emerged to the northeast at New Hope Church.

Venable returned to General Lee's side and relayed the somber news from Gordon. The old warrior knew that the fight was over and remarked, "Then there is nothing left me to do but to go and see General Grant, and I would rather die a thousand deaths."

Preparing for the end

The difficulties of battlefield communications and imprecise locating of responsible parties delayed cease-fire orders – as well as the fateful meeting of Grant and Lee in the parlor of the home belonging to merchant Wilmer McLean at Appomattox Court House – until sometime after 1pm on 9 April. Lee, expecting to meet his adversary sometime that day, had dressed in his finest uniform. General Longstreet found him that morning, Palm Sunday, a striking figure of military deportment. "He was dressed in a suit of new uniform, sword and sash, a handsomely embroidered belt, boots and a pair of gold spurs," Longstreet remembered years later. "At first approach, his compact figure appeared as a man in the flush vigor of 40 summers, but as I drew near, the handsome apparel and brave bearing failed to conceal his profound depression."

"THE MOMENT OF EXULTATION WAS SHORT-LIVED – AS THEY CRESTED A LOW RIDGE, THEY SAW UNION INFANTRY DEPLOYING INTO LINE OF BATTLE"

Another officer asked why Lee had dressed so formally, and the general replied, "I have probably to be General Grant's prisoner and thought I must make my best appearance."

As the day wore on, General Lee waited and slept for about an hour in the shade of an apple tree. He was awakened as two Union officers – Colonel Orville Babcock and Captain William Dunn – brought word of Grant's agreement to meet at a place of Lee's choosing. Colonel Charles Marshall, Lee's secretary and aide de camp, rode into the town to find an appropriate location for the talks. He encountered McLean, who first took the officer to a rundown house with no furniture. Marshall was unimpressed, and McLean then offered his own home. Marshall sent his aide, Private Joshua Johns, to bring Lee forward, and Babcock dispatched Dunn to summon General Grant. Within minutes, Lee, Babcock, and Marshall were seated in McLean's parlor, engaging in polite conversation while waiting for Grant to arrive.

Half an hour later, Grant walked through the front door. Lee rose, and the two shook hands while a group of Union officers, including Sheridan and Ord, waited outside. Grant

Union General Phil Sheridan led the cavalry that relentlessly pursued and blocked the escape of the Confederate army at Appomattox Court House

— Front Yard And Parlor —

WILMER MCLEAN WAS PRESENT WITH THE OPENING GUNS OF THE CIVIL WAR AND ITS CONCLUSION FOUR YEARS LATER

On the morning of 9 April 1865, Wilmer McLean was 51 years old, a veteran of the Virginia Militia, and an ironically prosperous war refugee. McLean had made money speculating in sugar and supplying the precious commodity to the Confederate military. A native of Alexandria, Virginia, he had married in 1853 and settled in the town of Manassas, Virginia, a few miles outside Washington, DC.

Merchant Wilmer McLean played host to the final drama at Appomattox Court House in April 1865

When the Civil War erupted, McLean's home became a focus of the First Battle of Bull Run, fought 21 July 1861. Confederate General PGT Beauregard commandeered the house for his headquarters. McLean was deeply disturbed by what he had seen. By the spring of 1863, he had moved his family 120 miles south, residing in a handsome two-storey home on the Richmond-Lynchburg Stage Road in the quiet town of Appomattox Court House, where he hoped the war would not disrupt their lives again. However, the conflict followed McLean, who allowed the historic surrender of the Army of Northern Virginia to take place in his home. From that day, he could rightly claim that the Civil War had begun in his front yard and ended in his parlor.

After the war, prosperity eluded the McLean family, who returned to Manassas in the autumn of 1867, and later to Alexandria. McLean tried to make a living, selling an artist's rendering of the surrender and working for the Internal Revenue Service. He defaulted on his bank loan, losing the Appomattox house in 1869, and died in Alexandria, aged 68, on 5 June 1882.

was disheveled and no doubt self-conscious of his appearance. Lee fairly glittered in his finery while Grant wore a dusty uniform that he had traveled in for some time.

"When I left the camp that morning I had not expected so soon the result that was then taking place, and consequently was in rough garb," Grant wrote in his memoirs. "I was without a sword, as I usually was when on horseback on the field, and wore a soldier's blouse for a coat, with the shoulder straps of my rank to indicate to the army who I was."

The surrender meeting

The conversation began pleasantly with Grant commenting that the two had briefly met while serving during the Mexican War nearly 20 years earlier. Grant remembered Lee, but there is some conjecture as to whether Lee could recall the meeting. Marshall said that Lee recognized Grant immediately, while Lieutenant Colonel Horace Porter, a Union staff officer, wrote that he heard Lee whisper that he could not remember what Grant looked like.

After a half hour, Lee turned the discussion back to the business at hand. "I suppose, General Grant, that the object of our present meeting is fully understood. I have come to meet with you in accordance with my letter to you this morning, to treat about the surrender of my army, and I think the best way would be for you to put your terms in writing."

Grant responded, "Yes, I believe it will."

The Union commander had motioned to have other officers enter the room, and they did, filing in quietly as Porter remembered "very much as people enter a sick-chamber when they expect to find the patient dangerously ill". Grant wrote down the framework of surrender in his order book and handed the book to Porter, who then passed it to Lee. The 58-year-old Confederate general wiped his glasses, moved a pair of candlesticks and a few books out of the way, and noted that the word "exchanged" had been omitted from the text. He searched for a pencil and then borrowed one from Porter, inserting the word in the appropriate space.

Twirling the pencil and tapping it on the small marble tabletop, he returned the pencil to Porter upon his departure, and the Union officer kept it, a prized possession, for the rest of his life.

Lee took special note that Grant was generous in stating that only public property was to be given up. Officers could keep their sidearms and baggage. He responded, "That will have a very happy effect." A moment later, he raised the prospect of Confederate soldiers keeping their horses for ploughing fields for a crop when they returned to civilian life. Grant at first replied that this was not possible, even after Lee noted that the horses were personal property and did not belong to the government. Then, Grant relented, his compassion and desire for reconciliation already shining through.

As the encounter neared its conclusion, the two commanders dutifully signed their respective documents. Lee pointed out that the Confederates were holding about 1,000 prisoners and that they had little or nothing to eat. Grant asked Sheridan if he could muster up some rations and then assured Lee that 25,000 would be coming forward. The food was intended both for the prisoners, who would soon be released, and the starving Confederate soldiers.

When formal matters were concluded, Grant introduced Lee to the Union officers gathered. Lee shook hands with those nearby and bowed towards those at a distance. At about 3pm,

A Post-surrender Frenzy

MEMENTOS OF THE SURRENDER AT APPOMATTOX COURT HOUSE WERE IN HIGH DEMAND IMMEDIATELY AFTER THE PROCEEDINGS

Shortly after the news of the surrender of General Lee and the Confederate Army of Northern Virginia to the Union forces under General Grant at Appomattox Court House had spread, souvenir hunters hacked the apple tree where Lee had napped, on the afternoon of 9 April 1865, into pieces. For good measure, several other nearby trees were dismembered as well.

When the meeting concluded at the McLean House, the homeowner watched helplessly as his belongings were dispersed in the possession of Union officers. General EOC Ord insisted on paying Wilmer McLean $40 for the table Lee had used, while General Phil Sheridan offered $20 for a table that had been beside Grant. When McLean refused to sell to Sheridan, the general reportedly took the table anyway and threw a $20 gold piece to the floor of the house. Sheridan later gave the table to General George Armstrong Custer as a gift to his wife, while Sheridan's brother procured a stoneware inkstand and another officer paid $10 for the pair of candlesticks Lee had moved in order to read Grant's terms of surrender. The chairs the generals sat in passed through several owners and finally made their way to the National Museum of American History in Washington, DC.

One mute witness to the surrender, a doll belonging to one of McLean's daughters, gained lasting fame. The doll was tossed around the house by several Union officers and finally taken by a young captain. It remained in the officer's family many years before being finally returned to Appomattox Court House.

The chairs used by Generals Grant (left) and Lee in Appomattox are now on display in the National Museum of American History in Washington, DC

In May 1865, a grand review of the victorious Union armies took place in Washington, DC

Lee walked to the porch, waited for his horse, Traveller, to be bridled, and pounded his right fist into his left hand as he looked down the valley towards his defeated army. As Lee mounted, Grant reached the porch, raising his hat in salute. Lee responded similarly from horseback, and the gathered officers followed suit.

With that, it ended. The Army of Northern Virginia would soon cease to exist, passing into history. The details of paroles, exchanges, and distribution of rations were left to subordinates.

Time to heal

In his memoirs, Grant reflected on the emotion of the moment. "I felt like anything but rejoicing at the downfall of a foe who had fought so long and valiantly, and had suffered so much for a cause, though that cause was, I believe, one of the worst for which a people ever fought, and one for which there was the least excuse."

As news of the surrender spread rapidly, Union artillery began firing in celebration. Grant was annoyed and quickly ordered it to cease. "The war is over; the rebels are our countrymen again; and the best sign of rejoicing after the victory will be to abstain from all demonstrations in the field." He dashed off a cable with news of the victory to Secretary of War Edwin M Stanton in Washington, DC. It was a masterpiece of understatement: "General Lee surrendered the Army of Northern Virginia this afternoon on terms proposed by myself. The accompanying additional correspondence will show the conditions fully."

While the drama played out at Appomattox, Confederate President Jefferson Davis had left Danville, where he had fled by rail, evacuating Richmond late on the night of 2 April, as the city burned and federal troops approached. He reached Charlotte, North Carolina, on 26 April, the same day that General Johnston surrendered his Confederate army to General William T Sherman after a campaign of maneuver northwards from Savannah, Georgia, the terminus of Sherman's famed 'March to the Sea'. Davis was arrested near Irwinville, Georgia, on 10 May. He was imprisoned at Fort Monroe in Virginia and indicted for treason, but never tried. He was released on bond for $100,000 to live out his days in Tennessee, Mississippi, and Louisiana.

The Civil War was over. Skirmishing did persist for weeks, and the final engagement of the conflict, generally accepted by historians, occurred at Palmito Ranch near Brownsville, Texas, 12-13 May 1865. Ahead lay years of 'reconstruction' and reconciliation. As the martyred President Lincoln had intoned in his second inaugural address just weeks earlier, it was time to "bind up the nation's wounds". ★

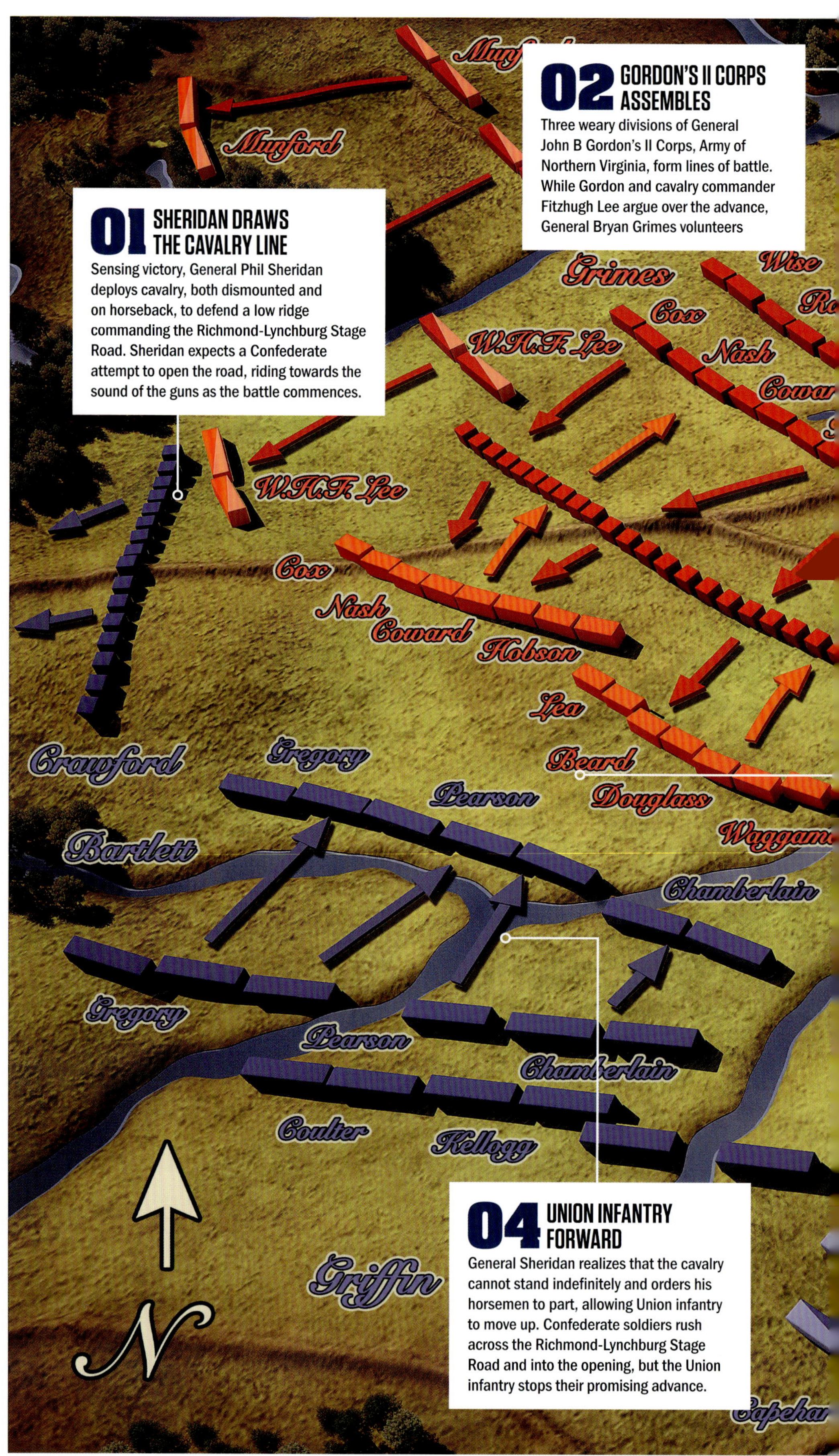

05 DISAPPOINTMENT AND DEFEAT

Generals Gordon and Fitzhugh Lee realize they cannot prevail against the array of Union infantry and begin to pull their forces back. Some of the Confederates disperse, hoping to escape the inevitable surrender of the Army of Northern Virginia.

03 DESPERATE CONFEDERATE ASSAULT

The Confederate attack gains some headway as the thin first line of Union cavalry begins to waver. Two Union cannon are captured by North Carolina cavalrymen. However, a stout second line of Union cavalry makes a tougher stand, slowing the rebel assault.

Image: Nicholas Forder

Booth is believed to have shouted 'Sic semper tyrannis', Latin for 'thus always to tyrants', after he leapt from the presidential box

THE ASSASSINATION OF ABRAHAM LINCOLN

The Civil War may have been over but the United States was thrown into disarray after what was meant to be a quiet night at the theater

WORDS **JACK GRIFFITHS**

The assassination of Abraham Lincoln sent shockwaves through a war-torn and divided nation. The president was shot on 14 April 1865 – five days after the American Civil War officially ended when Commander of the Confederate Army Robert E Lee laid down his arms to Union forces.

As the conflict had neared its conclusion, Union generals and politicians were confident of victory. A month before the end of the war President Lincoln made a speech outside the Capitol Building in Washington, DC. This came in the wake of his second term of presidency as he revealed his sadness at the toll of the conflict and his hope for a new united nation. Lincoln's words spoke for many but infuriated one man in the crowd – John Wilkes Booth. This was the final straw for the 26-year-old Confederate sympathizer and white supremacist, who finalized his plan to kill the president.

Booth was a famous actor of the era and a national celebrity. He was from a family of actors and would have fought for the South had he not promised his mother he wouldn't. During the war, with a group of co-conspirators, he attempted to abduct the president in exchange for Confederate prisoners of war. After this plan failed, he changed his mind and decided to kill Lincoln, fully believing that by assassinating the president he would help revitalize the Confederate war effort and prolong the Southern way of life.

A dark day

On 14 April, Good Friday, the president was enjoying a comedy at Ford's Theatre in Washington, DC. Lincoln was with his wife, Mary, and Union Army Major Henry Rathbone and his fiancée, Clara. The group was unguarded after bodyguard John Parker had slipped off to a saloon. Remarkably, this nearby bar was the same one where Booth had been downing some liquid courage just a few minutes before. Shortly after 10pm, a figure appeared at the rear of the presidential box. Blocking the door behind him, he had timed his

"LINCOLN'S WORDS SPOKE FOR MANY BUT INFURIATED ONE MAN IN THE CROWD – JOHN WILKES BOOTH"

Image: Getty

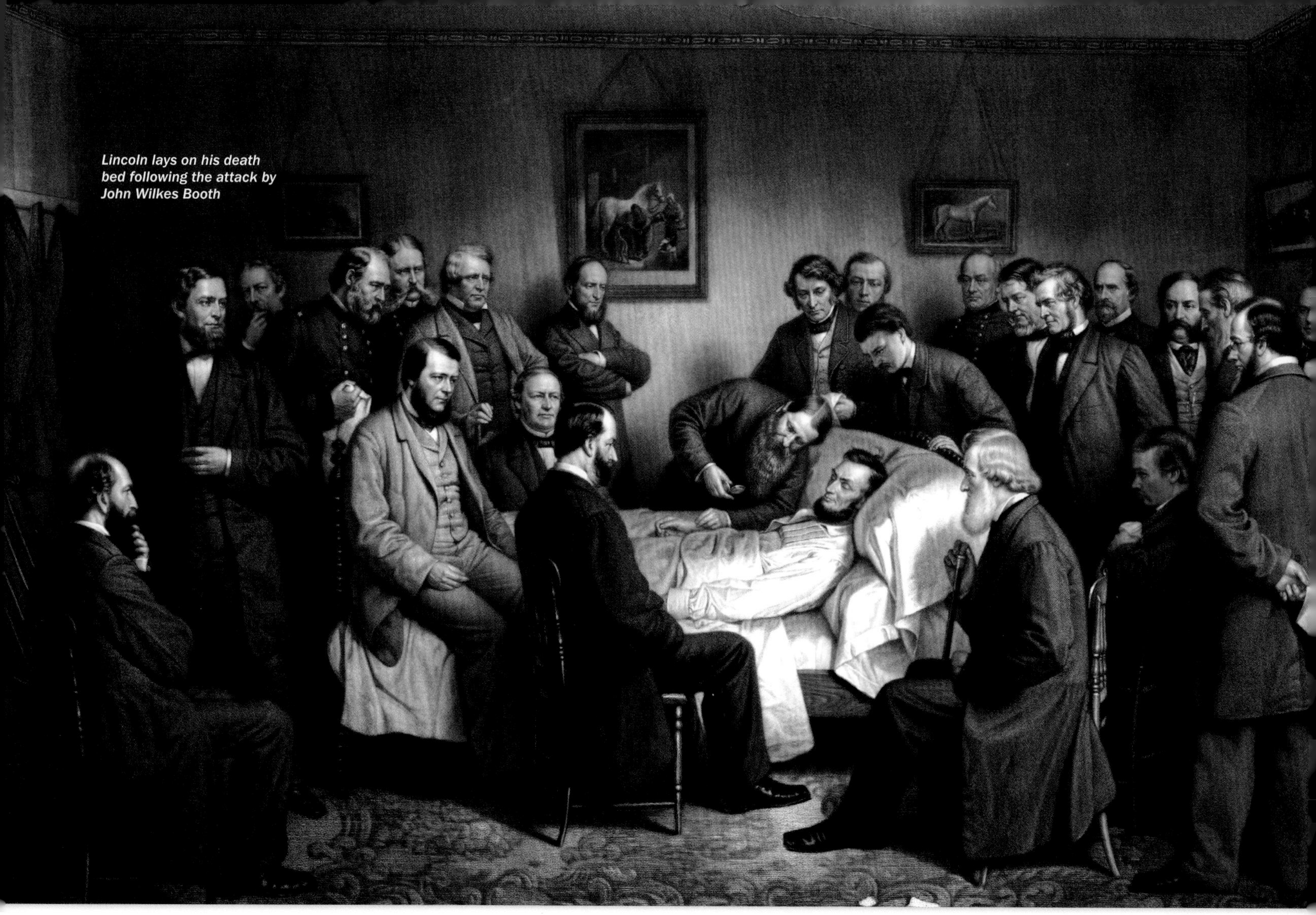

Lincoln lays on his death bed following the attack by John Wilkes Booth

John Wilkes Booth was a famous stage actor, who was also a Confederate sympathizer

entrance to coincide with what he knew would be a rapturous laugh from the audience, so as not to alert his target. Booth silently drew his single-shot Derringer pistol and nonchalantly and without hesitation, fired a bullet in the back of the president's head.

Mary recoiled in horror as her husband collapsed in his chair. Rathbone stood and attempted to apprehend Booth who slashed him on the shoulder with a concealed knife. To the horror of the crowd, the assassin dived onto the stage before making his escape through a side door.

The hunt for Booth

The stricken president was tended to by doctors who were in the audience. Despite their best efforts the bullet remained lodged in Lincoln's skull, and he died in a boarding house next door to the theater just after 7.15am the next morning. His killer meanwhile had taken off on horseback and made it to Maryland where he met up with co-conspirator, David Herold.

The hunt was on for Booth as he was tracked through Maryland and Virginia by federal troops. The road ran out for Booth and Herold, when they were finally located, after a 12-day manhunt, in a barn near Port Royal, Virginia. Herold surrendered but Booth, unyielding to the end, refused and either shot himself or was gunned down.

A telegram distributed to the press by the presidential office informed the American public of what had happened. Lincoln was by no means a universally popular figure, even in the Union, but many people paid their respects to his funeral train which passed through various towns on its way to his final resting place in Springfield, Illinois.

Vice President Andrew Johnson took up the role of president after Lincoln's death. One of his first actions was to trial all those involved in the plot to kill his predecessor. Eight conspirators were tried and were all found guilty of conspiracy to murder. Four were hanged, three were given life sentences, and one a six-year sentence. Justice had been done but a war-winning president was dead. Andrew Johnson was left to lead the post-war USA through the early stages of the Reconstruction and away from the memory of the bloodiest war ever to be fought on its soil. ★

BOOTH DIDN'T ACT ALONE AND OTHER HIGH-RANKING OFFICERS AND POLITICAL FIGURES WERE ALSO TARGETED IN A WIDER MURDER PLOT

The assassination of Abraham Lincoln was only one part of a larger operation that also involved killing the vice president and the secretary of state. Booth's associates in this plot were George Atzerodt, Lewis Powell, Edmund Spangler, and David Herold. The group often met at a boarding house owned by Mary Surratt, whose son was another acquaintance of Booth's.

Atzerodt was tasked with killing Andrew Johnson, while Powell and Herold would murder the secretary of state, William Seward. This would be completed at the same time on the same day in a triple hit against the Union. Booth would be aided in his assassination attempt by Spangler who was a stagehand at Ford's Theatre and would help him access all areas and leave as quickly as possible.

While Booth was etching himself into the annals of history in central Washington, Powell had barged his way into Seward's residence, past his bodyguard and into his bedroom where he repeatedly stabbed his target before fleeing on horseback with Herold.

"THIS WOULD BE COMPLETED AT THE SAME TIME IN A TRIPLE HIT AGAINST THE UNION"

Atzerodt, meanwhile, attempted to summon up some courage by downing drinks in a local bar. However, despite the alcohol consumption, he couldn't bring himself to do it.

As it turned out, Booth was the only one of the group to successfully kill his target after Seward miraculously recovered from his wounds. Herold was with Booth until the bitter end, helping him contact a doctor to fix his leg, which was broken when he fell onto the stage. And the pair remained together until they were tracked down by Union forces after a 12-day manhunt.

Mary Surratt was one of four conspirators to be hung and was the first ever woman to be executed by the US government

Image: Alamy, Getty

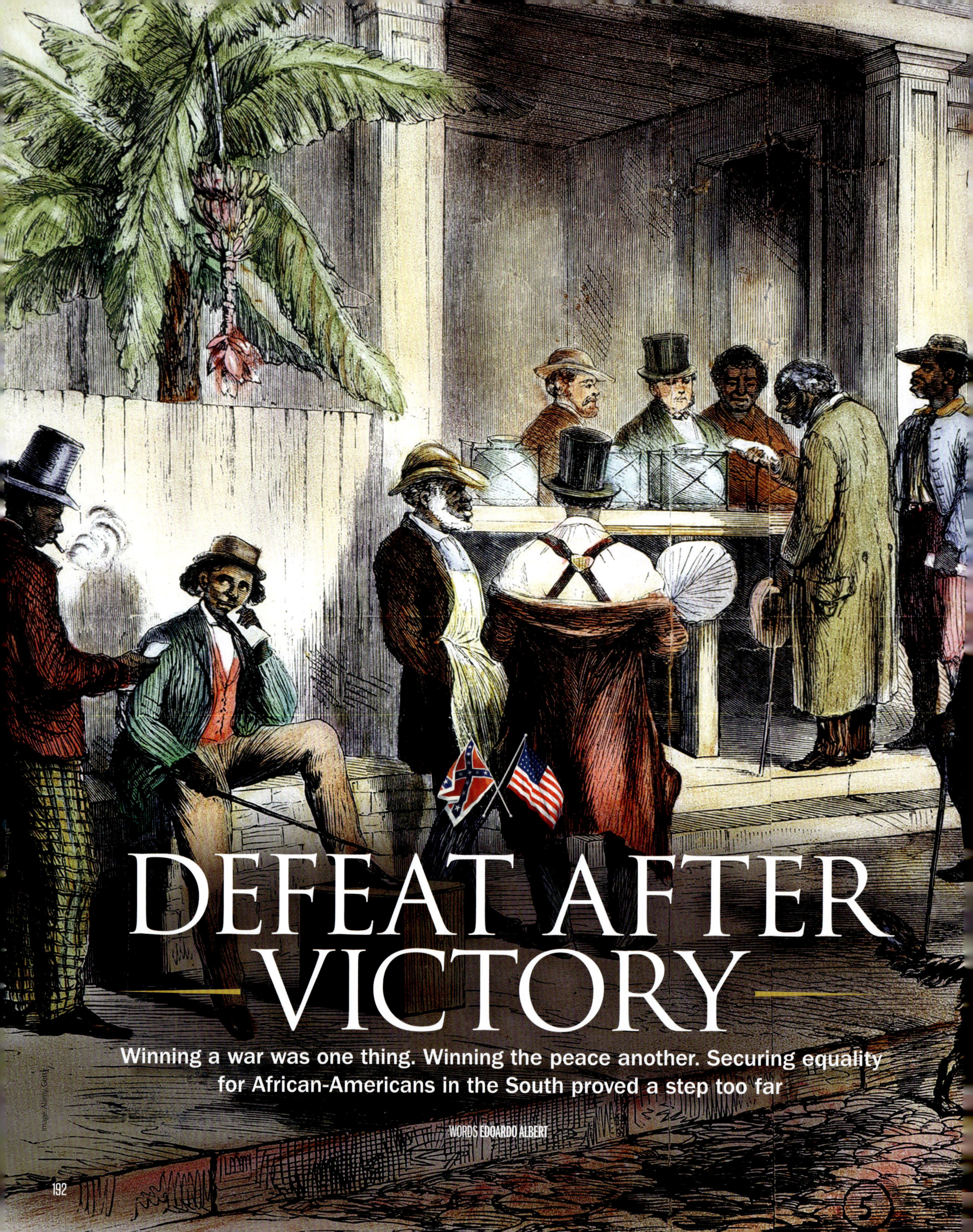

DEFEAT AFTER VICTORY

Winning a war was one thing. Winning the peace another. Securing equality for African-Americans in the South proved a step too far

WORDS EDOARDO ALBERT

Image: Alamy, Getty

Freedmen voting in elections in New Orleans in 1867

The Union had won the war. But could it win the peace? That was the great question that faced the winning side of the American Civil War following General Robert E Lee's surrender on 9 April 1865. Whatever hopes and plans the great architect of the Union victory, President Abraham Lincoln, had in mind had died with him when he was assassinated by John Wilkes Booth just five days later, on 14 April. Lincoln's vice president, the Southern Democrat Andrew Johnson, became president in his place.

President Lincoln had wanted clemency exercised towards the Confederate states as a way of re-establishing the Union, but President Johnson, a committed constitutionalist and equally committed racist, set about ensuring that the Southern states would have the freedom to govern themselves. As a result, the previously Confederate states began enacting a series of laws designed to put the newly freed black slaves back on the plantations and to keep them there.

While Andrew Johnson is frequently cited, by historians, as near the top of the list of bad American presidents, his personal story was as much an illustration of the American Dream as was Lincoln's. Both men had grown up in extreme poverty. Johnson's parents were illiterate and he never attended school. Self-educated, Johnson worked as a tailor before entering politics. There was much to admire about Johnson's life, little to applaud during his presidency.

In the immediate aftermath of the war, Johnson used his presidential powers to

***Above** The vice president, Andrew Johnson, became president after Lincoln's assassination. He is often ranked among the worst presidents in American history*

Above *The Battle of Liberty Place, 1874, when the White League attacked New Orleans' racially integrated police force*

Above *Ulysses S Grant, commanding officer of the Union forces during the Civil War and 18th president of the United States*

offer pardons to all the white citizens of the Confederate states, except for the leaders of the Confederacy and the major plantation holders, who had to petition personally for pardons. Johnson also proposed returning all land and property to dispossessed Southerners, with the exception of their human property: slaves were not to be restored.

The individual states also had to ratify the 13th Amendment to the Constitution, which outlawed slavery, while citizens of the South had to swear loyalty to the Union, and the states had to disavow secession from the Union and cancel the debts run up during the Civil War. They were generous terms, and it seems likely that Lincoln would have supported them. Indeed, when asked by a Union general how to treat the defeated enemy, Lincoln had replied, "Let 'em up easy."

However, it's unlikely that Lincoln would have acquiesced in the way Johnson did when it became clear that Southern states were using the freedom they had been given to try to ensure that freed slaves were kept in a condition as close to slavery as possible. Indeed, it was Johnson's belief that "white men alone must manage the South". The new Southern legislatures set about enacting laws that restored slavery in all but name: freedmen could only work as field laborers, black men without work could be sold to planters to work as laborers, and black children could be taken from their families.

Radical Reconstruction

The Republican-dominated Congress reconvened in December 1865. The president had already declared that Reconstruction was over, to the horror of the Republicans who had fought for the emancipation of the slaves. What's more, many former Confederate officials had been elected to serve in Congress, including even Alexander Stephens, the vice president of the Confederacy. However, when these Confederates presented themselves to Congress, the Clerk of the House refused to include them among the elected members.

In defiance of the Democrat president's obstructionism, the Republican Congress passed the Civil Rights Bill, which granted citizenship to all men "without distinction of race or color, or previous condition of slavery or involuntary servitude". However, presented with the Bill, President Johnson vetoed it. In defiance of the president, Congress voted to overturn Johnson's veto and the Civil Rights Act was passed into law on 9 April 1866.

In the South, meanwhile, white supremacist organization the Ku Klux Klan had been founded in Tennessee. Rising racial tensions led to three

***Above** While denied political rights, black churches became established in the South, serving as an important focus for community life and hope*

days of rioting in Memphis, Tennessee, which saw 48 people, almost all black, killed.

An increasingly radical Congress proposed the 14th Amendment to the Constitution, an amendment that defined a United States citizen as simply someone born in or naturalized to the United States, and sent it to the states for ratification, with the demand that the Southern states ratify the amendment as the price of being re-admitted to the Union. In the Congressional elections of the fall of 1866, voters returned a House of Congress full of radical Republicans determined to restart Reconstruction. Such was their majority in Congress that President Johnson could no longer obstruct their program. Congress proceeded to pass a series of Reconstruction Acts, dividing the South into five military districts under army control and forcing them to accept black suffrage. This began what came to be called Radical or Congressional Reconstruction, which lasted until 1877.

During most of this period, the Republican Party controlled most of the Southern states. To enact the Reconstruction Acts, many Northerners headed to the South – soldiers, teachers, and businessmen. They came to be called 'carpetbaggers' after their suitcases made from stitched-together carpet. On the Southern side, the locally born white

The Colfax Massacre

THE BLOODIEST AND MOST SIGNIFICANT VIOLENCE OF THE RECONSTRUCTION ERA

The 1872 elections in Louisiana were evenly split between Republicans and Democrats. In the aftermath, with rumors swirling of paramilitary groups taking control of local parishes, a black militia force, led by Civil War veteran William Ward, took control of the courthouse of Grant Parish in April 1873. As white supremacist forces gathered, Ward left on 11 April to seek help from the state governor. Two days later, white supremacist forces, armed with a cannon, opened fire on the courthouse. After a brief firefight, the black defenders surrendered.

After giving themselves up, however, a massacre took place, with somewhere between 60 and 150 of the black militia being killed. The murders generated newspaper headlines across the country and federal forces eventually arrested 97 men for the crime. Fearing that a trial for murder before a state court would see the accused's acquittal, however, the authorities instead charged them with breaking the Enforcements Act. When the case was appealed to the Supreme Court, the court found for the defendants, stating that the Enforcements Act applied only to states, not to individuals. As a result, the perpetrators of the massacre escaped unpunished. For black people in the South, it seemed clear, there was now no redress against corrupt and biased local courts. With the passing of the first Jim Crow laws, the re-segregation of the South was firmly in place.

"FOR BLACK PEOPLE IN THE SOUTH, IT SEEMED CLEAR, THERE WAS NOW NO REDRESS AGAINST CORRUPT AND BIASED LOCAL COURTS"

Although the massacre provoked outrage, as demonstrated by this illustration from Harper's Weekly, *its aftermath was a stepping stone to segregation*

Image: Getty

An illustration of the Ku Klux Klan preparing to lynch a man that they regarded as a collaborator

Republicans were called 'scalawags', and were mainly small farmers. Finally, local black people overwhelmingly voted Republican in an effort to end the racial segregation of the South and to gain some economic and political power. Black Americans were elected to Congress and the Senate, and many served in state legislatures and as the everyday elected officials in the South, from sheriffs to justices of the peace. For a society that had based itself upon segregation, this black emancipation came as a tremendous shock. For many white Southerners, it seemed that their black slaves had suddenly become their political masters – and they weren't happy about it.

Through 1867 and 1868, most of the Southern states were re-admitted to the Union (Georgia, the last, was re-admitted in 1870) and, on 28 July, the 14th Amendment to the Constitution was ratified. President Johnson, who had escaped impeachment by the narrowest of margins (one vote in the Senate, Congress having voted to impeach) was denied a shot at re-election by the Democrats, who chose Horatio Seymour, who had served as governor of New York, as their nominee for the presidential elections. For their part, the Republicans nominated General Ulysses Grant, the military architect of the Union victory in the Civil War. Grant won the election – though the margin was tight. It was the votes of newly enfranchised black men that provided the Republicans with the necessary votes to win.

Votes for all?

With a Republican President, Congress and Senate, legislators in Congress passed the 15th Amendment to the Constitution, which stipulated that all men were entitled to vote, regardless of race, color or previously having been a slave, and sent it off to the states for ratification. The amendment was a response to the increasing levels of violence in the South, where white supremacist organizations were trying to stop black emancipation. The first among these was the Ku Klux Klan, which targeted freed black slaves and Republicans with threats, violence, and murder. However, as reports of the violence reached Washington, Congress passed the Enforcements Act, which allowed the federal government to protect the rights of black citizens when their local legislatures failed to do so. The third of the Enforcements Acts, which was known as the 'Ku Klux Klan Act' and passed in

"FOR MANY WHITE SOUTHERNERS, IT SEEMED THAT THEIR BLACK SLAVES HAD SUDDENLY BECOME THEIR POLITICAL MASTERS – IT WAS A TREMENDOUS SHOCK AND THEY WEREN'T HAPPY ABOUT IT"

Many teachers from the North went to the South to educate and train the newly freed slaves

1871, targeted the Klan and, by its effective application, destroyed this first iteration of the Ku Klux Klan as an organization. However, local Democrats, seeking to overturn Republican rule and effect racist legislation in state assemblies, started similar organizations that served as the enforcement arm of the Democratic Party, eventually helping it to return to power in the South.

Jim Crow laws

While radical Reconstruction had begun with great idealism and high hopes, it was eventually tarnished as corrupt. Political scandals in the North served to taint many officials, while rumors of the corruption of black government officials in the South began to spread. By the time President Grant won re-election in 1872, the political will for and popular patience with Reconstruction was beginning to run out. The war had ended seven years earlier, and the attention of voters and politicians was turning elsewhere.

Despite continuing violence in the South – about 150 black men being killed in the Colfax Massacre of 13 April 1873 – the Democrats won a Congressional majority in 1874. By 1876, among the Southern states, only Louisiana, Florida, and South Carolina were under Republican control. With control of the House, and most Southern state legislatures, the Democrats began passing the series of racist statutes that became known collectively as the Jim Crow laws, ensuring continuing racial segregation in the South. These laws remained in place until 1963.

While the Republicans – who had fought so hard for black emancipation – won the war, it was the Democrats, with their dogged defense of white supremacy, who won the peace. ★

***Above** Republican candidates sought to link their Democratic election rivals with organizations such as the Ku Klux Klan. This was often true*

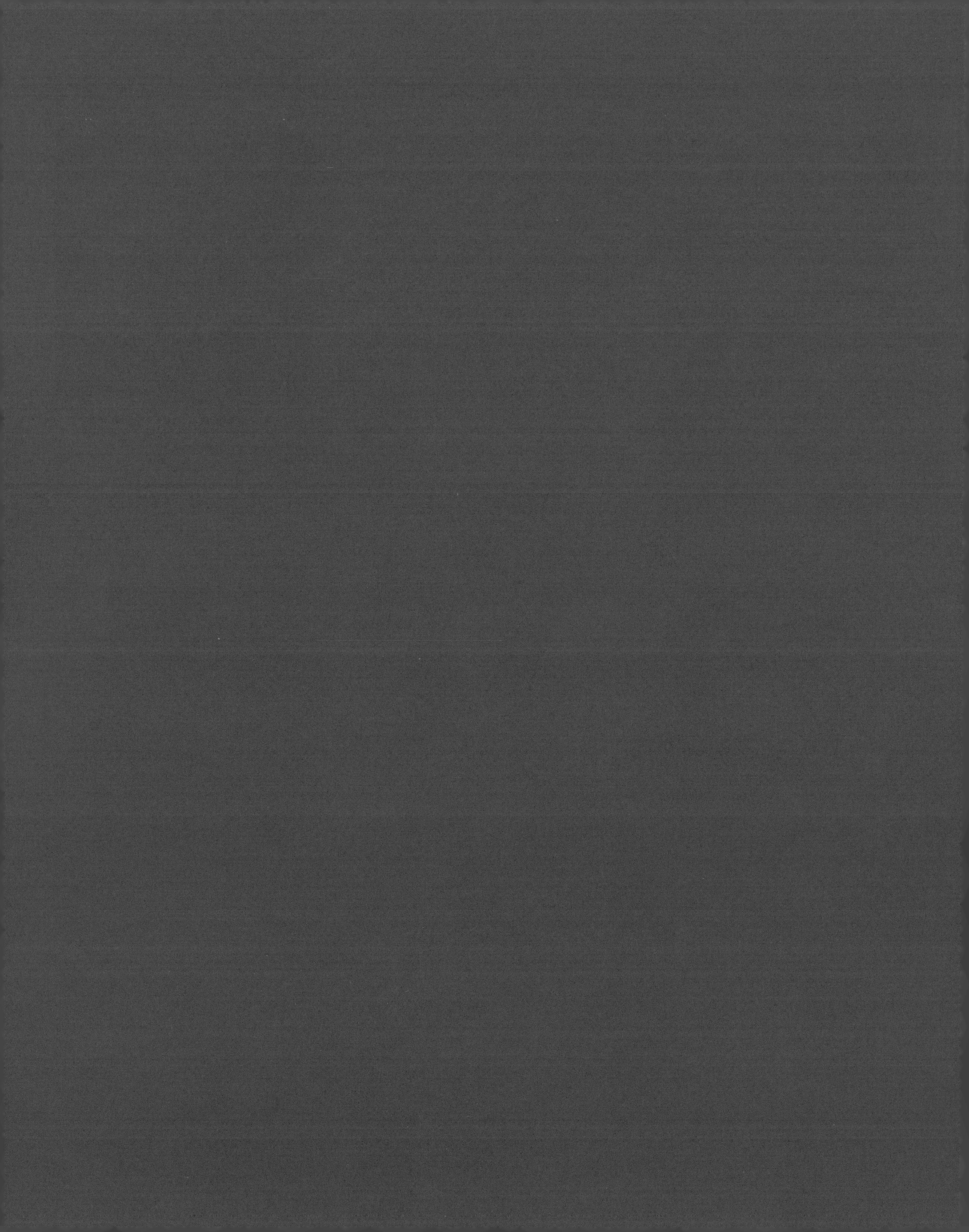